Physical Activity and Psychological Well-Being

The 'feel-good' effect of physical activity is often reported by exercisers but has not been sufficiently recognised in health services and health promotion. In the modern world of stress and inactivity there is an increasing need to assess the potential benefits of physical activity for our mental health. *Physical Activity and Psychological Well-Being* provides a research consensus on the relationship between physical exercise and aspects of mental health. Whilst reviewing and integrating relevant information, the book also considers physical activity in relation to the different aspects of mental health:

- anxiety
- depression
- mood and emotion
- self-esteem
- cognitive functioning
- psychological dysfunction

Physical Activity and Psychological Well-Being is an important resource and foundation for those in health services, health psychology, clinical psychology, psychiatry and sport and exercise settings for promoting the benefits of physical activity for improving mental health. The text is also invaluable reading for undergraduate and postgraduate students in sport and exercise science.

Stuart J.H. Biddle is Professor of Exercise and Sport Psychology at Loughborough University, **Kenneth R. Fox** is Professor and Head of Exercise and Health Sciences at the University of Bristol, **Stephen H. Boutcher** is Reader in Psychophysiology at De Montfort University.

Physical Activity and Psychological Well-Being

Edited by Stuart J.H. Biddle, Kenneth R. Fox, Stephen H. Boutcher

London and New York

First published 2000
by Routledge
11 New Fetter Lane, London EC4P 4EE

Simultaneously published in the USA and Canada
by Routledge
29 West 35th Street, New York, NY 10001

Routledge is an imprint of the Taylor & Francis Group

Typeset in Times by
Florence Production Ltd, Stoodleigh, Devon
Printed and bound in Great Britain by
Biddles Ltd, Guildford and King's Lynn

British Library Cataloguing in Publication Data
A catalogue record for this book is available from the British Library

Library of Congress Cataloging-in-Publication Data
Physical activity and psychological well-being / edited by Stuart J.H. Biddle,
Kenneth R. Fox, Stephen H. Boutcher.
     p.cm.
Includes bibliographical references and index.
    1. Exercise—Psychological aspects. 2. Mental illness—Physiological
aspects. I. Biddle, Stuart. II. Fox, Kenneth R., 1949– III. Boutcher,
Stephen H. (Stephen Hugh), 1949–
RA781.P562 2000
613.7′1′019—dc21   00–028617

ISBN 0–415–23481–6 (hbk)   ISBN 0–415–23439–5 (pbk)

Contents

Figures

Tables

Contributors

Professor Stuart J.H. Biddle is Professor of Exercise and Sport Psychology at Loughborough University where he is associated with the British Heart Foundation National Centre for Physical Activity and Health and the Institute of Youth Sport, both within the Department of Physical Education, Sports Science and Recreation Management. He was President of the European Federation of Sport Psychology 1991–1999, and in 1998 was awarded Distinguished International Scholar of the Association for the Advancement of Applied Sport Psychology. He is the inaugural Editor-in-Chief of the journal *Psychology of Sport & Exercise*. Professor Biddle's research interests are in motivational influences on health-related physical activity and exercise, as well as emotional and other psychological outcomes of physical activity; and he enjoys cycling to work.

Professor Kenneth R. Fox is Professor and Head of Exercise and Health Sciences at the University of Bristol. His research interests include exercise and physical self-perceptions, the role of physical activity in obesity prevention and treatment, and health-related behaviour change interventions. Publications include the edited text *The Physical Self: From Motivation to Well-being* (Champaign, IL: Human Kinetics, 1997) and the *Physical Self-Perception Profile Manual* (DeKalb, IL: Northern Illinois University, Office for Health Promotion, 1990) as well as papers on exercise focusing on motivation, obesity, and well-being.

Dr Stephen H. Boutcher is currently Director of the Physical Activity and Health Research Unit at De Montfort University. His research focuses on the effect of physical activity on the mental and cardiovascular health of hypertensives, older men and women, and individuals with arthritis. He has extensive experience of publishing and is a member of the Editorial Board of the *Journal of Sport & Exercise Psychology*. Prior to his return to the UK, Dr Boutcher was a staff member of universities in the United States and Australia.

Guy Faulkner is currently a researcher in exercise psychology at Lough-borough University. After graduating in physical education at the University of Sydney, Australia, Guy completed a Masters degree in Sport and Exercise Psychology at the University of Exeter, England, before lecturing in Higher Education for three years. Research interests are mainly in physical activity and mental health and its promotion. The role of exercise as an adjunctive treatment for schizophrenia is also of particular interest and he has published on this topic in the *Journal of Sport & Exercise Psychology* and the *Journal of Mental Health*.

Professor Nanette Mutrie is a Visiting Researcher at the MRC Social and Public Health Sciences Unit at Glasgow University and is affiliated to the Centre for Exercise Science and Medicine at the university. She has researched ways of increasing active living in both clinical populations and the community. Recent publications have addressed the psychological benefits of physical exercise for women, physical activity and its link with mental, social and moral health in young people and exercise adherence issues for clinical populations. Professor Mutrie is an Accredited Sport and Exercise Psychologist with the British Association of Sport and Exercise Sciences (BASES) and was Chair of the BASES psychology section for three years until 2000. She is also an elected member of the European Federation of Sport Psychology's Managing Council. In an effort to enjoy the mental health benefits of activity, she plays squash and walks with her dog.

Dr Attila Szabo is Senior Lecturer in Sport and Exercise Psychology at The Nottingham Trent University having been a researcher in Canada and Hungary. His research interests focus on exercise and effect, exercise dependence and deprivation, and Internet-based research.

Professor Adrian Taylor is the Alexander Chair of Health and Physical Activity at De Montfort University. He spent ten years at the University of Brighton before moving to De Montfort in 2000. On behalf of the British Association of Sport and Exercise Sciences he has led the development of a Department of Health-funded National Quality Assurance Framework for GP exercise referral schemes, and a national audit of work with older people, sport and exercise in higher education. Adrian has published and presented on physical activity interventions in primary care, psychological aspects of sports injury rehabilitation, and exercise and mental health. He is currently leading a three-year project looking at stress reactivity and exercise among trainee musicians.

Acknowledgements

The editors would like to thank the following for their valued input to this project:

- Somerset Physical Activity Group and Somerset Health Authority, in particular Trudy Grant
- British Association of Sport & Exercise Sciences, in particular Dr Andy Smith
- The British Psychological Society
- All members of the Academic Symposium for their helpful feedback on earlier drafts of chapters
- Guy Faulkner (Loughborough University) for his editorial work.

1 The case for exercise in the promotion of mental health and psychological well-being

Kenneth R. Fox, Stephen H. Boutcher, Guy E. Faulkner and Stuart J.H. Biddle

Exercise and community health

There is now a worldwide acceptance among medical authorities that physical activity is an important element of healthy living (WHO, 1995). Syntheses of studies (Berlin & Colditz, 1990; Powell, Thompson, Caspersen, & Kendrick, 1987) have indicated that sedentary lifestyles carry at least twice the risk of serious disease and premature death. This is on a par with the relative risk of hypertension and hyperlipidemia and not far behind smoking and has led to suggestions that inactivity should be considered the fourth primary risk factor for coronary heart disease and stroke. Sedentary living is also the most prevalent risk factor with around 40% of the middle-aged and elderly population taking part in infrequent or no moderate to vigorous physical activity (Sports Council/HEA, 1992).

The public burden of inactivity is therefore high and activity promotion could provide a cost-effective strategy for public health improvement (Morris, 1994). In the US it has been estimated that inactivity results in one third of all deaths from CHD, colon cancer and diabetes (Powell & Blair, 1994). The strength of the evidence has led to a US Surgeon General's Report entitled *Physical Activity and Health* (1996) calling for nationally driven initiatives to promote physical activity. In the UK, the Health of the Nation Task Force on Physical Activity produced the consultation paper *More people, more active, more often* (Department of Health, 1994b). Also, the Health Education Authority expert consensus conference was held to determine the recommended amount of activity for health and targets for physical activity promotion (Killoran, Fentem, & Caspersen, 1994). Policy documents and agendas for physical activity promotion were also produced by organisations such as the National Forum for Coronary Heart Disease Prevention (1995).

Since that time, substantial amounts of public funds have been provided through the Health Education Authority to deliver *Active for Life*, a public media and community support campaign to promote physical activity. This has finished now and in its latter phases had a more specific focus on groups such as young people, women, and ethnic minorities. For instance, a consensus conference, recommendations document and book summarising existing literature (Biddle, Sallis, & Cavill, 1998) has been produced concerning young people and physical activity. A similar campaign has been launched by the Health Education Board for Scotland.

This rapid boom in interest in the role of physical activity in health has not only taken place at the central policy-making level. There have also been significant initiatives at grass roots level since the early 1980s. For example, many schools and local education authorities have been attempting to promote children's physical activity through a greater emphasis on health in the curriculum and through schemes to promote walking and cycling to school. Leisure services have teamed up with primary health care units to develop exercise prescription schemes. These mushroomed in the 1990s (see Fox, Biddle, Edmunds, Bowler, & Killoran, 1997) largely in the absence of rigorous evaluation but have thrived because of a general belief in their efficacy and value by patients and personnel. In contrast, the use of exercise in secondary care has been slow and mainly restricted to cardiac rehabilitation. Similarly, commerce and industry in Britain have not mirrored the tremendous growth in corporate wellness programmes seen in the United States.

In summary, developments in the use of exercise as a medium for health promotion have been built on increasingly sound evidence from epidemiological and well-controlled training studies (see HEA, 1995; and Pate et al., 1995, for summaries) as well as a grass roots interest among various groups of professionals. It is clear that the case has been constructed around the impact of exercise on reducing the risk of *physical* health problems such as CHD, some cancers, obesity, diabetes, and to a lesser extent musculo-skeletal problems such as low back pain and osteoporosis. To date, much less attention has been paid to the contribution of exercise to the prevention and treatment of the increasingly burgeoning problem of *mental* disorders, illnesses, and general mental malaise.

The mental health problem

The 1995 Health Survey for England showed that 20% of women and 14% of men may have at some time suffered mental illness. It has been estimated that one in seven adults in the UK will suffer some form of psychiatric morbidity at some point in their lifespan. Even among children it has been estimated that up to 20% will suffer mild and 7–10% moderate to severe mental health problems that hinder normal development (Kurtz, 1992) and there is evidence of a worsening trend, particularly in socially disadvantaged populations (Rutter & Smith, 1995).

The most prevalent psychiatric disorder is depression, affecting 5–10% of the population of most developed countries (Weismann & Klerman, 1992), with some estimates suggesting that 20% of the population will be affected by 'depressive disorders' at one time in their lives (Richards, Musser, & Gerson, 1999). It is more common in the older middle-aged and elderly populations with the result that 20% of consultees in primary care in Britain have recognisable degrees of symptomology (Paykel & Priest, 1992). In addition, more than half with mental health problems seek help from their GP yet GPs have no specialised training in this area (Richards et al., 1999). Treatment is generally through serotonin-enhancing pharmaceuticals. Less common is the use of psychotherapy, sometimes incorporating stress management techniques and occasionally exercise.

Such prevalance is not without great cost. The Department of Health (1996) estimated that in 1992–93, 17% of expenditure in the health services that amounted to more than £5 billion was spent on mental illness and disorders. In 1992, the Office of Health Economics estimated costs of treating depression at £333 million, which included £55 million for drugs, £250 million for hospitalisation, and £28 million for primary care consultations. Wider cost implications were estimated at £6 billion when social services provision, sickness and invalidity benefits, and loss of productivity were included. Cooper and Cartwright (1996) estimated that half of all absenteeism due to sickness is stress related. The Department of Health (1996) estimated that 15% and 26% of days of certified incapacity in men and women respectively were due to mental disorders.

Problems with mental health are also associated with suicide ideation, suicide attempts, and successful suicides, contributing to human distress and further service costs. There are also increasing signs that less than optimal mental well-being is common in the population. The impact of emotional distress, low self-esteem, poor body image, chronic anxiety and stress that is not diagnosed as a clinical disorder has not been possible to estimate. However, it adds to the demands of primary care and social services, is linked to drug abuse problems, alcoholism and increased absenteeism from work. Furthermore, mental well-being is a critical element of quality of life.

Recently, the Department of Health acknowledged the problems of increasing mental illness and poor mental well-being in their White Paper *Saving Lives: Our Healthier Nation* (1999) and wrote 'The national strategy must reflect more than just the absence of physical disease and be a basis for efforts which acknowledge a more rounded idea of good health'. The promotion of mental health has been included as one of four health targets in the proposed national health contract so that regional and local strategies will be developed to address the problem. As part of this contract, new primary care groups consisting of multi-professional teams are being established. In promoting mental health, these groups will have to consider a broader range of approaches that can be incorporated within local health improvement programmes.

Physical activity and the promotion of psychological well-being

Although it is clear that the case for exercise in reducing physical illness is well established, there has also been a growing interest in the contribution of exercise to the alleviation of the problems of mental illness. Specifically, there has been increasing consideration of the role of exercise as

- a therapy for the treatment of mental illness and disorders;
- a means of coping and managing mental illness;
- a means of improving quality of life for the mentally ill; and
- a means of preventing the onset of mental health problems.

In addition, there is a growing recognition of a widespread mental malaise in the general public that is expressed as mild depression, low self-esteem, high stress and anxiety and poor coping. This has been accompanied by institutional and cultural reductions in physical activity levels and it has been suggested that increases in exercise participation may have a substantial impact on the incidence of sub-clinical levels of mental ill health among the general public. This has accompanied a greater focus, at the demand of the research councils and National Health Service funding bodies, on the assessment of quality of life and related constructs such as life satisfaction and mental well-being.

These concerns have been reflected in an increasing interest in research and policy concerning exercise and mental health. In 1987 the US National Institute of Mental Health consensus workshop statements regarding the contribution of exercise to mental health were published in a book by Morgan and Goldston (1987). This comprehensive summary of the literature has since been followed and updated by others such as Biddle and Mutrie (1991), Leith (1994) and more recently Morgan (1997), and several published narrative and meta-analytical reviews. There have also been further consensus conferences which have, at least in part, addressed the mental benefits of exercise, the most notable of these being the 'Physical activity, health and well-being' conference held in Quebec in 1995 (see Biddle, 1995; Blair & Hardman, 1995) and the San Diego conference on adolescence and physical activity (see Sallis & Patrick, 1994). Additionally, in a review of the treatment of depression in primary care services, the Centre for Health Economics (Freemantle et al., 1993) recommended the funding of research into the effectiveness of non-drug therapies, particularly for those who do not respond well to medication.

Accordingly, either in terms of clinical or non-clinical conditions, exercise may offer substantial potential alone or as an adjunct in improving the mental well-being of many individuals. There are five important benefits that are associated with the potential use of exercise in such a role. First, exercise is cheap. Second, exercise carries negligible deleterious side-effects. Third, exercise can be self-sustaining in that it can be maintained by the individual once the basic skills have been learnt (Martinsen, 1993). Fourth, given that many common non-drug treatments, such as cognitive behavioural therapy, can be expensive and often in short supply (Mutrie, this book), there is much to commend other strategies. The need for treatment in psychiatry can never be fully met by health professionals. Promoting exercise could reach a broader audience of individuals who cannot access therapy or would prefer not to use medication. Greater time and effort could also be targeted at more acute and complex cases by mental health services. Finally, given the inherent physical benefits, exercise should be promoted regardless of any impact on mental health. In particular, the physical health needs of psychiatric clients are poorly served (McCarrick, Manderscheid, Bertolucci, Goldman, & Tessler (1986). These benefits have important implications for the quality of life of many individuals as well as the financial burden imposed on the NHS by mental ill health.

In some countries, the evidence for exercise and mental health has already been accepted and formalised into delivery systems. In Belgium, for instance, psychomotor therapy to treat depression and anxiety is now established in the health system. Unfortunately, in the UK it remains unusual for mental health services to use exercise as a therapy or preventive medium. Furthermore, the case for exercise and its potential to improve the general mental well-being of the population and prevent mental illness has either not been widely publicised or seen as a priority by health services, a situation paralleled in the US, where exercise is also not a more popular treatment option despite the supportive evidence (Tkachuk & Martin, 1999). One reason for this lack of recognition may be the ineffective diffusion of such research to other health professionals, which this book seeks to rectify.

Purposes of this book

Somerset Health Authority (SHA) has commissioned this series of papers. SHA through its appointed officers and the Somerset Physical Activity Group are already committed to physical activity promotion. Notably they have developed the first recognition/accreditation and scientific advisory system for exercise prescription in the UK. SHA has also seen the potential for exercise in the promotion of mental as well as physical health and already has promotion and research projects underway. They saw a need to update and summarise existing evidence for the case of exercise and mental health enhancement. This is particularly timely in the light of the recent Department of Health White Paper (DoH, 1999) that has targeted mental health as one of four key health outcomes in the national health contract. In relation to mental health, exercise is specifically suggested as a strategy that 'people' can participate in for improving mental health.

The purpose of these chapters is therefore to provide an updated overview of the case for exercise and the promotion of psychological well-being. Leading researchers have been recruited to produce chapters on the effects of exercise on anxiety and stress, depression, mood and affect, self-perceptions including self-esteem, cognitive performance and also the negative effects of exercise on psychological well-being. Attention has been directed at (a) treating mental illness and disorders, and (b) enhancing psychological well-being in the general public. Priority has been given to evidence from randomised controlled trials, large scale epidemiological studies, and meta-analytic reviews. Authors have been asked to summarise their findings in tables and closing sections featuring 'what we know' and 'what we need to know' statements. A closing chapter draws together key findings and implications for further research and practice.

Throughout, attention has been paid to the relevance of findings to health service commissioners and providers and every effort has been made to present the information in familiar terminology. The Consensus statements that were adapted from this work have been supported by professional and governing bodies such as the BPS (British Psychology Society), BASES (British Association of Sport and Exercise Sciences) and Exercise England. The strong evidence base exists! It is hoped that this resource will be valuable for practitioners in 'making the case' for physical activity and mental health at a local and national level.

In closing, it is important to acknowledge a range of other conditions for which exercise has been suggested as a therapeutic possibility and that are not covered fully in this book. For example, exercise has been suggested as an adjunctive therapy for schizophrenia (see Faulkner & Biddle, 1999), developmental disorders (see Gabler-Halle, Halle & Chung, 1993), somatoform disorders (see Tkachuk & Martin, 1999), substance abuse disorders such as alcohol dependence and drug addiction (see Mutrie, 1997) and smoking cessation (see Ussher, Taylor, West & McEwen, in press). Additionally, promising research on the effects of exercise on sleep (see Youngstedt, O'Connor, & Dishman, 1997) is emerging. These areas have been given limited treatment here largely because they are emergent areas of research or an insufficient amount of research has been conducted to warrant reliable conclusions. However, they point to the exciting and as yet untapped potential exercise may offer within the growing field of mental health promotion.

Definitions

Throughout the papers, the following definitions apply.

Affect (emotion): specific feeling states generated in reaction to certain events or appraisals.

Anorexia nervosa: a psychological disorder characterised by excessive weight loss through dieting and over-exercising motivated by a false perception of fatness.

Anxiety: an emotional state, typified by a cognitive component (e.g. worry, self-doubt and apprehension) and a somatic component (e.g. heightened awareness of physiological responses such a heart rate, sweaty palms and tension). Anxiety can also be described as a relatively stable disposition to be anxious across multiple situations and the term used is trait anxiety.

Bulimia: an eating disorder in which binge eating is followed by self-induced vomiting or purging.

Clinically defined depression: a level of depression that has been diagnosed with standard instruments (e.g. above 16 on the Beck Depression Inventory) and/or clinical interviews (e.g. satisfying criteria from the Diagnostic and Statistical Manual of Mental Disorders IV).

Commitment to exercise: the degree of dedication or devotion to an adopted exercise behaviour.

Deprivation sensations: (see *withdrawal symptoms*).

Exercise: a subset of physical activity that is volitional, planned, structured, repetitive and aimed at improvement or maintenance of an aspect of fitness or health.

Exercise addiction: a condition in which exercise becomes the most important component of one's life; exercise is performed even when other commitments are more important or against medical advice; a process that has negative consequences on both the individual and her/his environment including career and personal relationships (see also *exercise dependence* and *obligatory exercising*).

Exercise dependence: a behavioural process in which the need for exercising is so strong that it controls the individual's life with several identifiable symptoms such as salience, euphoria, exercise tolerance, withdrawal symptoms, conflict, relapse, loss of control over life activities and exercise behaviour, identifiable negative consequences, risk of self-injury, social withdrawal, lack of compromise, and denial but awareness of the problem (see also *exercise addiction* and *obligatory exercising*).

Exercise deprivation: the forced need to abstain from exercising due to other commitments or injury that often results in negative psychological and/or physical symptoms (see also *withdrawal symptoms*).

Mood: the global set of affective states we experience on a day-to-day basis.

Negative addiction: a term used to contrast *positive addiction* and it refers to the harmful effects of socially endorsed behaviours, such as exercise or work, when they are performed in a compulsive manner.

Obligatory exercising: used as a synonym to *exercise addiction* and *exercise dependence*; the individual loses control over exercise whilst the latter takes control over the individual (see also *exercise addiction* and *exercise dependence*).

Physical activity: an umbrella term describing any bodily movement produced by the skeletal muscles resulting in energy expenditure.

Physical fitness: a multidimensional indicator of several functional capacities such as cardiovascular endurance, muscular strength, or mobility, which in varying degrees are a result of genetics and stage in the lifespan, as well as physical activity levels.

Positive addiction: often confounded with *commitment to exercise*, the term refers to compulsion with a socially accepted behaviour such as exercise or work in contrast to socially condemned behaviours such as alcohol or drug abuse (see also *commitment to exercise)*.

Primary exercise dependence: a behavioural process in which exercise performed in a compulsive manner represents an end in itself to achieve something positive such as euphoria and/or to avoid something negative such as withdrawal symptoms (see also *exercise dependence* and *secondary exercise dependence* and *withdrawal symptoms*).

Psychological dysfunction: undesirable state of mental well-being that has adverse effect(s) on the individual's normal daily functioning.

Secondary exercise dependence: a behavioural process in which exercise performed in a compulsive manner represents a means to achieve another objective such as weight loss (see also *exercise dependence* and *primary exercise dependence*).

Self-esteem or *self-worth*: the awareness of good possessed by the self and represents how positive individuals feel about themselves in general.

Self-perception: an umbrella term that denotes all types of self-referring statements about the self ranging from those that have specific content to those that express general feelings.

Social physique anxiety: anxiety or over-concern about one's physical appearance in situations in which comparison (in physical appearance) with others is inevitable.

Sport: physical activity that involves structured competitive situations governed by rules. In mainland Europe, the term 'sport' is often used in the wider context to include all exercise and leisure-time physical activity.

Stress: has been defined in many ways but an interactional perspective is assumed within this book. As a result of appraisal of perceived capabilities and demands associated with sources of stress (stressors) stress manifests itself in emotional states, and physiological, psychological and behavioural responses.

Withdrawal symptoms: psychological and physical symptoms one experiences when a planned exercise session is missed; they are more severe in people addicted to exercise and may surface even after missing a single bout of planned exercise (see also *exercise deprivation*).

2 Physical activity, anxiety, and stress

Adrian H. Taylor

Stress-related disorders have been widely recognised. The Department of Health (DoH) estimated that in 1994 80 million working days were lost due to anxiety and depression, at a cost of £5.3 billion. In addition, NHS expenditure on the treatment of anxiety and depression has been estimated at over £1 billion. Stress has been linked to all current Department of Health (Our Healthier Nation) priority areas including cancer, coronary heart disease/stroke, accidents, and mental health/suicide (DoH, 1999).

A growing body of literature has focused on the relationship between physical activity (PA), stress and anxiety (Landers & Petruzzello, 1994), and yet in a recent review of the effectiveness of mental health promotion interventions, only three studies were identified that had focused on the use of exercise (Tilford, Delaney, & Vegells, 1997). The notion that physical fitness somehow protects people from the stress of daily life is not a new one. For example, Kobasa, Maddi and Pucetti (1982) reported that executive businessmen, operating in a high stress environment, who both participated in an aerobic exercise programme and had a 'hardy' personality had a reduced frequency of illness. The purpose of this review, therefore, is to examine the evidence for using exercise for the prevention and treatment of anxiety disorders.

The review will begin with definitions of stress, anxiety and PA and a brief introduction to their interrelationships. The chapter will then focus on the evidence for these relationships from, firstly, a synthesis of qualitative and quantitative reviews, and then from a systematic review of recent research studies. This will be followed by statements concerning 'what we know' and 'what we need to know', and how our existing knowledge may influence future interventions and professional practice among those seeking to enhance mental health.

Definitions of stress, anxiety and physical activity

Sources of stress (stressors) in our daily lives are rarely just objective, such as extreme heat or noise. The interactional perspective on stress suggests that stress arises from an imbalance between our perceived capabilities and perceived situational demands (Cox, 1985). Stress manifests itself in emotional states, as well as physiological, psychological and behavioural responses. The emotional state, anxiety, reflects negative cognitive appraisal, typified by worry, self-doubt and apprehension (i.e. cognitive anxiety). State (situational) anxiety may also be elevated due to increased awareness of physiological responses to stress (i.e. somatic anxiety). As an example, phobic anxiety may only occur in response to specific circumstances in which a person perceives a lack of control or uncertainty. An individual may also have a tendency to become anxious across many situations and this predisposition has been termed trait anxiety. Both state and trait anxiety, because they are largely cognitive phenomena, have usually been assessed using questionnaires. However, anxiety has also been inferred from measures of physiological arousal (e.g. blood pressure).

For the purposes of this review, physical activity is defined as gross movement of sufficient intensity and duration to potentially increase aerobic or anaerobic capacity. Forms of movement such as those involved in yoga, t'ai chi and stretching exercises are not included. However, the review will consider the effects of such movement forms on anxiety when included in a study as a comparison treatment intervention.

The role of physical activity in anxiety prevention and treatment

The main concern in the prevention and treatment of anxiety is that performance in a wide range of daily tasks may suffer (e.g. examination failure; serious accidents), and that enduring anxiety may lead to chronic health problems, such as fear of social interaction or even suicide. This review will focus mostly on the effects of physical activity on self-reported anxiety, with reference to some physiological measures where understanding of underlying processes is enhanced. Typically, the chronic effects of exercise training (over weeks to months) on trait anxiety have been examined. One proposed mechanism for such effects is from the accumulated doses of single exercise sessions. Acute exercise studies have therefore focused on changes in anxiety from pre to post single exercise sessions. Both chronic and acute exercise studies have employed research designs to determine the specific effects of exercise by comparing changes in anxiety with either control groups or alternative treatment groups.

In a related area of research, the effects of exercise on psychophysiological reactivity to stress have also been examined. The main questions have been: (1) Does fitness level influence reactivity to stress? (2) Does fitness training (chronic exercise) reduce reactivity to stress? (3) Does a single (acute) session of exercise reduce reactivity to stress? Most studies have used laboratory simulation of stress (e.g. cognitive tasks performed under pressure) to answer these questions. The main implication of this work is that regular exercise may attenuate the response to daily stressors

(Selye, 1956) which for the most part require no such physiological reactivity since the coping response rarely requires a fight or flight. Prolonged inappropriate response to stressors may result in cardiovascular, metabolic and immunological changes linked to chronic health problems such as hypertension, diabetes mellitus and other diseases of maladaptation (Selye, 1956).

Review of reviews

The PA, stress and anxiety literature has advanced to the point where there are reviews of reviews (Landers & Petruzzello, 1994; Gauvin & Spence, 1996). The two papers cited have reviewed 29 and 57 reviews, respectively, revealing great variability in completeness. For the purposes of the present chapter, computerised search techniques (see later) and cross-checking in recent research papers were conducted. Reviews (articles and book chapters) were classified as qualitative (without meta-analysis) or quantitative (with meta-analysis). The findings from the latter are shown in Table 2.1.

Strength of exercise effects from meta-analyses

Meta-analyses have become an increasingly acceptable way to provide a summary of both the strength of relationships between variables of interest and also to identify the key moderator variables that might influence the strength of such relationships (e.g. gender differences). As a guideline, effect sizes (ES), usually determined through the calculation of differences between an exercise and control group or from pre- to post-exercise intervention, of up to 0.39, 0.40–0.69, and above 0.69, are generally described as reflecting a small, moderate and large effect, respectively (Thomas & Nelson, 1996).

The reviews shown in Table 2.1 indicate that exercise has a low to moderate anxiety-reducing effect across different populations and that there are some important moderator variables. While some original research studies have been reviewed in more than one of the reviews in Table 2.1, each one offers a distinct focus.

Calfas and Taylor (1994) identified only 11 studies concerned with young people that prevented further identification of moderator variables in the meta-analysis. The anxiety-reducing effect of exercise was minimal, but only four studies involved a control group and a further four had a poor conceptual basis for inclusion in the review.

In contrast, Long and Van Stavel (1995) included 40 studies involving healthy adults (those over 18 years). There was a moderate anxiety-reducing effect (ES = 0.45) among exercise groups engaged in activity with a dosage sufficient to increase aerobic fitness. This effect was slightly reduced (ES = 0.36) when contrasting change with other non-aerobic exercise groups. The effects seemed to be stronger for those reporting greater stress and among adults rather than college students. No other moderators were identified.

McDonald and Hodgdon (1991) limited their review to 22 studies that demonstrated aerobic fitness gain. Interestingly, the ES for reduction in trait anxiety was lower (ES = 0.25) than the previous review. Anxiety-reducing effects were only apparent for males and young/middle-aged participants.

Kugler, Seelbach and Kruskemper (1994) also restricted their review to studies in which the exercise was of sufficient dosage to increase fitness, but only among cardiac rehabilitation patients ($n = 13$ studies). The overall ES was again small (0.31) with no identified moderator variables.

Petruzzello, Landers, Hatfield, Kubitz and Salazar (1991) provided the most comprehensive meta-analysis, with over 100 studies examining the effects of both acute and chronic exercise on psychological self-report measures and psychophysiological indices of stress. The overall ES ranged from low (0.24) to moderate/high (0.65), with greater effects on self-report measures from chronic exercise and greater effects on psychophysiological measures from acute exercise. A number of moderator variables were identified which inform us of the most likely subject, exercise, and methodological characteristics that influence the strength of relationships.

For self-report measures, chronic exercise reduced trait anxiety more when: exercise sessions lasted 21–30, or more than 40, minutes (in comparison to < 21); the training period was more than 15 weeks (in comparison to < 10). Studies involving random or matched assignment showed the greatest anxiety-reducing effects. In terms of acute effects, state anxiety was reduced more when the exercise was aerobic and it lasted 21–30 minutes (in comparison to < 21); and the ES was determined from within-subject comparison from pre- to post-exercise as opposed to changes from pre- to post-exercise being compared with other anxiety-reducing treatments.

For psychophysiological measures combining chronic and acute exercise effects, there were more likely to be reductions in skin conductivity, electromyography (EMG), and central nervous system (CNS) measures when exercise intensity was 40–59% of heart rate max/VO_2max (compared to 70–79%); exercise duration was less than 31 minutes; participants were 18–30 years of age; there was no random assignment to exercise; and a within-subject, pre- to post-exercise design was used.

In the most notable review on the psychophysiological reactivity to stress, Crews and Landers (1987) conducted a meta-analysis involving 34 studies. The findings generally indicated reduced reactivity to stressors (in terms of heart rate, systolic and diastolic blood pressure, skin conductivity, muscle tension and self-reported psychological symptoms), or faster recovery following a stressor, for those who were fitter or improved their fitness with training, or had just undertaken a single exercise session, compared with a baseline measure or a control group.

Table 2.1 Summary of key meta-analytic review papers

Author	No. of studies	Number of effect sizes	Delimitations of review	Overall ES	Key moderators
Calfas & Taylor, 1994	10 non-clinical 1 clinical	Not given	Various searches & cross-checking, 11–21 year olds	0.15	Insufficient studies so did qualitative review
Crews & Landers, 1987	34	92 from 1,449 participants	Reactivity to stressors clearly stated	0.48	No follow-up analysis due to heterogeneity in ES. But larger ES for published, chronic, random assigned studies
Kugler et al., 1994	13	Not given	Only studies designed to improve fitness in post MI/angina/cardiac patients No combined interventions	0.31	None (only considered duration of training and time for follow-up). Smaller n related to greater ES
Long & Van Stavel, 1995	40	76.	1975–93 Only studies with Type = gross, freq. = 2/3 p.w. Duration = 20 mins, > 6wks Only >18 yrs, healthy No x-sectional designs	w. gp = 0.45 b. gp = 0.36	Low-stressed = 0.28 v High-stressed = 0.51 Student = 0.16 v Adult = 0.53 No effect of gender, anxiety measure, training length or freq. of exercise (p.w.), study drop-out, leader background, aerobic v non-aerobic, random assignment, publication type, follow-up

Table 2.1 (continued)

Author	No. of studies	Number of effect sizes	Delimitations of review	Overall E.S.	Key moderators
McDonald & Hodgdon, 1991	22 12 A state 17 A trait 3 TMAS	Not given	1973–89 Only studies with fitness gain – ACSM aerobic guidelines – A state/trait & TMAS	A state = 0.28 (0.31m/0.16f) A trait = 0.25 (0.28m/0.07f)	No effect for females No effect for older (cf. young & middle age) Design not important (pre-exp. had smaller ES)
Petruzzello et al., 1991	104	408 from 3,048 participants	Fully reported, up to 1989	A state = 0.24	Aerobic > non-aerobic Within 5s = 0.47 and cardiac rehab = 0.48
				A trait = 0.54	<21mins = –0.12, > 20min = 0.41 No effect for 18–30 yr olds < 10 wks = 0.16, > 10 wks= 0.36 to 0.63 random > intact groups
				phys. = 0.56 (acute = 0.65) (chronic = 0.40)	GSR/EMG/CNS> SBP/DBP/HR 40–59% > 70–79% <31 mins = 0.77, > 30 mins = 0.29 random < intact or single gp repeated 18–30 > 45 yrs+

Notes:

Per week (p.w.); state anxiety (A state); trait anxiety (A trait); Taylor Manifest Anxiety Scale (TMAS: Taylor, 1953); galvanic skin response (GSR); electromyography (EMG); central nervous system (CNS); systolic blood pressure (SBP); diastolic blood pressure (DBP); heart rate (HR); within-group comparison (w. gp); between-group comparison (b. gp); male (m); female (f); myocardial infarction (MI); American College of Sports Medicine (ACSM); physiological (phys.); effect size (ES); pre-experimental design (pre-exp.).

Qualitative reviews

There have been many qualitative (narrative) reviews, varying in scope and rigour. Perhaps one of the most comprehensive involved 56 studies concerned with chronic exercise and self-reported anxiety (Leith, 1994; also see Leith & Taylor, 1990). Overall, 73% of the studies reported anxiety-reducing effects. Leith suggested that the only exercise characteristic to influence the outcome was duration. Chronic exercise lasting nine or more weeks fairly consistently led to greater reductions in trait anxiety.

Criteria for selecting original sources for the present review

The present review involved a systematic on-line computer search of Medline, CINAHL, Psychinfo, and Sport Discus. The following key words were used in the searches: exercise, physical activity, physical fitness, anxiety, and psychological stress. Review and original research literature was also checked for additional references. Sources were limited to full refereed journal articles, this excluding abstracts, conference proceedings, book chapters, and dissertations. Because the most comprehensive review of the field (Petruzzello et al., 1991) included sources up to 1989, a decision was made to limit the search to articles appearing from 1989 onwards. No sources were excluded on the basis of research design. The review also includes papers which have considered the effects of exercise on specific sub-domains of anxiety [e.g. test anxiety, treadmill and dyspnea anxiety among Coronary Obstructive Pulmonary Disease (COPD) patients, self-presentational anxiety, such as physical appearance anxiety and social physique anxiety (Leary, 1992)]. Previous reviews have not included these but reducing such types of anxiety may have important consequences on future behaviour and well-being.

Limitations of the search

Previous reviews have included studies using the anxiety/tension scale from the Profile of Mood States (POMS) questionnaire. An editorial decision, on behalf of the overall project, was made to include these studies in the chapter on exercise and mood (Biddle, this volume). For the most part, only studies that included a standardised, readily available anxiety measure were reviewed.

Studies involving multifaceted interventions were excluded. For example, a number of cardiac rehabilitation programmes included exercise, stress management and cognitive-behavioural counselling. While such programmes are common they also make interpretation of mental health changes impossible to attribute to exercise alone.

Studies that focused on exercise in a form not normally prescribed for the general population were also excluded. For example, some studies focused on changes in competitive state anxiety from before to after a sports competition, or responses to maximal exercise testing.

This review will therefore consider whether literature from 1989 to the present has confirmed and clarified our understanding of:

1 The anxiety-reducing effects of chronic physical activity.
2 The anxiety-reducing effects of acute physical activity.
3 The effects of chronic and acute physical activity on reactivity to stress.

The effects of chronic exercise

Cross-sectional studies

The 11 studies identified (Aldana, Sutton, Jacobson, & Quirk, 1996; Brandon & Loftin, 1991; Frederick & Morrison, 1996; King & Cotes, 1989; Lobstein, Ismail, & Rasmussen, 1989; Martinsen, Strand, Paulsson, & Kaggestad, 1989; Muraki, Maehara, Ishii, Ajimoto, & Kikuchi, 1993; Nouri & Beer, 1989; Stephens, 1988; Stewart et al., 1994; Szabo, Brown, Gauvin, & Seraganian, 1993) vary considerably in terms of quality. A typical research design has involved the comparison of anxiety levels between less and more active, or less and more fit, using a wide range of activity measures or fitness tests. Clearly, such a pre-experimental design may offer little in the way of causal evidence for the anxiety-reducing effects of exercise, in comparison with quasi and true experimental designs (Campbell & Stanley, 1963). Nevertheless, some large cross-sectional studies (e.g. Stephens, 1988) have provided good generalisability (if weak internal validity), or may offer an initial insight into stronger associations among subsets of the population not previously identified.

Summary of cross-sectional studies

The largest study (Aldana et al., 1996), of over 32,000 individuals enrolling in a health insurance screening programme, used the Strain Questionnaire (Lefebvre & Sanford, 1984). A self-report activity survey was used to determine typical energy expenditure levels which was then used to dichotomise participants into high and low active. The less active were twice as likely to report high stress levels. However, a causal relationship cannot be inferred. It may well be that less anxious individuals were attracted to physical activity and exercise, more than were anxious individuals. Also, studies that have contrasted high and low fit people are severely limited by the fact that fitness measures are partly genetic and partly behaviour-related. Only a few studies examined both activity levels and fitness measures.

Design of longitudinal studies

The 27 studies involving some form of exercise intervention over a period of time are summarised in Table 2.2. A typical design has involved one or more measures of anxiety at baseline, followed by a period of exercise over weeks or months, and one or more follow-up assessment(s) of anxiety. In order to control for a variety of alternative explanations for anxiety-reducing effects, a comparison has been made with a control group receiving either no intervention or a placebo group receiving an inactive intervention with equal contact time. Some studies have also contrasted the anxiety-reducing effects of exercise and other stress management interventions. All but five studies assessed fitness, using a variety of standardised testing protocol, at baseline and after the training period.

Findings from longitudinal studies

Nine (33%) of the studies in the present review reported no anxiety-reducing effects on one or more of the self-report measures administered. Two of these studies appeared to have inadequate power to detect anxiety reductions (see Kugler et al., 1994 for a discussion on sampling sizes in this field of research).

PARTICIPANT CHARACTERISTICS

Previous reviews have been critical of exercise scientists for using convenient samples of college students. Indeed, 32% of the 56 studies involving chronic exercise reviewed by Leith (1994) included college students. In the present review only 15% involved college students, demonstrating a new focus on older populations. Over 25% of the studies included participants over 60 years of age. Unfortunately, there has been no increase in the concern for under 18-year-olds, with only one study identified since 1988 (Norris, Carroll, & Cochrane, 1992). A variety of unhealthy groups were studied, including four with cardiovascular disease, one with cancer, one with COPD, and six with mild to severe mental disorders. Almost all the studies involved initially inactive individuals. There was no difference in the number of males and females in the studies.

RESEARCH DESIGN

There appears to have been an increase in the proportion of studies that have employed random assignment. The present review revealed 67% compared with about 40% using random assignment in the reviews by Petruzzello et al. (1991) and Leith (1994). Of the nine studies that showed no anxiety-reducing effect, one involved an intact group comparison and the other eight involved random assignment. This suggests that there is

Table 2.2 Longitudinal relationship between physical activity and anxiety

Author(s)	Participants	Design	Comparison group	Duration	Type of exercise	Fitness change (Δ)	Anxiety measure	Outcome/ comments
Altchiller & Motta, 1994	38f/5m 32yrs (20–67)	Pre/post – Post/post r.a. to 2 grps	1. Aerobic ex. (AE) 2. Non-aerobic (NAE) (calisthenics)	8 wks	70–85% (AE only) 3 × p.w.	N/A	TAI	Only AE ↓ TAI (ES = -0.60) Limitations: AE grp initially less anxious Only 48% adherence to AE
Bartlewski, Van Raalte, & Brewer, 1996	43f college	Pre-post 2 intact grps	1. Aerobic ex. (AE) 2. Psychology class (C)	10 wks	High impact aerobics class	N/A	SPAS	AE ↓ SPAS (ES = 0.54 cf. control = -0.10)
Blumenthal et al., 1991	50m/51f 67yrs (60–83) inactive, healthy	Pre-post r.a. to 3 grps	1. Aerobic ex. (AE) 2. Yoga (Y) 3. Wait-list control (C)	16 wks (3 gps) + 16 wks (gp 1) + 6 mth	1. 70% HR, 30 min aerobic, + 30 mins non-aerobic, 3 × p.w. 2. Yoga = 60 min, 2 × p.w.	Only AE grp at 16 wks	TAI	No ↓ TAI (for f or m)
Brown et al., 1995	69f/66m 53 yrs (40–69) inactive, healthy	Pre-post r.a. to 5 grps	1. Mod. int. walk (MW) 2. Low int. walk (LW) 3. (2) + relaxation (LWR) 4. t'ai chi (TC) 5. No ex. control grp	16 wks	1. 65–75% HR, 30–40 mins, 3 × p.w. 2. 45–55% HR, 40-50 mins, 3 × p.w. 3. As 2 with relaxation tape 4. 45 mins, 3 × p.w.	Only in MW & LW	TAI	No ↓ TAI (for any grp)
Carrieri-Kohlman et al., 1996	26f/25m 67 +/- 7yrs mod-severe COPD patients	Pre-post-post r.a. to 2 grps then both did home based ex. prog.	1. Aerobic ex. (AE) 2. Self efficacy enhancement (SE) + 1	5 wks + 8 wks	1. 12 sessions over 4–6 wks 70–85%, 20–30 mins 2. (1) + coaching (nurse-led + video) 3. Home walk, 70%, 20 mins, 4 × p.w.	AE & SE	SAI TRANX DA	AE & SE ↓ all measures (at 5 and 13 wks)

Table 2.2 (continued)

Author(s)	Participants	Design	Comparison group	Duration	Type of exercise	Fitness change (Δ)	Anxiety measure	Outcome/comments
Cramer, Nieman, & Lee, 1991	50f 34 yrs (20–45), inactive, healthy	Pre-during-post r.a. to 2 grps	1. Walking 2. No ex. control	15 wks	Walking = 60% HR, 45 mins, 5 × p.w. Supervised on outdoor route	Only Ex. grp	SAI	Walking ↓ SAI (at 6 wks only) Δ SAI not related to Δ fitness
Dixhoorn et al., 1990	147m/9f 56 yrs (36–76) MI patients	Pre-post r.a. to 2 grps	1. Aerobic ex. (AE) 2. Aerobic ex. + therapy	5 wks (AET)	AE = 70% peak HR, 30 mins, 7 × p.w. cycle erg. AET = additional 60 mins p.d. of relaxation and breathing	Both grps ↑ 50%	TAI	No ↓ TAI (for either grp)
Fisher & Thompson, 1994	54f 23 yrs (17–45) low appearance evaluation	Pre-post r.a. to 3 grps	1. Control 2. Ex. therapy 3. Cog.-behav. therapy	6 wks	2. Aerobic and weight – 1 supervised and 2 home sessions p.w. 3. 6 × 1 hr sessions on stress, relaxation, image etc.	N/A	PASTAS	Both therapy grps ↓ PASTAS
Jambor et al., 1994	30 29 yrs (20–45) inactive	Pre-post 2 non-equivalent grps	Ex. v quiet rest	8 wks	60–90%, 15–45 mins, 3 × p.w. aqua running program	Ex. Grp ↑	Mod. CSAI-2	Ex. & rest ↓ cognitive and somatic anx.
King et al., 1993	357 m, f 57 yrs (50–65) inactive, healthy	Pre-post r.a. to 4 grps	1. No ex. control 2. Vig. group ex. 3. Vig. home ex. 4. Mod. home ex.	12 mths	Vigorous ex. = 73–88%, aerobic, 3 × p.w. Moderate ex. = 60–73%, 30 mins, 5 × p.w. Group ex. = at an ex. centre	Gains 2, 3, & 4	TMAS PSS	2, 3, & 4 ↓ TMAS and PSS Higher adherence – more ↓ TMAS and PSS Δ anxiety not related to Δ fitness or body wt. Home based gp. did ↑ ex.

Study	Sample	Design	Conditions	Duration	Exercise protocol	Effect	Measure	Findings
Kugler et al., 1990	35m 32–66 yrs cardiac rehab.	Pre-post r.a. to 4 grps (from wks 7–14 post MI)	1. Ex. advice control 2. Hospital based 3. Hospital + home cycle 4. Hospital + home walk	8 wks	2. 75%, 20 mins, 3 × p.w., cycle erg. 3.1 (hospital) + 2 (home) p.w., cycle 4. 1 (hospital) + 2 (home) p.w., cycle + walk	Gains 2, 3, & 4	TMAS	3 & 4 ↓ TMAS but small n
Martinsen, Hoffart, & Solberg, 1989	70 m, f 39 yrs anx. patients	Pre-post r.a. to 2 grps	1. Aerobic ex. (AE) 2. Non-aerobic ex. (NAE)	8 wks	1. 70%, 60 mins, 3 × p.w., walk/jog 2. Strength & flexibilty exercises plus rehabilitation	Only AE grp	CPRS PARS ACS	AE and NAE ↓ anxiety Δ fitness *not* related to Δ anx.
Martinsen, Sandvik & Kolbjørnsrud 1989	89 m, f 40 +/-7 yrs psych. in-patients sedentary	Pre-post-post	None	8 wks + 12 mths	50–70%, 60 mins daily, ski, cycle, walk, jog, aerobics + normal treatment	yes	SRT	↓ anxiety (particularly alcohol abusers and depressed) after 8 wks and 12 mths 65% adherence > greater ↓ anxiety
McAuley et al., 1995	58f,56m 55 yrs (45–64) inactive, healthy	Pre-post	None	20 wks	Brisk walking, 15–40 mins, 3 × p.w., supervised	N/A	SPAS	↓ SPAS – related to: ↓ hip circ. for females, ↑ initial outcome expectancy, ↑ self efficacy (walking), being male, but *not* adherence to ex. or age
Mock et al., 1997	46f 49 yrs (35–65) inactive, newly diagnosed, breast cancer	Pre-post alternately assigned to 2 grps	1. Walking (W) 2. No ex. control (C)	3 wks	1. Walking, 20–30 mins, 4/5 × p.w. self-directed with limited therapist contact	No Δ	VAS	Walking ↓ anxiety 86% ex. adherence
Norris, Carroll, & Cochrane, 1990	77m 20–50 healthy policemen	Pre-post Intact grps	1. Aerobic ex. (AE) 2. Non-aerobic ex. (NAE) 3. Control	10 wks	AE = 45 min, 3 × p.w., run, aerobic NAE = 30 min, 3 × p.w., weights	Only AE ↑	JSQ	AE ↓ job stress

Table 2.2 (continued)

Author(s)	Participants	Design	Comparison group	Duration	Type of exercise	Fitness change (Δ)	Anxiety measure	Outcome/ comments
Norris, Carroll, & Cochrane, 1992	30f, 30m 13–17 yrs, healthy	Pre-post 4 intact grps r.a. to 4 conditions	1. Vig. ex. 2. Mod. ex. 3. Flexibility (NAE) 4. Control	10 wks	1, 2, 3 = 25–30 mins, 2 × p.w., 70–75% (vig.), 50–60% (mod.)	Only vig. ex. ↑	MAACL-A PSS	Vig ex. ↓ MAACL-A Vig ex. ↓ strength of stress-anxiety relationship
Norvell & Belles, 1993	43 m 33 +/- 8yrs, healthy policemen	Pre-post r.a. to 2 grps (3rd group = ex. drop-outs)	Ex. v wait list controls	16 wks	Ex. = 12 station circuit, 20 mins, 3 × p.w.	ex. grp ↑	PSS SCL-90-A	Ex. ↓ anx. and PSS
Norvell, Martin, & Salamon, 1991	43 f 59 +/- 6yrs inactive, healthy	Pre-post r.a. to 3 grps	1. Aerobic ex. (AE) 2. Passive ex. (PE) 3. No ex. control	12 wks	AE = 70–85%, 30 mins, 2 × p.w. PE – on exercise tables	only AE grp ↑	PSS SCL-90-A	*No* ↓ Anx./PSS But ↑ in fitness related to ↓ PSS
O'Connor et al., 1995	19f, 13m college inactive, healthy	Pre-post r.a. to 2 grps	Ex. v no ex. control	8 wks	Ex. = 60–85%, 30 mins, 3 × p.w. aerobics	only Ex. grp ↑	SAI	*No* ↓ anx. (pre-post on maximal ex. test)
Pierce, Madden, et al., 1993	90 m,f 45 yrs (29–59) mild hypertensives	Pre-post r.a. to 3 grps	1. Aerobic ex. (AE) 2. Non-aerobic ex. (NAE) 3. Wait-list control	16 wks	AE = 70%, 35 mins, 3 × p.w. walk/jog NAE = circuit, weights, flexibility, 30 mins, 2/3 × p.w.	only AE grp ↑	SAI TAI	*No* ↓ SAI/TAI
Pistacchio, Weinberg & Jackson, 1989	301 m, f college healthy	Pre-post	Post hoc comparisons to identify determinants	10 wks	60%, 20–30 mins, 3 × p.w. aerobics class	N/A	TAI	*No* ↓ in anxiety overall but ↓ TAI predicted by initial ↑ ex. self efficacy & ↑ TAI
Sexton, Maere, & Dahl, 1989	28f/25m 38 yrs (19–60) neurotic inpatients	Pre-post-post r.a. to 2 grps	1. Walking (W) 2. Jogging (J)	8 wks + 6 mths	Both = 70%, 30 mins 3/4 × p.w., unsupervised after leaving hospital (4–5 weeks)	J ↑ at 8 wks J & W ↑ at 6 mths	BPRS, + SCL-90-A. + & STAI	W and J ↓ Anx. Δ fitness (pre-6 mths) related to 6 mths anxiety More drop-outs from jogging

Study	Sample	Design	Groups	Duration	Exercise details	Fitness	Scale	Results
Steptoe et al., 1989	33 m,f 37 +/- 9 yrs (20–60) anxious, overweight	Pre-post-post r.a. to 2 grps	1. Aerobic ex. (AE) 2. Non-aerobic ex. (NAE)	10 wks + 3 mths	AE = 60–65%, 20 mins, jog/walk NAE = weight training + flexibility Both did 1 supervised and 3 unsupervised p.w.	AE ↑	TAI POMS	At 10 wks – AE ↓ POMS (no ↓ in TAI) At 3 mths – AE ↓ POMS and TAI 70% adherence to supervised session
Topp, 1989	49 m,f college healthy	Pre-post 3 intact groups (classes)	1. Aerobic ex. (AE) 2. Relaxation (R) 3. Controls	7 wks	AE = running, 3 × p.w. R = 30 mins, 3 × p.w.	AE ↑	TAQ	AE and R ↓ test anxiety Δ fitness *not* related to Δ anx.
Veale et al., 1992	42f, 23m 35 yrs (19–58) depressed outpatients	Pre-post r.a. to 2 grps	1. No ex. controls 2. Aerobic ex. (AE)	12 wks	AE = running, 3 × p.w.	AE ↑	TAI	AE ↓ TAI Δ fitness related to Δ anx. 71% adherence to ex.
Worcester et al., 1993	173 m 54 +/- 2yrs <70 yrs post MI patients	Pre-post-post r.a. to 2 grps (over 3 yrs)	1. Low ex. (NAE) 2. High ex. (HE)	8 wks + 12 mths	LE = low intensity, calisthenics and intermittent 60 mins, 2 × p.w. HE = high intensity, 60 mins, 3 × p.w. aerobic ex.	Only HE ↑ at 8 wks	SAI	*No* ↓ SAI for LE or HE at 8 wks or 12 mths

Notes:

Per week (p.w.); Spielberger State & Trait Anxiety Inventory (SAI & TAI: Spielberger et al., 1983); Taylor Manifest Anxiety Scale (TMAS: Taylor, 1953); Physical Appearance State and Trait Anxiety Scale (PASTAS: Reed et al., 1991); Treadmill anxiety (TRANX); Dyspnea anxiety (DA); Profile of Mood States (POMS: McNair et al., 1971) – Tension/Anxiety scale only; Modified Competitive State Anxiety Inventory (Mod. CSAI-2: Martens et al, 1990); Visual Analogue Scale (VAS); Symptom Rating Test (SRT); Comprehensive Psychopathological Rating Scale (CPRS); Phobic Aviodance Rating Scale (PARS); Agoraphobic Cognitions Scale (ACS); Perceived Stress Scale (PSS); Social Physique Anxiety Scale (SPAS: Hart et al., 1989); Multiple Affect Adjective Check List – Anxiety (MAACL-A: Zuckerman & Lubin, 1965); Test Anxiety Questionnaire (TAQ: Sarason, 1975); Hopkins Symptom Check List (SCL-90: Derogatis, 1980); Job Stress Questionnaire (JSQ: Seamonds, 1982); Brief Psychiatric Rating scale (BPRS); within-group comparison (w.gp); between-group comparison (b.gp); male (m); female (f); myocardial infarction (MI); coronary obstructive pulmonary disease (COPD); effect size (ES); N/A Not assessed; random assignment (r.a.); ergometer (erg.); circumference (circ.). NB. Scales without citations are described in the respective sources shown in the table.

ier bias in the publishing process (i.e. studies involving randomised
signs are more likely to be published when there are no anxiety-reducing
effects) or that anxiety-reducing effects are less likely to be observed in
carefully controlled studies; a point which cannot be resolved easily. There
appears to have been an increase in the proportion of studies with longer
periods of training and follow-up assessments. Petruzzello et al. (1991)
reported only 7% of studies involving training periods over 15 weeks
compared to 26% in the present review. Encouragingly, four studies also
included a follow-up assessment.

The shortest study (3 weeks) by Mock and colleagues (1997) used a visual
analogue scale to assess anxiety. They found significantly reduced anxiety
among a group of newly diagnosed breast cancer patients assigned to a self-
directed walking programme with only limited nurse contact (compared
with a no exercise control group of similar health status). Interestingly,
while there were only small increases in fitness for the walking group, there
were small losses in fitness for the control group. Another relatively brief
training study (just 5 weeks) by Dixhoorn, Duivenvoorden, Pool, &
Verhage (1990) involved 156 post-MI patients who either did just daily
exercise or daily exercise and relaxation therapy. Neither group reduced
anxiety despite exceptionally large gains in fitness of 50%.

EXERCISE CHARACTERISTICS

The majority of the studies appeared to be concerned with increasing
aerobic fitness, with at least one group in 22 studies following American
College of Sports Medicine (ACSM, 1991) guidelines for frequency (3 times
per week), intensity (*c.* 60–90%) and duration (at least 20 minutes). Six
studies did not report complete information about the exercise dose. This
should not necessarily be seen as a criticism as studies involving free-living
exercise in a natural environment are obviously very difficult to monitor,
and yet may well be most favoured by participants. Only two studies
reported some exercise sessions lasting less than 20 minutes (within a range
from 15 to 45 minutes) and both involved progression from shorter to
longer sessions over time. This is supported by the fact that of the 22 studies
reporting assessment of aerobic fitness change, only one (Mock et al., 1997)
failed to find an increase. Perhaps this is not surprising given the inactive
status of participants in the majority of studies. Interestingly, of the nine
studies reporting mixed or no anxiety-reducing effects, eight (the other did
not report fitness change) reported fitness gains for the exercise groups. Of
the seven studies which specifically examined the effects of fitness change
on anxiety change, only three found a positive relationship. This confirms
previous reviews (e.g. Leith, 1994).

If aerobic fitness gain is not essential for anxiety reduction, is there a
difference between the effects of non-aerobic and aerobic exercise? From
only two non-aerobic studies identified in the meta-analysis of Petruzzello

et al. (1991) there was no evidence for anxiety-reducing effects. In the present review, only one study (Martinsen, Hoffart, & Solberg, 1989) out of seven (see Table 2.2) involving a non-aerobic exercise group (e.g. calisthenics, flexibility, circuit training, weight training), reported an anxiety-reducing effect. This study involved initially anxious hospital inpatients, and the non-aerobic group was involved in not only strength and flexibility exercises, but also relaxation therapy. Both these facts may have influenced the findings.

It is also important to consider adherence to exercise, since any anxiety-reducing effect is unlikely to remain if the treatment is discontinued. Only a few studies examined whether greater adherence was related to greater effects, or whether specific intervention groups differed in their adherence levels. There are, of course, important methodological implications too if only those likely to reduce anxiety remain in a study. King, Taylor, & Haskell (1993) reported that those who did more exercise reduced their scores more on the Taylor Manifest Anxiety Scale and the Perceived Stress Scale over a 12-month period. Interestingly, those in vigorous and moderate home-based exercise groups had higher levels of adherence (compared with group-based supervised sessions). Martinsen, Sandrik and Kolbjornsrud (1989) also identified a positive relationship between adherence and anxiety reduction. In a study comparing the effects of walking and jogging on neurotic hospital inpatients, Sexton, Maere and Dahl (1989) reported reduced anxiety for both groups but better adherence to the walking programme.

OTHER MODERATORS

One criticism of the literature is that it may be impossible to separate the real effects of exercise on anxiety from expected effects (Ojanen, 1994). In other words, will exercise reduce anxiety even if participants don't expect it to? Only a few studies have attempted to control for expectancy (e.g. Steptoe, Edwards, Moses, & Mathews, 1989). In an interesting study by McAuley, Bane, Ruddolph and Lox (1995), those with higher initial expectancy reduced their social physique anxiety (SPA) more than those with lower expectancy. Similarly, those with greater belief in their ability to walk (self-efficacy) also reduced SPA by more. In the past, researchers have focused on objective exercise and group characteristics in search of moderators. The work by McAuley et al. reflects an increasing concern for the psychosocial factors which may determine the strength of the anxiety-reducing effects. For example, Wankel (1993) discussed the importance of enjoyment during exercise as a determinant of changes in mental health outcomes.

TREATMENT COMPARISONS

If aerobic exercise reduces anxiety, are these effects greater than other anxiety-reducing interventions? Only four studies addressed this question.

The alternative treatment included, yoga, t'ai chi, cognitive-behavioural therapy, and relaxation. Fisher and Thompson (1994) reported enhanced scores on the Physical Appearance State and Trait Anxiety Scale, among females with low appearance evaluation, following either exercise therapy or cognitive-behavioural therapy after six weeks. Topp (1989) also reported reduced test anxiety after seven weeks of either aerobic running or relax-ation. Blumenthal et al. (1991) and Brown et al. (1995) reported no reduction in anxiety (using Spielberger's Trait Anxiety Inventory) following either aerobic exercise or alternative therapies (see Table 2.2). These findings confirm Petruzzello et al.'s (1991) review that suggested aerobic exercise has no greater benefit in reducing anxiety than alterna-tive anxiety-reducing treatments. However, only aerobic exercise groups increased cardiovascular fitness. There are, of course, many other health benefits known to result from physical activity, such as reduced risk of cardiovascular disease, osteoporosis, and colon cancer (Bouchard, Shephard, & Stephens, 1994).

There is clearly a need for more studies to compare exercise and other treatments but if the anxiety-reducing effects are similar, unsupervised exercise could be a cheaper alternative. Adherence to different treatments should also be considered.

Mechanisms for anxiety-reducing effects of chronic exercise

A number of mechanisms have been proposed in the literature, including the development of more positive affect and cognitions associated with lower anxiety. These might involve positive mood states, self esteem and perceptions of the physical self, and perceptions of control over behaviours and outcomes (see Biddle, this volume; Fox, this volume). Exercise train-ing may also develop enhanced coping resources, and social networks which may, in turn, reduce anxiety. While fitness changes appear not to be essen-tial for anxiety reduction, it is likely that improved physical health status will enhance health-related quality of life and reduce fear and anxiety often associated with ageing (Rejeski, Brawley, & Schumaker, 1996). Improved health status may be due to enhanced immunological, cardiovascular, neu-rological and physical functioning associated with physical activity.

A further suggested mechanism is through the accumulated effects of single exercise sessions. The next section will examine the effects of a single exercise session on state anxiety.

The effects of acute exercise

The 24 studies involving a single exercise session are summarised in Table 2.3. Changes in self-reported anxiety are shown together with psycho-physiological measures (e.g. blood pressure) which provide an insight into some of the mechanisms for anxiety-reduction effects.

Only three studies failed to show an anxiety-reducing effect on self-report measures (Head, Kendall, Ferner, & Eagles, 1996; O'Connor, Petruzzello, Kubitz, & Robinson, 1995; Youngstedt, Dishman, Cureton, & Peacock, 1993) from pre- to post-exercise. Eight of the nine studies that reported effect sizes showed greater anxiety-reducing effects of exercise than the overall mean effect size (0.24) reported in the meta-analysis by Petruzzello et al. (1991).

PARTICIPANT CHARACTERISTICS

It is clear that most studies involved convenience samples with only four not involving college students. Twenty studies involved males and 12 included females. Only single studies were located involving each of the inactive, physically challenged or high test-anxious people. The research, therefore, offers little generalisability to the general population of adults and special groups. The only study (Petruzzello, Jones, & Tate, 1997) to compare active with inactive individuals revealed anxiety-reducing effects for both (from 6 to 30 minutes post-exercise) with greater effects for the active (ES = 1.04) than the inactive (ES = 0.56). Anxiety increased during exercise among the inactive group, suggesting a need for practitioner support and different cognitive strategies used by the exercise neophyte.

RESEARCH DESIGN

Most studies (14) involved within-subject designs (i.e. participants were tested in all conditions, serving as their own control), while three studies involving random assignment to different groups, three had intact groups, and three had no control group. Nine studies involved comparison with a non-exercise control group/condition and two also contrasted the effects of exercise with another anxiety-reducing treatment.

Across the 24 studies, anxiety was measured between 0 and 120 minutes post exercise, with 14 studies using more than one measurement time. Petruzzello et al. (1991) reported the lowest ES (though not significantly less) for assessments up to 5 minutes post-exercise and yet five studies in the present review only measured anxiety immediately after exercise.

EXERCISE CHARACTERISTICS

The studies finding no anxiety-reducing effects were all unique in terms of exercise characteristics, and the findings largely confirm previous literature (Petruzzello et al., 1991). Head and colleagues (1996) reported that participants had not reduced anxiety 15 minutes after a 60 minute low intensity treadmill walk. In the study by O'Connor and colleagues (1995), trained participants performed maximal fitness tests under two different protocol. Although Petruzzello et al. identified no detrimental effect of

Table 2.3 Effects of acute exercise on anxiety

Author(s)	Participants	Design	Comparison group	Exercise characteristics	Anxiety measure	Outcome/comments
Berger & Owen, 1992	74, m, f college healthy	Pre-post (0 mins) Intact class or pool grps r.a. to swim/record	1. Pool (swim) 2. Pool (record keeping) 3. Class control	1 = 81%, 20 mins, in pool	SAI	Swim and recording ↓ Anx. (i.e. 'time out' support) Only women ↓ Anx.
Brown, Morgan, & Raglin, 1993	10 m, f college Physically challenged	Pre-post (2/3 mins) Within subj. r.a. to both conditions	Ex. v quiet rest	Aerobic cycle or treadmill	SAI Phys: BP	Quiet rest ↓ SAI, SBP, DBP Ex. ↑ SBP, ↓ SAI
Crocker & Grozelle, 1991	85, f college healthy	Pre-post (0 mins) r.a. to 3 grps	1. Aerobic ex. (AE) 2. Autogenic relaxation (AR) 3. Control (C)	AE = 70–80% HR, 20 min, aerobic program AR = 30 mins C = free to wander for 30 mins	SAI	AE and AR ↓ SAI No gender differences
Dishman, Farquhar, & Cureton, 1994	23 m college healthy	Pre-post (1 min) between 2 grps	1. low fit (VO$_2$ = 43ml. kg.min.) 2. High fit (VO$_2$ = 57 ml. kg.min.)	Preferred intensity (no difference in RPE between fitness level) 20 mins, cycle erg.	SAI	Ex. ↓ SAI (only for high fit)
Doan et al., 1995	52 m, f college healthy, high test-anxious	Pre-post (0 mins) r.a. to 3 grps	1. Aerobic ex. (AE) 2. Relaxation (R) 3. Control (C)	AE = moderate, 15 mins, cycle erg. R = blindfold, relaxation tape C = magazine reading	MAACL	AE ↓ MAACL (ES) = –0.80 cf. control) R ↓ MAACL (ES) = –0.70 cf. control)
Head et al., 1996	20 m college healthy	Pre-post (15 mins) Within subj. r.a. to all 5 conditions Double blind	1. Placebo 2. & 3. Low/high propranolol 4. & 5. Low/high metoprolol	50%, 60 mins, treadmill walk with placebo drug or 2 types of betablockers (low/high dose)	SAI	No ↓ SAI (for ex. & drug conditions)

Study	Sample	Design	Conditions	Exercise protocol	Measures	Results
McAuley, Mihalko, & Bane, 1996	34, m, f college healthy all 3 conditions	Pre-during-post (0, 15 mins) Within subj. r.a. to 3 conditions	1. Lab ex. (LE) 2. Natural environment ex. (NEE) 3. Control (C)	1. & 2. RPE = 14-16, 20 mins, aerobic 3. Quiet rest	SAI	LE ↓ SAI (ES = -0.82) NEE ↓ SAI (ES = -0.60) Somatic items ↑ during, ↓ after ex. Cog. items ↓ during & after ex.
O'Connor & Davis, 1992	14 m college healthy	Pre-post (10, 20 min) Within subj. r.a. to all 4 conditions	1. 0800 hrs 2. 1200 hrs 3. 1600 hrs 4. 2000 hrs	Ex. at each time = 70%, 20 mins treadmill run	SAI Phys: BP	Ex ↓ SAI and SBP (at both 10 and 20 mins post ex.) No effect of time of day
O'Connor et al., 1993	14 f college healthy	Pre-post (1-120 mins) Within subj. r.a. to all 4 conditions	1. Control 2, 3, 4. Weight training	2, 3, 4 = 6 exercises × 10 reps × 3 sets, 30 mins at different loads (2 = 40%, 3 = 60%, 4 = 80% of max.)	SAI Phys: BP HR	No ↓ HR and BP Pre-post (120 min): 40% ↓ SAI (ES = -0.25) 60% ↓ SAI (ES = -0.58) 80% ↓ SAI (ES = -0.43)
O'Connor et al., 1995	16 m college healthy	Pre-post (2, 10 mins)	None	2 min stages to maximum intensity	SAI	Max. ex. ↓ SAI (ES = -0.68 at post-2 min, -0.98 at post-10 min)
O'Connor et al., 1995	12 m 28 yrs trained	Pre-post (10 mins) Within subj. r.a. to both conditions	2 protocols for max. test	1. 3 min stages to maximum 2. 5 min stages to maximum	SAI	No ↓ in SAI for either protocol. ES = -0.14 to 0.52
Petruzzello & Landers, 1994a	19 m college active	Pre-post (10-30 mins)	None	75%, 30 mins, treadmill run	SAI Phys: EEG	Ex. ↓ SAI (at 10-30 min post) Ex. ↑ left frontal activation (cf. right frontal) S's with initial ↑ left sided activation ↓ SAI more (at 30 min post)
Petruzzello & Landers, 1994b	16 m college active	Pre-post (0-30 mins) Within subj. r.a. to both conditions	1. 15 min ex. 2. 30 min ex.	Both at 75%, treadmill run	SAI	Both conditions ↓ SAI (at 10, 20, 30 mins). ES = -0.53 to -0.96 (less at 10 mins)

Table 2.3 (continued)

Author(s)	Participants	Design	Comparison group	Exercise characteristics	Anxiety measure	Outcome/comments
Petruzzello et al., 1993	20 m college active	Pre-post (0–30 mins) Within subj. r.a. to all 3 conditions	1. Cooler situ 2. Normal situ 3. Warmer situ	All at 75%, 30 mins treadmill run	SAI	All 3 conditions ↓ SAI (at 20 & 30 mins post). ES = −0.52 to −0.98) (less at 10 mins with ↑ SAI for warmer situ) Δ core body temp. not necessary for Δ SAI
Petruzzello et al., (1997)	18 active 12 inactive college	Pre-during-post (6–30 mins)	Active v inactive	RPE = 13, 24 mins, cycle erg.	SAI	Both grps ↓ SAI (at 6–30 mins). ES = −1.04 (active) ES = −0.56 (inactive) No. diff. bet. grps but inactive ↑ SAI during ex.
Petruzzello & Tate, 1997	20 m,f college trained	Pre-post (0–30 mins) Within subj. r.a. to all 3 conditions	1. No ex. control 2. 55% $\dot{V}O_{2max}$ 3. 70% $\dot{V}O_{2max}$	30 mins, cycle erg.	SAI Phys: EEG	55% and control didn't ↓ SAI 70% ex. ↓ SAI (at 5 and 10 min post) predicted by greater relative left frontal activation pre-ex.
Raglin & Wilson, 1996	25 m,f 24 yrs trained	Pre-post (5, 60, 120 mins) Within subj. r.a. to all 3 conditions	1. 40% $\dot{V}O_{2max}$ 2. 60% $\dot{V}O_{2max}$ 3. 70% $\dot{V}O_{2max}$	20 mins, cycle erg.	SAI	All conditions ↓ SAI (at 60 and 120 mins post) 70% ex ↑ SAI (at 5 min post) but only S's with a low pre-ex. SAI
Raglin, Turner, & Eksten, 1993	25 m,f college trained	Pre-post (0, 20, 60 mins) Within subj. r.a. to both conditions	Cycling v wt. training	70–80%, 30 mins	SAI Phys: BP	Only cycling ↓ SAI (at 60 min post) *No* ↓ DBP
Rejeski, Hardy, & Shaw 1991	30 m college healthy	Pre-during-post (10 mins)	None	75%, 15 mins, treadmill run	SAI AD-ACL	ex ↓ SAI (at 10 min post) ex ↓ AD-ACL (energetic arousal) ex ↑ AD-ACL (tiredness & calmness)

Study	Sample	Design	Conditions (Ex. v waiting grp)	Intensity	POMS	Findings
Roth, 1989	40 active, 40 inactive m, f college healthy	Pre-post (15 mins) r.a. to 2 grps	Ex. v waiting grp	Ex. = 60–80% (6–8 mins) + 50–65% (12–14 mins)	POMS	Ex ↓ Anxiety/tension (for both active and inactive)
Szabo et al., 1998	40 runners	11.9 active days compared with 9.1 inactive days	Runners studied in situ	Active days = 8 km in 40.6 mins on average	SAI	SAI lower on days when participants ran, cf. didn't run.
Tate & Petruzzello, 1995	20 m, f college active	Pre-during-post (5–30 mins) Within subj. r.a. to all 3 conditions	1. No ex. 2. 55% 3. 70%	30 mins, cycle erg.	SAI AD-ACL	ex. ↑ SAI (during ex.) Only 70% ex. ↓ SAI (at 30 min post). ES = −0.39 55% & 70% ex. ↓ AD-ACL (energetic arousal) during & post
Trine & Morgan, 1997	30 m, f 41 yrs (m) 34 yrs (f) runners	Pre-post (5–15 mins) Within subj. r.a. to all 3 conditions	1. 0600 hrs 2. 1100 hrs 3. 1600 hrs	Preferred intensity, run on indoor track. No diff. between conditions	SAI Phys: HR, BP	ex. at all times ↓ SAI and DBP. No effects of time of day, preferred time to run, or gender
Youngstedt et al, 1993	11 m college fit	Pre-post (15, 25 mins) Within subj. r.a. to all 4 conditions	1. Cycling in warm water 2. Cycling in cold water 3. Sitting in warm water 4. Quiet rest	70%, 20 mins	SAI Phys: BP, EEG	No ↓ SAI or EEG (alpha, beta, theta wave) 1 & 3 ↓ mean BP (at 15 & 25 mins post ex.)

Notes:

Per week (p.w.); State & Trait Anxiety Inventory (SAI & TAI: Spielberger et al., 1983); Profile of Mood States (POMS: McNair et al., 1971) – Tension/Anxiety scale only; Multiple Affect Adjective Check List – Anxiety (MAACL-A: Zuckerman & Lubin, 1965); Activation-Deactivation Adjective Check List (AD-ACL): Thayer, 1967; male (m); female (f); effect size (ES); random assignment (r.a.); ergometer (erg.); physiological measure (phys.); systolic & diastolic blood pressure (SBP & DBP); electroencephalography (EEG); Ratings of Perceived Exertion (RPE: Borg, 1973). Under design column, time(s) in brackets is time(s) of post-assessment(s) after exercise ends.

high intensity exercise (> 80%) on anxiety reduction, O'Connor's study suggests that there is a ceiling at which benefits can be gained. They reported some non-significant increases in anxiety 10 minutes after exercise (ES = 0.52). Youngstedt et al. (1993) also reported no reduction in state anxiety but participants cycled in a pool, a rather unnatural environment, to test the effects of temperature, as an anxiety-reducing mechanism.

Recent attention has focused on the effects of the exercise environment on anxiety reduction. McAuley, Mihalko, and Bane (1996) revealed that both exercising in a laboratory and in a natural environment reduced anxiety. O'Connor and Davis (1992), and Trine and Morgan (1997), investigated the effects of time of day on anxiety reduction. They both concluded that time of day, whether it be actual or different from preferred time, had no influence.

Only two studies involved weight training. Raglin, Turner and Eksten (1993) compared weight training with cycling and found only the latter led to a reduction in anxiety. This confirmed Petruzzello et al's (1991) meta-analysis, albeit with very few studies. However, O'Connor, Bryant, Veltri and Gebhardt (1993) compared a non-exercising control group with weight training, holding repetitions constant but setting intensity at 40%, 60% and 80% of one maximum repetition. ESs were −0.25, −0.58, and −0.43, but only 120 minutes after exercise completion.

TREATMENT COMPARISONS

Only two studies (Crocker and Grozelle 1991; Doan, Plante, DiGregorio, & Manuel, 1995) compared the anxiety-reducing effects of an aerobic exercise group with a relaxation group. Both groups reduced anxiety compared with the control group, thereby supporting Petruzzello et al.'s meta-analytic findings.

Mechanisms for anxiety-reducing effects of acute exercise

A number of physiological changes occur from pre- to post-acute exercise and these have been suggested as possible mechanisms for anxiety-reducing effects. These include temperature increase, increased beta endorphins, reduced muscle tension, increase in parasympathetic activity, and reduced excitability of the central nervous system. The findings largely confirm those revealed by Petruzzello et al. (1991) in that exercise-related anxiety-reducing effects are associated with changes in psychophysiological measures, although these are less apparent for blood pressure and heart rate measures.

Another proposed mechanism for anxiety-reducing effects has been the 'time-out' or 'distraction' hypothesis. In support of this, Brown, Morgan and Raglin (1993) reported reduced anxiety following both quiet rest and exercise (following earlier studies by Raglin & Morgan, 1987, and Ruck & Taylor, 1991). This suggests that any distracting activity may result in reduced anxiety. However, it may be that some forms of exercise (perhaps with greater external stimulation such as music) may provide a greater guarantee that distraction will occur, and of course there are other benefits from physical activity. The anxiety-reducing effects of exercise may also last longer.

Effects of exercise on reactivity to stress

Summary of findings from cross-sectional exercise studies

Nine of the fourteen cross-sectional studies reviewed since 1989 showed that fit and/or active individuals were less reactive to psychosocial stressors. Due to a variety of possible confounding factors, this literature will not be reported in detail here (Blaney, Sothmann, Raff, Hart, & Horn, 1990; Boutcher, Nugent, & Weltman, 1995; Buckworth, Dishman, & Cureton, 1994; Choi, & Salmon, 1995; Czajkowski et al., 1990; de Geus, Lorenz, van Doornen, de Visser, & Orlebeke, 1990; de Geus, Lorenz, van Doornen, & Orlebeke, 1993; Graham, Zelchner, Peacock, & Dishman, 1996; Houtmann, & Bakker, 1991; Long, 1991; McCubbin, Cheung, Montgomery, Bulbulian, & Wilson, 1992; Sothmann, Hart, & Horn, 1991; Steptoe, Moses, Mathews, & Edwards, 1990; Van Doornen, & de Geus, 1989).

Summary of findings from chronic exercise studies

Twelve studies, published since 1988, were identified which compared reactivity to and/or recovery from a psychosocial stressor pre- and post-training. A summary of these studies is shown in Table 2.4.

All studies showed improvements in aerobic fitness over periods from 5 to 16 weeks with the exception of one that examined the effects of exercise withdrawal. This study lasted only one week and showed no change in reactivity (Szabo & Gauvin, 1992). Six studies showed no effects and six showed some positive effect of training on psychological and physiological measures during and/or after a stressor. Given the wide variety of exercise training in terms of frequency, intensity and duration, the nature of the stressors (i.e. passive v. active response, novel v. familiar, natural v. simulated), and the indices of psychophysiological reactivity, it is difficult to draw conclusions. However, Claytor (1991) suggested that reactivity differences were only likely to be observed when the task was familiar. In another recent review, Sothmann et al. (1996) suggested that more studies were needed involving clinical populations with compromised stress systems (e.g. depressed, anxious, etc.), and studies to examine gender differences given that the neuroendocrine stress response may be different for males and females. They also suggested that consideration of how exercise training may impact on both the sympathetic and parasympathetic response should be considered more in the future.

Table 2.4 Effects of chronic exercise on psychosocial stress reactivity

Author(s)	Participants	Design	Stressor	Exercise characteristics	Anxiety measure	Outcome/comments
Blaney et al., 1990	14 m 42 yrs (35–50) healthy active	Pre (T1) – post (T2) 16 wks self-select to 2 grps	Stroop test (18 mins)	Ex. training group ↑ $\dot{V}O_{2max}$ from 45→53 ml.kg⁻¹.min⁻¹ Control grp = 42 & 43 ml.kg⁻¹.min⁻¹	SAI TAI Phys: ACTH, cortisol, HR	No Δ in reactivity or recovery on all variables, from T1 to T2
Blumenthal et al., 1990	37 m 42 yrs (30–52), healthy, Type As	Pre (T1) – post (T2) over 12 wks r.a. to 2 grps	Maths task 3 × 5 min blocks	Aerobic ex. (AE) grp ↑ $\dot{V}O_{2max}$ by 14% Strengths training (ST) grp by 3% ↑ $\dot{V}O_{2max}$	Phys: HR, BP, E, NE, RPP	AE less reactive (HR, DBP, E) from T1 to T2 AE recovered faster from T1 to T2 cf. ST grp
Calvo, Szabo, & Capafons, 1996	21m, 58f college, healthy	(pre (T1) – post (T2) over 12 wks r.a. to 2 grps	Speech, maths, fine motor task	Control = waiting list (with some contact) Ex. grp = Combined strength, flexibility & endurance training, $\dot{V}O_2$ ↑	1. Overt behaviour 2. CSAQ 3. HR	Ex. grp reduced 1 & 2 from pre-post and cf. control grp. Ex. grp had faster HR recovery, post-stress
de Geus et al., 1990	22 m college inactive, healthy	Pre (T1) – post (T2) over 7 wks r.a. to 2 grps	1. Memory search task 2. Tone avoidance task 3. Cold pressor test	Aerobic ex. grp ↑ $\dot{V}O_{2max}$ from 46.6 → 51.9 No. ex. grp didn't change	Phys: HR, RR, PEP, RSA SAI	No Δ in reactivity or recovery on all variables from T1 to T2

Study	Sample	Design	Stressor/Task	Training	Measures	Results
de Geus et al., 1993	62 m 33 yrs (24–40) inactive, healthy	Pre (T1) – mid (T2) – post (T3) over 12 + 12 wks r.a. to 2 grps self select to 2 grps	1. Memory search task 2. Tone avoidance task 3. Cold pressor test	Training + training grp: $\dot{V}O_{2max} = 47 \to 52 \to 54$; Training + de-training grp: $\dot{V}O_{2max} = 47 \to 51 \to 50$; No training + training grp: $\dot{V}O_{2max} = 45 \to 45 \to 52$; No training + no train. grp: $\dot{V}O_{2max} = 44 \to 43 \to 44$	Phys: HR, BP, TPR, PEP	Training ↓ HR and DBP overall but not reactivity to stressors; No sig. moderators
Kubitz & Landers, 1993	24 m,f college healthy	Pre (T1) – post (T2) r.a. to 2 grps (AE, C)	Pre-stress – recovery at T1 and T2 Stressor = Stroop test (3 min) and maths (3 min)	AE = 60–80%, 40 mins 3 × p.w., 8 wks, cycle erg. C = 8 wks	SAI Phys: HR, RSA, BP, EEG	No training effects on SAI or BP; Ex. training ↓ HR and changed RSA and alpha laterality during stressor
LaPerriere et al., 1990	50 m 18–40 yrs inactive, healthy, HIV risk	Pre-post ex. r.a. to 2 grps then HIV test	Notification of HIV test results	Ex. = 80% (3 mins) + 60–70% (2 mins) 45 mins, 3 × p.w., aerobic fitness gains over 5 wks control = no. ex.	POMS Phys: immune profile	Only controls with +ve HIV results ↑ anx. (ie. ex. attenuated anxiety response to natural stressor). Also supported by immune profile results
Sherwood, Light, & Blumenthal, 1989	27 m 41 yrs (33–56) Type A's	Pre (T1)-post (T2) over 12 wks r.a. to 2 grps	Letter response task in competition with others (5 mins)	Aerobic training grp ($\dot{V}O_{2max} = 34 \to 38$) Strength training grp ($\dot{V}O_{2max} = 34 \to 35$)	Phys: HR, BP, TPR, CO	AE training for hypertensives ↓ DBP, HR, TPR and DBP reactivity to stressors
Stein & Boutcher, 1992	33 m 46 +/– 6 yrs inactive, healthy	Pre (T1)-post (T2) over 8 wks r.a. to 2 grps	1. Passive responding 2. Push button Stroop 3. Verbal Stroop (11 mins total)	Aerobic training (peak $\dot{V}O_2 = 2.9$–3.3 l.min^{-1}) No ex. controls (no change)	Phys: HR, BP, R-R int, PTT, TWA, RWA, Temp	Training ↓ HR overall and reactivity to stressors; No change in other variables

Table 2.4 (continued)

Author(s)	Participants	Design	Stressor	Exercise characteristics	Anxiety measure	Outcome/comments
Steptoe et al., 1990	20m, 55f 39 yrs (18–60) inactive. healthy	Pre (T1) – post (T2) over 10 wks r.a. to 4 grps	Easy and hard problem solving (6 mins each)	Vig. aerobic (est. $\dot{V}O_{2max}$ ↑ 22%) Mod. aerobic (est. $\dot{V}O_{2max}$ ↑ 12%) Weight training (est. $\dot{V}O_{2max}$ ↑ 6%) No ex. control (no change)	Phys: HR, BP, RR TAI	Training → no change in TAI No diff in reactivity to stresors in any variable
Steptoe, Moses et al., 1993	3 m, 29 f 37 +/- 9 yrs (20–60) anxious, overwght	Pre (T1) – post (T2) over 10 wks matched 2 grps	Easy and hard problem solving (6 mins each) Raven's progressive matrices	Mod. aerobic ex. ($\dot{V}O_{2max} = 41 \rightarrow 48$) Non-aerobic ex. (no change)	Phys: HR, BP, SCL	AE training – no differences in reactivity to stressors in any variable from T1 to T2
Szabo & Gauvin, 1992	16 m, 8 f college v. active, healthy	Pre (T1) – post (T2) over 1 week r.a. to 2 grps	Math task (5 min)	1. Regular ex. grp 2. Ex. withdrawal grp	Phys: HR	Ex. withdrawal had no effect on HR reactivity to stressor

Notes:
Pulse transit time (PTT); skin temperature (Temp); Pre-injection period (PEP); Cardiac output (CO); Norepinephrine (NE); T-wave amplitude (TWA); R-wave amplitude (RWA); Skin conductance level (SCL); Total peripheral resistance (TPR); diastolic blood pressure (DBP); Respiration rate (RR), Epinephrine (E); Rate pressure product (RRP); inter heart beat interval (R-R int); respiratory sinus arrhythmia (RSA); electroencephalography (EEG); adrenocorticotrophic hormone (ACTH); State & Trait Anxiety Inventory (SAI & TAI: Spielberger et al., 1983); Cognitive–Somatic Anxiety Questionnaire (CSAQ: Calvo et al., 1990); Profile of Mood States (POMS: McNair et al., 1971); random assignment (r.a.); group (grp); weeks (wks); years (yrs); male, female (m, f); Stroop test requires fast response only when rapidly presented word matches colour of word.

Summary of findings from acute exercise studies

Fourteen studies, published since 1988, were identified that compared reactivity to and/or recovery from a psychosocial stressor following a single exercise session. A summary of these studies is shown in Table 2.5.

Only four studies failed to show a reduction in reactivity to a stressor following exercise. Exercise sessions lasted between 10 and 120 minutes, and were performed at between 28–80% of maximum heart rate. The stressors were largely brief (3–5 minutes duration) and included both passive and active responses. A wide range of biochemical, cardiovascular, psychological and cerebral measures were employed. All studies involved healthy participants, mostly of college age.

As examples of the type of study showing a positive outcome, Rejeski, Thompson, Brubaker and Miller (1992) reported that exercising on a cycle ergometer for 40 minutes at 70% of maximum heart rate, followed by 30 minutes of rest before a public speech, led to less increase in systolic and diastolic blood pressure during the stressor, in comparison with a non-exercising control condition. Also, Steptoe, Kearsley and Walters (1993) compared a light exercise group with groups exercising on a cycle ergometer at 50% and 70% of their maximum oxygen uptake. They reported lower systolic blood pressure following the public speech among the 70% group compared with the light exercise group.

Implications for the researcher

The review conducted provides ideas for further research. In the broadest terms, research should examine the anxiety-reducing effects of exercise among specific sub-groups of the population and more carefully consider the social context in which exercise takes place. Hopefully we can determine, through experimental manipulation of cognitive processes such as self-evaluation, how the exercise practitioner can increase the anxiety-reducing effects of PA.

Many questions remain about the importance of reducing psychophysiological reactivity to psychosocial stressors through exercise training or a single session of exercise. For example, Carroll, Smith, Sheffield, Shipley and Marmot (1995) suggested that reactivity to a psychological stressor only accounted for 1% of the variance in blood pressure 4.9 years later when controlling for initial blood pressure among a large sample. However, the authors did accept that the follow-up period was rather short, and that reactivity among a younger sample may better predict hypertension in later life. Clearly, an implication is that more prospective studies are necessary to examine how exercise may serve as a mediator in the development of hypertension, particularly among those with a predisposition to physiologically react more strongly to psychosocial stressors.

Table 2.5 Effects of acute exercise on psychosocial stress reactivity

Author(s)	Participants	Design	Stressor	Exercise characteristics	Anxiety measure	Outcome/comments
Boone et al., 1993	8 41 +/- 7 yrs borderline hyper-tensives	Within subj. randomly ordered to (ex. or no ex.) then pre-during-post stressor	Stroop test (5 min)	Ex. = 60%, 60 mins, treadmill No ex. = quiet rest, 60 mins Both followed by 10 mins rest	Phys: BP, HR	Ex. ↓ MAP, SBP & DBP reactivity to stressor
Doan et al., 1995	52 m,f college, healthy high test-anxious	r.a. to 3 grps (AE, R, C) then pre-post stressor	IQ test (3 min)	AE = mod, 15 mins, cycle erg. R = blindfold, relaxation tape C = magazine reading	MAACL	C ↑ MAACL (cf. AE & R) Effects of AE greater for m (cf. f)
Flory & Holmes, 1991	18 f college healthy	Within subj. (AD + SP) then (15 mins) pre-post stressor	Study period (40 mins)	AD = 28%, 20 mins dance SP = 40 mins 'studying'	MAACL Phys: HR, BP	No diff in MAACL at post task AD ↑ HR (cf. SP)
Hobson & Rejeski, 1993	80 f college healthy	Within subj. randomly ordered to C, 10, 25 & 40 min then pre-during stressor	Modified Stroop test (3 min) following 20 mins rest	C = no ex. control 10 & 25 & 40 mins. ex. on cycle erg at 70%	Phys: BP	40 min ex. ↓ DBP & MAP reactivity to stressor cf. no ex. condition No effects for 10 & 25 min conditions
Jin, 1992	96 m, f 36 yrs healthy from t'ai chi clubs	r.a. to 4 grps (TC, TC-V, W,C). Within subj. (MS + ES) then treatment	MS = math & tests (60 mins) ES = horror film (60 mins) On different days	TC = t'ai chi, 60 mins TC-V = t'ai chi video, 60 mins W = walking, 60 mins, 6 km/h C = neutral reading	SAI Phys: HR, BP, CA	All 4 grps ↓ cortisol Only TC ↓ SAI (cf. control) but not after expectancy effects controlled Longer post treatment period needed

Study	Sample	Design	Stressor	Exercise protocol	Measures	Results
Kubitz & Pothakos, 1997	28 m, f college healthy	r.a. to 2 ghrps (AE, C) then (5 min) pre-post stressor	Vigilance task (15 mins)	AE = 75–80%, 15 mins, cycle erg. C = relaxation tape	AD-ACL Phys: EEG	AE ↓ beta & ↑ alpha & theta waves. AE ↑ AD=ACL. All effects only after ex. and at 5 mins in stressor
Perronet et al, 1989	7 m 23 yrs healthy	Pre-post Within subj. r.a. to both conditions	Stroop test (3 mins)	1. 53%, 120 mins, cycle erg. 2. rest (120 mins)	Phys: HR, BP, E, NE	Ex ↓ E (by 50%)
Rejeski, Gregg, et al., 1991	12 m 31 yrs (23–38) highly trained cyclists	Within subj. randomly ordered to C, LE, HE, then pre, during, and post stressor	Modified Stroop test (2 × 3 mins) following 30 mins rest	C = no ex. control LE = 50%, 30 mins, cycle erg. HE = 80%, 60 mins, cycle erg.	Phys: HR, BP	HE had ↓ SBP during stress (cf. LE & C). LE & HE had ↓ DBP during stress (cf. C). HE < LE < C on MAP during stressor. No differences post stressor
Rejeski et al., 1992	48 f 25–40 yrs low & mod. fit, healthy	Within subj. random ordered to C, Ex., then pre-during-post stressor	Modified Stroop test 3 mins) + Public speech (3 mins) following 30 mins rest	C = no ex. control Ex. + 70% HR, 40 mins cycle erg.	Phys: HR, BP MAACL-R- Anxiety Anxiety – self report	Ex. had ↓ SBP & DBP during stressors (cf. C). Ex. had fewer & less intense anx.-related thoughts prior to speech (not Stroop). Ex. had no effect on recovery rates or MAACL
Roth, 1989	40 active 40 inactive, m, f, college healthy	Stressor 1 then r.a. to ex. v control then stressor 2	Numerical tasks	Ex. = 60–80% (6–8 mins) + 50–65% (12–14 mins) Control = waiting	Phys: HR, BP POMS	Ex. had no effect on HR and BP reactivity to stressors stressors. No diff. between active v inactive or fit v unfit
Roy & Steptoe, 1991	30 m college healthy	r.a. to 3 grps (C, LE, HE) then pre-during-post stressor	Numerical tasks (4 × 5 mins) following 20 mins rest	C = no ex. control LE = 25 Watts, 20 mins, cycle erg. He = 100 Watts, 20 mins, cycle erg.	SAI Phys: HR, BP CSAQ	No effects on SAI & CSAQ. C > LE > HE on SBP, DBP, HR reactivity to stress

Table 2.5 (continued)

Author(s)	Participants	Design	Stressor	Exercise characteristics	Anxiety measure	Outcome/comments
Sedlock & duda, 1994	58 f college healthy	4 grps then pre-during-post stressor	Numerical task (5 mins) follwing 20 mins rest	1. High TAI / low fit 2. Low TAI / low fit 3. High TAI / high fit 4. Low TAI / high fit All grps = 50%, 15 mins, cycle erg.	Phys: HR ASDS	Fitness level had no mediating effect on reactivity or recovery to a stressor following ex. High TAI had higher HR and ASDS post stressor
Steptoe, Kearsley, & Walters, 1993	36 inactive 36 active 27 yrs (20–35), m	r.a. to 3 grps (C, LE, HE) then pre-during-post stressors	Numerical tasks (5 mins) + Public speech (3 mins) mixed order, following 30 mins rest	C = light ex. control LE = 50%, 20 mins, cycle erg. HE = 70%, 20 mins cycle erg.	Phys: HR, BP, BRS POMS	Only HE had lower SBP during and post maths (cf. C), lower SBP post speech (cf. C), lower BRS & DBP post maths (cf. C) No differences for HR No diff. between active v inactive
Szabo et al., 1993	9 m healthy	Within subj. to both ex. or film then during stressors	1. Numerical task (3 mins) 2. Stroop test (3 mins)	Ex. = 60%, 30 mins cycle erg. Film = control = neutral	SAI Phys: HR, BP, E, NE	Ex. had no effect on reactivity to stressor

Notes:

Pulse transit time (PTT); skin temperature (Temp); Pre-injection period (PEP; Cardiac output (CO): Norepinephrine (NE); T-wave amplitude (TWA); R-wave amplitude (RWA); Skin conductance level (SCL); Total peripheral resistance (TPR); Respiration rate (RR); Epinephrine (E); Rate pressure product (RRP); inter heart beat interval (R-R int); systolic/diastolic blood pressure (SBP/DBP0; heart rate (HR); Mean arterial pressure (MAP); electroencephalography (EEG); Baroceptor reflex sensitivity (BRS); State & Trait Anxiety Inventory (SAI & TAI: Spielberger et al., 1983); Cognitive–Somatic Anxiety Questionnaire (CSAQ: Calvo et al., 1990): Multiple Affect Adjective Check List (MAACL: Zuckerman & Lubin, 1965); Profile of Mood States (POMS: McNair et al., 1971); Adjective Semantic Differential Scale (ASDS: Hull et al., 1984); Activation-Deactivation Adjective Check List (AD-ACL: Thayer, 1967; random assignment (r.a.): male, female (m, f).

Implications for the exercise practitioner

The physical benefits of exercise have received the greatest attention in the past. This review provides ample evidence to support the use of exercise for the reduction of trait anxiety over a period of time, and for the anxiety-reducing effects of a single exercise session. While it appears clear that exercise of an aerobic rhythmic type is most beneficial, other social factors need to be carefully considered to maximise the benefits.

Exercise sessions and programmes should provide a distraction from worry and anxiety-inducing thoughts and provide the exerciser with a sense of mastery and achievement. If an anxious exerciser feels threatened or under evaluation in an exercise setting then these perceptions should be discussed with an exercise leader with appropriate exercise counselling skills. To avoid social anxiety, exercise testing and programming should involve individual contact and goal setting in an environment that supports positive change in self-perceptions. The promotion of physical activity for anxiety reduction should be discussed and exercise sessions incorporated into daily living. It may be that individuals find less motivation to exercise during more intense periods of stress (e.g. prior to exams or deadlines). An exercise counsellor/leader should identify such risks of inactivity and emphasise the importance of exercise for stress management.

There is some evidence that improvements in fitness can have a cross-training effect, enabling the more fit to physiologically react less and recover more quickly from stressors. The accumulated effects of reduced reactivity may result in lower levels of stress-related fatigue from normal occupation-related activities and other psychosocial demands. The implications of this are that individuals may feel less tired through enhanced recovery from daily stressors. They may also be less likely to cope with stress by other means such as smoking and alcohol consumption. There is some evidence that physical activity may be linked to reduced cravings for a cigarette and improved success in smoking cessation (Ussher, Taylor, West, & McEwen, in press).

Implications for the health analyst and policy maker

Despite the minimal reference to physical activity in a recent review of the effectiveness of different mental health promotion interventions (Tilford et al., 1997), there is considerable evidence, from rigorously designed and conducted research, supporting the anxiety-reducing effects of physical activity. Evidence for a variety of physiological, psychological and social mechanisms has partially supported the logical supposition that these effects will occur. While the effects may be similar to other non-medication anxiety treatments, the simplicity of promoting physical activity, such as walking, and at low cost, makes the promotion of physical activity for the treatment of various types of anxiety appealing.

A supervised exercise programme, such as in an exercise prescription scheme, may provide an important setting for the initiation of an anxiety-reducing intervention if the exercise practitioner has an adequate understanding of the anxiety-reducing mechanisms involved.

In conclusion, summary statements of 'what we know' and 'need to know' will be presented.

What we know

- The literature suggests a low-to-moderate anxiety-reducing effect of physical activity, with some studies suggesting a potentially greater effect.
- Studies have fairly consistently shown that a period of exercise training can reduce trait anxiety.
- Single exercise sessions will result in reductions in state anxiety.
- The research evidence comes from studies employing various designs but the stronger effects are shown by randomised controlled trials.
- The limited number of comparisons between physical activity and other medication-free anxiety treatments suggest comparable anxiety-reducing effects.
- Single sessions of moderate exercise can reduce short-term physiological reactivity to and enhance recovery from brief psychosocial stressors.
- Exercise training has successfully reduced trait anxiety across a wide range of sub-groups in the population, including active and inactive, anxious and non-anxious, healthy and unhealthy individuals (e.g. undergoing cardiac rehabilitation, or with cancer, COPD, and a variety of mental disorders), and in both males and females.
- Exercise training has been used successfully to reduce trait anxiety in a wide range of clinical and non-clinical settings. However, some anxiety disorders (e.g. panic disorder with agoraphobia) may not respond to exercise training.
- Exercise training appears to have the greatest trait anxiety-reducing effects when the duration is at least 10 weeks (with greatest benefits over 15 weeks).
- Trait anxiety-reducing effects are not dependent on changes in physical fitness.
- Single (acute) exercise sessions appear to have the greatest state anxiety-reducing effects when the exercise type is aerobic and rhythmic.

What we need to know

- There has been relatively little examination of the anxiety-reducing effects of PA for young people.
- There is scope for better understanding of how special groups (e.g. the obese with social physique anxiety; asthmatics and COPD patients who experience fears about breathing; older people with a fear of falling) may benefit from a programme of exercise.
- Only a few studies have examined the trait anxiety-reducing effects of exercise with sessions less than 20 minutes.
- We need to know more about the long-term effects of accumulated doses of activity (in line with current recommendations for physical activity for cardiovascular disease prevention).
- Only a few studies have examined the long-term anxiety-reducing effects (i.e. over 4 months) of PA. We need to know, for example, whether a 10 week exercise programme will have lasting anxiety-reducing effects, and if not what dose of exercise is necessary to maintain the effects.
- We know little about the anxiety-reducing effects of short bouts (<15 minutes) of free-living, unsupervised aerobic physical activity, which can be most easily integrated into an active lifestyle, as a low-cost intervention.
- We know little about the anxiety-reducing effects of non-aerobic exercise such as weight and circuit training.
- Few studies have examined the influence of social interactions on anxiety in the exercise setting. We need to know whether exercise practitioner manipulations of self-efficacy, outcome expectancy, perceived competence, goal setting, feedback, attentional focus and perceived exertion and enjoyment can increase anxiety-reducing effects, particularly among inactive and inexperienced exercisers.
- The cost-effectiveness of physical activity as an anxiety treatment has not been considered. Studies need to compare PA with other anxiety-reducing interventions, not only in terms of anxiety reduction (which appears to be similar) but also in terms of cost. Related to this would be careful consideration of adherence to the respective interventions.
- Fitness change has been extensively investigated as a mediator in the PA–anxiety relationship, with equivocal findings. Other possible mediators should be investigated including correlates of trait anxiety such as hardiness/mental toughness, and coping resources.

- Adherence to exercise training appears to be greater when it is of moderate intensity (e.g. walking), and integrated into an active lifestyle. Nevertheless, we need to know much more about the determinants of adherence to free-living and facility-based exercise programmes.
- Further evidence is needed to show how improved fitness may reduce cardiovascular, neuroendocrine, and cerebral reactivity to and recovery from psychosocial stressors.

Effects of a single session of exercise on state anxiety

- Most studies have examined anxiety-reducing effects among college-age participants in laboratory settings. We need to know more about the effects of a single session of exercise in naturalistic settings, such as in workplace gyms following anxiety-evoking work, or in schools prior to or after examinations.
- Studies have generally shown limited anxiety-reducing effects from a session of resistance exercise, but this may be due to limited follow-up periods. We need to know if the anxiety-reducing effects are observed later than 2 hours post-exercise before dismissing this form of activity.
- Few studies have examined the effects of low–moderate intensity physical activity (e.g. slow walking). We need to know more about the minimum intensity necessary for anxiety-reducing effects.
- We need to know more about the anxiety-reducing effects of different lengths of exercise sessions, particularly comparing shorter (5–10 minute sessions) with longer sessions (20–30 minutes).

Effects of exercise training on reactivity to stress

- Few studies have examined how people with low stress buffering capabilities (e.g. the depressed, anxious) can reduce their reactivity to and enhance recovery from stressors with exercise training.
- Few studies have examined the effects of low–moderate intensity physical activity on stress reactivity; most have focused on improving aerobic fitness.
- Few studies have examined the effects of exercise on naturally occurring stressors which may elicit more intense stress reactions and emotions such as anger, hostility, helplessness, and fear.

Effects of acute physical activity on reactivity to stress

- We need to know more about the dose (intensity and duration) of exercise necessary for reducing reactivity, and how affective outcomes from exercise interact with reactivity.
- We need to know how exercise can impact on naturally occurring stressors, in terms of reactivity

Acknowledgements

Sincere thanks are expressed to Dr Helen Carter for her tireless assistance in collecting the material and preparing the tables in the manuscript while completing her Ph.D at the University of Brighton.

3 The relationship between physical activity and clinically defined depression

Nanette Mutrie

This review aims to provide a comprehensive picture of what we know about the relationship between physical activity and clinically defined depression. It will cover epidemiological evidence, evidence from meta-analytic reviews and will highlight key studies in the area. Discussion is included on whether or not a case can be made for a causal link between physical activity and depression. Finally, what we know, what we need to know, and what future research and practice should focus on will be itemised.

Introduction

According to the NHS Health and Advisory Service (1995), one in seven adults in the UK will suffer some form of psychiatric morbidity and the prevalence of mental health problems among children is estimated at up to 20% with 7–10 % having moderate to severe problems which prevent normal functioning (Kurtz, 1992). Depression is one of the most common psychiatric problems. An estimated 20% of consultees in primary care report symptoms of depression (Paykel & Priest, 1992). In terms of workplace incidence of depression it has been suggested, by analysing American employee health insurance data, that depression is the most common complaint with a higher prevalence in women than men (Anspaugh, Hunter & Dignan, 1996). It has been estimated that clinically defined depression affects 5–10% of the population of most developed countries (Weismann & Klerman, 1992). Taken together this evidence suggests a large and expensive burden in healthcare resources in the treatment of depression.

Definitions of depression range from episodes of unhappiness, which affect most people from time to time, to persistent low mood and inability to find enjoyment that would probably be classified as clinical depression. In addition, depression may be secondary to other medical conditions such as alcohol addiction. Most cases of depression are treated in general practice but more severe cases are referred to psychiatric services. In the UK, drugs continue to be the most frequently used treatment for depression although psychotherapy and ECT are also used (Hale, 1997). Hale (1997) states that all anti-depressant drugs are equally effective given correct dosage and six to eight weeks of treatment. The common usage of drugs clearly has cost implications and while non-drug treatment, such as weekly sessions of cognitive behavioural therapy, may be suitable for a number of patients, it is often in short supply and is also costly.

A recent overview of depression and its treatment in the UK did not mention the value of exercise at all (Hale, 1997). Over the past 20 years the literature in the area of physical activity/exercise and mental health has been growing, but as Dishman (1995) points out the evidence has not apparently persuaded mental health agencies, such as the American Psychiatric Association, to endorse the role of exercise in treating mental illness such as depression. This is in contrast to coronary artery disease in which inactivity is now recognised as a primary risk factor (Pate et al., 1995). Perhaps the evidence for the role of exercise in treating and preventing mental illness is not convincing or perhaps the mental health literature is suffering from a dualist tendency to treat the mind (mental health) and body (physical health) as separate issues and therefore fail to see as a priority the mental outcomes of a physical treatment such as exercise (Beesley & Mutrie, 1997).

Patients often report that they do not want drugs (Scott, 1996) and yet drugs are the most common treatment for depression. Patient choice is, therefore, another aspect of the treatment of depression that suggests it is worthwhile to pursue the possibility of the use of exercise. Exercise could be a reasonable option which has few negative side effects and could be cost-effective in comparison to both drug and non-drug options such as psychotherapy.

McEntee and Halgin (1996) reported that while many psychotherapists believe in the therapeutic value of exercise, very few (around 10%) recommend exercise to their clients. From their survey of 110 practising psychotherapists they concluded that one of the major reasons for the reluctance to discuss exercise was that it was perceived as inappropriate. Exercise was perceived as being very directive and perhaps dealt with better by physicians or physical recreation specialists: 'Many therapists simply do not see their work as pertaining to the body, and they believe that most clients come to therapy to discuss psychological ailments, not physical or exercise-related ones' (McEntee & Halgin, 1996, p. 55). It would therefore seem that there is much work to be done to convince those who deliver mental health services to focus on the links between mind and body and to look more positively on the role of exercise in mental health issues.

Definition of clinically defined depression

One issue that has plagued our understanding of the relationship between physical activity and depression is the lack of agreement amongst researchers of criteria that define depression. Many previous reviews have included cases of 'depression' that would not reach clinically defined criteria and may be better defined as transitory negative affect. In this chapter, only clinically defined depression will be included; that is, patients will have sought help for their symptoms and a diagnosis made via standard instruments or interviews. The most common questionnaire used, especially in exercise studies, is the Beck Depression Inventory (BDI) (Beck, Ward, Mendelsohn, Mock, & Erbaugh, 1961). Moderate depression on the BDI is defined as a score of 16 or above. However, many exercise studies have included individuals with scores lower than 16 at baseline which would be considered as a transitory or normal score; such studies will not be included in this review. In terms of clinical interview, diagnosis of depression is made via criteria listed in the Diagnostic and Statistical Manual of Mental Disorders (DSM-IV) (American Psychiatric Association, 1994) or the International Classification of Diseases (ICD-10) (World Health Organisation, 1993). In research studies, the Research Diagnostic Criteria are often used (Spitzer, Endicott, & Robins, 1978).

Depression often occurs with other chronic diseases and mental disorders and such cases may well be included but all will have met the criteria for clinical depression. In this review, and throughout the text (see Chapter 1), physical activity is used as the term to describe any form of activity resulting in energy expenditure while exercise is used to describe systematic programmes of activity, which are often supervised. Thus in discussing epidemiological evidence physical activity will be the term which is used, but when discussing treatment the term exercise is more appropriate.

Epidemiological evidence

We owe a great debt to the work of Morgan (see Morgan, 1994) who pioneered much of the initial research into the role of exercise and mental health. It was perhaps his early findings that fitness levels for both male (Morgan, 1968, 1969) and female (Morgan, 1970b) psychiatric patients were lower than non-hospitalised controls, which led to experimental work in using exercise as part of a treatment regime for such patients. Martinsen, Strand, Paulson and Kaggestad (1989) replicated these findings, with Norwegian psychiatric patients. Morgan (1970a) also showed that patients admitted to a psychiatric hospital, but discharged in a short period of time (on average 61 days), had higher levels of muscular endurance on admission than patients with similar initial levels of depression who remained in hospital for longer (at least one year). Such cross-sectional data raised intriguing questions about whether lack of exercise can cause depression or whether depression causes lack of exercise, and whether increasing fitness levels could influence recovery. There were also methodological questions about the relative contribution of genetics and motivation in the fitness estimates that were obtained. However, some of these early questions have now been answered. In the next section, the review of epidemiological evidence suggests that depression is indeed associated with low activity/fitness and that those who maintain activity are less likely to develop depression.

The strongest epidemiological evidence comes from four prospective studies that have followed cohorts over time. In all of the studies depression was clinically defined and in one study depression was diagnosed by psychiatric interview (Weyerer, 1992). Statistical adjustments for potential confounding variables, such as age and socio-economic background, were also made in each of the studies.

Farmer et al. (1988) reported a follow-up of 1,497 respondents to a large survey with particular regard to activity and depression. This study showed that, over a period of eight years, women who had engaged in 'little or no' activity were twice as likely to develop depression as those who had engaged in 'much' or 'moderate' activity. The effects of age, employment, income, education and chronic medical conditions were all statistically accounted for. There was no significant association over the same time period for men, but for those men who were depressed at baseline, inactivity was a strong predictor of continued depression at the eight-year follow-up.

Camacho, Roberts, Lazarus, Kaplan and Cohen (1991) also found an association between inactivity and incidence of depression in a large population from Alameda County in California who provided baseline data in 1965 and were followed up in 1974 and 1983. Physical activity was categorised as low, medium or high. In the first wave of follow-up (1974) the relative risk (RR) of developing depression was significantly greater for both men and women who were low active in 1965 (RR 1.8 for men, 1.7 for women) compared to those who were high active. There is some evidence for a dose-response relationship with those who were moderately active in 1965 showing lower risk of developing depression than those who were low active (see Figure 3.1).

In the second follow-up in 1983, four categories of activity status were created. These categories are shown in Table 3.1 and are defined as follows:

1   those who were low active in 1965 and remained low in 1974 (low/low);
2   those who had been low active in 1965 but had increased activity level in 1974 (low/high);
3   those who had been high active in 1965 and decreased activity by 1974 (high/low);
4   those who had been high active at both times points (high/high).

Those who were inactive in 1965 but had increased activity in 1974 were at no greater risk of developing depression in 1983 than those who had been active at both times points (the reference group for computing the odds ratio). This perhaps suggests a protective effect of physical activity.

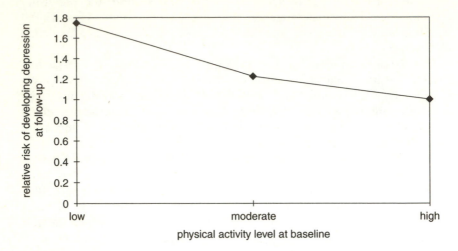

Figure 3.1 Relative risk of developing depression at follow-up from different levels
of baseline physical activity (adapted from Camacho et al., 1991).

None of the odds ratios computed for risk of depression in 1983 showed
significant differences between the four activity categories. The largest
odds ratio, however, was for those who had relapsed from activity in 1965
to inactivity in 1974. They were 1.6 times more likely to develop depression in 1983 than those who had maintained activity, but it must be
remembered that this odds ratio did not reach significance. The authors
note, however, that this odds ratio was relatively unaffected by adjustments for age, sex, physical health, socio-economic status, social support,
life events, anomie, smoking status, relative weight, 1965 level of depression and alcohol consumption. This led them to believe it is a robust
finding. Given that only 137 people were in this category, it is perhaps
not surprising that the odds ratio did not reach significance. However, the
evidence from the 1974 follow-up did provide statistically significant
evidence that low activity preceded the reported depression.

Table 3.1 Changes in physical activity status and subsequent depression (from
Camacho et al., 1991)

Activity status 1965–74	Odds ratio for developing depression in 1983	Confidence interval for odds ratio
1 low/low	1.22	0.62–2.38
2 low/high	1.11	0.52–2.21
3 high/low	1.61	0.80–3.22
4 high/high	1.00	Reference group

Paffenbarger, Lee and Leung (1994) have reported similar findings from the Harvard Alumni studies that followed men for 23–27 years. In that study men who engaged in three or more hours of sport activity per week at baseline had a 27% reduction in the risk of developing depression at follow-up compared to those who played for less than one hour per week. When the authors combined the various indices of physical activity (sports play, walking, stair climbing) evidence for a dose-response relationship emerged; those who had expended 2,500 kcal or more per week were 28% less at risk of developing clinically recognised depression than men who expended less than 1,000 kcal/week. Those who expended between 1,000 and 2,499 kcal/week had a 17% reduction in risk compared to the least active group. This dose-response trend was significant and is illustrated in Figure 3.2 in terms of relative risk. These findings also suggest that inactivity precedes depression.

All of these studies have been conducted on North American populations but Weyerer (1992) showed that in a community sample from Bavaria ($n = 1,536$), the physically inactive were 3.15 times more likely to have depression than those who were regularly active. All were interviewed by a research psychiatrist and 8.3% were identified as depressive using a clinical scale. There was some evidence for a dose-response relationship since those reporting only occasional physical activity were 1.55 times more likely to have depression than those who were regularly physically active, although this was not statistically significant. This cross-sectional data is open to the criticism that the relationship is created because the depressed are inactive. The strongest counter to this argument, which we have seen in the three studies already reviewed, is follow-up data which

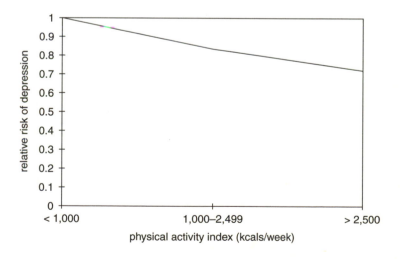

Figure 3.2 Relative risk of developing depression at follow-up from different levels of physical activity at baseline (adapted from Paffenbarger et al., 1994).

shows the least active are most at risk of developing depression at a later point in time. However, low physical activity was not a predictor of depression at a five-year follow-up to this study. The time scale of the Weyerer follow-up (1992) was shorter than any of the other studies and this may be the reason for this apparent difference in results.

All four of these studies show an association between activity and depression with the least active having the greatest incidence of depression. In three of the four studies follow-up data suggest that inactivity at baseline is predictive of developing depression at follow-up. This suggests that inactivity precedes depression. It is important to reiterate that other possible variables, such as physical health status, were accounted for since people may well be inactive because they are disabled or prevented from taking part in activity because of a medical condition. However, there are other reasons such as lack of social skills or socio-economic status that could also predict both inactivity and depression that may not have been fully accounted for. Hopefully, there will be more epidemiological data of this nature that will help us form a picture of the time course of the onset of depression in relation to inactivity and allow for further exploration of variables that predict inactivity and depression. In particular, longitudinal studies are required to elucidate the possible benefits and risks of involvement in PA for youth or adult psychological functioning. Steptoe and Butler (1996) suggested that this could be done with British data from a cohort study initiated in 1970 which they have already used to show a positive association between sport participation and emotional well-being for the cohort during adolescence. Thus the epidemiological data are strongly suggestive of a protective effect from activity but yet more data are required. A final point to note is that there is no evidence to suggest that increasing physical activity or exercise increases the risk of depression.

Meta-analyses

Two meta-analytic reviews of exercise as a treatment for depression have provided further substantial evidence for positive effects (McDonald & Hodgdon, 1991; North, McCullagh, & Tran, 1990). Both report effect sizes of around one half of a standard deviation of change in depression scores which suggests that exercise does have an anti-depressant effect. Calfas and Taylor (1994) report a small meta-analysis of five randomised control trials (RCT) on healthy and psychologically 'at risk' adolescents. They reported an effect size of -0.38 for exercise on depression, although the small number of studies involved means that this must be a cautious conclusion.

The outcomes of meta-analytic reviews are subject to the quality of the input. Dishman (1995) suggests that averaging results from studies with different designs and methods of measurement is not helpful and concludes that there are too few studies with similar features to warrant confidence in the results of meta-analysis in this area. In addition, the issue of whether depression has been clinically defined is particularly important for this chapter. In fact very few studies included in the meta-analyses by North et al. (1990) or McDonald and Hodgdon (1991) had clinically diagnosed individuals.

Craft and Landers (1998) have addressed this issue and conducted a meta-analysis confined to those with clinically defined depression. This meta-analysis included 30 studies, many of which were unpublished dissertations. The average effect size (ES) was −0.72. Further analysis of the moderating variables showed that the effect sizes for mode of exercise (aerobic versus non-aerobic) did not differ, and there was no difference between exercise treatment and psychotherapeutic or behavioural interventions. However, there was a greater ES for those initially classified as moderate to severe in depression compared to those classified as mild to moderate. The results of Craft and Landers' meta-analysis are therefore very encouraging. However, even with a well conducted meta-analysis such as this one, some of Dishman's (1995) criticisms remain since in some of the comparisons (e.g. with different entry level of depression) there are very few studies. It seems best, therefore, to also look at individual studies in detail rather than relying solely on meta-analytic conclusions.

Key studies

Most narrative reviews in this area (e.g. Biddle & Mutrie, 1991; Byrne & Byrne, 1993; Gleser & Mendelberg, 1990; Martinsen, 1989; Morgan, 1994) make cautious positive conclusions but note the methodological limitations of many studies and this criticism has been echoed many times (Dishman, 1995). However, with the exception of Martinsen (1989, 1993, 1994), reviews have included non-clinically defined depression and Morgan (1994) noted that one of the most reliable findings in this area is that exercise will not decrease depression in those who are not depressed in the first place. It would seem appropriate, therefore, to examine all studies in which exercise has been used to treat clinically defined depression and to limit the discussion to studies which have the best design features.

Literature was searched using BIDS, accessing Social Science Citation Index and Embase which searches medical literature, PsychLit, Firstsearch and Sport Discus. All studies from 1970 onwards which could be located incorporating random assignment of subjects to groups and including a clinically defined measure of depression were reviewed. This process excludes some well-designed studies, such as McCann and Holmes (1984), because depression levels were below 16 on the BDI. The key studies are summarised in Table 3.2.

Table 3.2 Randomised controlled studies of exercise treatment for clinically defined depression

Authors/location	Participants	Design	Treatment groups	Measures	Results (statistically significant at 0.05)
Greist et al. (1979) USA	n = 28 (15 women), RDC criteria for depression	10 weeks of treatment, 1 and 3 month follow-up	1. 10 sessions of time-limited psychotherapy 2. time-unlimited psychotherapy; 3. running with a leader 3 × 30–45 mins/week	SCL	The running treatment was as effective as the two psychotherapy treatments
Klein et al. (1985) USA	n = 74 (53 women), mean age 30 years, recruited via media, RDC criteria for depression	12 weeks of treatment and 1, 3 & 9 month follow-up	1. running with a leader, 2 × 45 mins/week 2. group meditation, 2 hours/week 3. group therapy, 2 hours/week	SCL and psychiatric interview	The running treatment was as effective as the other two treatments
Martinsen et al. (1985) Norway	n = 43, mean age 40 years, hospitalised depressives, clinical assessment by DSM-III	9 weeks of treatment	1. exercise group, aerobic training, 50–70% max. VO_2, 1 hour, 3/week 2. control group, occupational therapy, 1 hour, 3/week	BDI; predicted max. VO_2	The exercise group decreased depression scores and increased fitness more than the control group
Doyne et al. (1987) USA	n = 40 (all women) recruited through mass media; mean age 29 years; clinical assessment by RDC	8 weeks of treatment; 1, 7, 12 month follow-up	1. aerobic group (running); 4/week 2. non-aerobic group (weight-lifting); 4/week 3. waiting list control group	BDI; HRSD; cardiovascular fitness (METS) from sub-maximal test	Both exercise conditions reduced depression more than waiting list control. Levels of depression remained lower than baseline to 1 year follow-up
Fremont & Craighead (1987) USA	n = 49, recruitment via advertisement BDI scores of 16 and above	10 weeks of treatment and 2 month follow-up	1. cognitive therapy 1 hour/week 2. running with a leader, 3 × 20 mins/week 3. both cognitive therapy and running.	BDI	All three groups improved. Improvements maintained at 2 month follow-up

Study	Sample	Duration	Intervention	Measures	Results
Mutrie (1988) UK	n = 24 (20 women), mean age 42 years, clinical assessment by GP diagnoses and BDI scores of 16 and above	8 weeks of treatment; assessment at 4 weeks, 8 weeks and 20 week follow-up	1. aerobic exercise conducted at home (walk/jog) 3 × 20–30 mins/week 2. non-aerobic strengthening and stretching exercise conducted at home, 3 × 20–30 mins/week 3. no treatment for 4 weeks, then combination of aerobic and non-aerobic exercise, 3 × 20 mins/week	BDI, POMS, standard step-test for aerobic fitness, standard sit-up test for strength	After 4 weeks only the aerobic group made significant reductions on BDI. After 8 weeks all groups decreased BDI scores and these scores were maintained at 20 weeks with no group differences. There were no group differences in fitness test results with no change noted at 4 weeks and all groups improving by 8 weeks
Martinsen, Strand et al. (1989) Norway	n = 99 (63 women), mean age 41 years, hospitalised depressives, RDC classification	8 weeks of treatment	1. aerobic training, 3 × 1 hour/week 2. strength & flexibility training, 3 × 1 hour/week	Montgomery-Asberg rating scale, BDI, predicted $\dot{V}O_2$ max.	Both groups decreased depression scores. Only the aerobic group made gains on max. $\dot{V}O_2$
Veale et al. (1992) Trial 1 UK	n = 83 (53 women) mean age 36 years, clinical assessment by CIS	12 weeks of treatment	1. standard treatment 2. aerobic exercise (3/week running) adjunctive to standard treatment	CIS, BDI, predicted $\dot{V}O_2$ max.	Exercise group reduced depressive symptoms (CIS) and trait anxiety more than standard group despite incomplete adherence by some S's
Veale et al. (1992) Trial 2 UK	n = 41; clinical assessment by CIS	12 weeks of treatment	each group received standard treatment and either: 1. aerobic exercise (3/week) or 2. non-aerobic exercise (stretching, yoga) (3/week)	CIS, BDI, predicted $\dot{V}O_2$ max.	Both exercise groups showed similar changes to that seen in study 1 above. No differences between groups on any measures
Bosscher (1993) Netherlands	n = 24 (12 women), mean age 34 years, hospitalised depressives, RDC	8 weeks of treatment	1. standard movement therapy of mixed games and exercises, 50 mins 3 × week 2. running 45 mins 3 × week	SDS	Only the running group showed significant decreases in depression although scores still above entry level criteria. No fitness measures taken

Notes:
RDC (Research Diagnostic Criteria: Spitzer, Endicott & Robins, 1978) DSM-III (Diagnostic and Statistical manual of Mental Disorders: American Psychiatric Association, 1980) SCL (Symptom Checklist: Derogatis, Lipman & Covi, 1973) BDI (Beck Depression Inventory: Beck, Ward Mendelsohn, Mock & Erbaugh, 1961) HRSD (Hamilton Rating Scale: Hamilton, 1960) POMS (Profile of Mood States: McNair, Lorr & Droppleman, 1971) CIS (Clinical Interview Schedule, Goldberg, Cooper, Eastwood, Kedward, Shepherd, 1970) SDS (Zung depression scale, Zung, Richards & Short, 1965).

Conclusions from key studies

The first and obvious conclusion from Table 3.2 is that more studies are required. Only three could be found which had been conducted in the 1990s. It is also concluded that both internal and external validity are high, given that only those studies with good design features were included, and given that they have been conducted in North America and Europe, all with similar results. Table 3.2 also shows that exercise programmes (both aerobic and non-aerobic) can reduce clinically defined depression and that the reduction of depression is of the same order as that found for a variety of standard psychotherapeutic treatments. Furthermore, these anti-depressant effects are feasible in a short time frame (4–8 weeks) and persist from 2 months to 1 year. These findings seem to be very similar to those from meta-analyses and thus add confidence to the meta-analytic conclusion that exercise can have a substantial anti-depressant effect.

What we do not know is the comparative effects of exercise treatment with drug treatment. This seems surprising given that drugs are the most common treatment for depression in the UK, and it is also surprising that so few studies have been conducted in the UK. The studies in Table 3.2 have mean ages of participants between 29 and 42 years suggesting that exercise effects for depression levels for youth or older adults have not been studied. Only one study on the use of exercise as an adjunctive treatment in clinically diagnosed mental illness in children was found (Brown, Welsh, Labbe, Vitulli, & Kulkarni, 1992), but it was excluded from the table of key studies since it did not reach the design criteria. Similarly, a well-designed study (McNeil, LeBlanc, & Joyner, 1991) of exercise and social contact with older adults was excluded since the adults were entered into that study with scores below 16 on the BDI. In addition, we do not know much about adherence levels to exercise especially in the follow-up phases. Some studies do report this but in most cases the details are missing.

It is clearly difficult to conduct studies with good design features in this area. Even by selecting those studies with random assignment to treatment conditions, methodological difficulties remain which limit the strength of the conclusions. These difficulties include:

- achieving a big enough sample to ensure statistical power (could the findings of 'no difference' between some conditions be a Type 2 statistical error?);
- equalising time in contact with professionals in the different treatment conditions;
- avoiding resentful demoralisation in a no-treatment group or a group given the 'routine' as opposed to the 'new' treatment;
- controlling for the effects of the positive characteristics of an exercise leader;
- conducting long term follow-up; and

- finding adequate measures of the variables of interest including fitness changes.

The next stage for research must attempt to overcome these methodological difficulties.

How good is the evidence for an anti-depressant effect from exercise?

It is still difficult to conclude that there is a causal link between exercise and reduction in depression because there are many peripheral issues (such as the effect of an exercise leader, or a class effect) associated with most of the successful programmes. There are also relatively few experimental studies. However, given the more recent addition of epidemiological data to the discussion it may be appropriate to use Hill's (1965) classic criteria for deciding whether there is an association or a causal link between observed illness (in this case depression) and some environmental condition (in this case exercise status). Hill (1965) suggested eight criteria which can be used to help scientists and practitioners decide if a causal interpretation of evidence can be made. I will use these eight criteria to look at the evidence for an anti-depressant effect of exercise.

Strength of association

The first of Hill's criteria is strength of the association. Meta-analytic studies show an effect size of 0.53 – 0.72 for exercise on depression. Epidemiological studies suggest a relative risk of around 1.7 for the inactive reporting depression at a later date. This evidence is not quite as strong as that for exercise and coronary heart disease, where range of relative risk of between 1.5 to 2.5 for the inactive have been reported (Pate et al., 1995). Nevertheless, the exercise effect for depression does show strength of association.

Consistency

The second of Hill's criteria is consistency where the question is whether or not the association between exercise and depression has been shown in different places, with different people, at different times and in different circumstances. If we look at Table 3.2 we can see that experimental evidence has been found in the US, UK, and other parts of Europe. The same is true for the epidemiological evidence. Men and women have been included, the data spans three decades of work, and the circumstances include community, hospitals and primary care settings. It does indeed seem that the findings are consistent.

Specificity

Specificity, the third of Hill's criteria, refers to whether or not other associations exist between the conditions and the disease. Hill argues that specificity, which is limiting the conditions to the disease, for example smoking and lung cancer, strengthens the argument for causation. In exercise studies specificity does not exist. Depression is not the only condition that has been linked to inactivity. Indeed, others have shown a link between exercise and all-cause mortality (Blair et al., 1989), and depression has been shown to have more than one contributing factor (Kaplan, Roberts, Camacho, & Coyne, 1987). However, while Hill argued that if specificity exists it strengthens the argument for causation, he also argued that if specificity is not present other criteria might supply additional evidence and it is not a fatal flaw in the case.

Temporal sequence

The fourth of Hill's criteria is temporal sequence. In order to conclude that there is a causal link between inactivity and depression we must be able to judge whether or not inactivity precedes the onset of depression. Early cross-sectional studies could not answer this because it was equally likely that depression preceded inactivity. However, at least three prospective population studies have shown that the inactive are more likely to develop depression. Thus there is some evidence for the temporal sequence which strengthens the case for causation.

Dose-response

Hill's fifth criterion is evidence for a dose-response curve or biological gradient. Two of the prospective epidemiological studies showed a dose-response gradient with the least active at baseline being most at risk of developing depression at follow-up, while the most active had the lowest risk. In terms of experimental studies there is insufficient evidence at present to suggest that different doses of exercise produce different psychological outcomes. Although both aerobic and non-aerobic exercise have produced an anti-depressant effect, almost all the aerobic exercise has been based on moderate intensity (60–75%) levels with a typical 3 times per week, 20–60 minute prescription. However, it has also been noted that negative effects in terms of mood occur in athletes who far exceed the typical prescription (Morgan, 1994). Thus the evidence for a dose-response curve is modest. There is obviously a need for additional data to complete this imperfect picture.

Plausibility

The sixth criterion is biological plausibility. Here we are looking for the explanation of the observed association. There is considerable agreement that the underlying mechanisms that relate to the positive effects from exercise on mental illness are not yet known (Biddle & Mutrie, 1991; Morgan & Goldston, 1987; Plante, 1993). Several possible mechanisms, including biochemical changes such as increased levels of endorphins, and psychological changes such as an increased sense of mastery, have been proposed (La Forge, 1995; Petruzzello, Landers, Hatfield, Kubitz, & Salazar, 1991). The studies showing an anti-depressant effect for non-aerobic exercise suggest that an improvement in aerobic fitness is not a key issue. However, objective measures of all possible fitness parameters (aerobic, strength, flexibility and body composition) should be included in studies to provide evidence that the exercise programme has had the desired fitness effect and to shed light on potential mechanisms.

The fact that we do not know which mechanism operates should not prevent us saying that they remain 'plausible'. Dishman (1995), in his excellent review of this topic, concludes that our lack of knowledge about the biological plausibility of the association between exercise and mental health is a major shortcoming in the literature. It is likely that this short-coming contributes to the lack of acceptance of the role of exercise by psychiatrists (Hale, 1997). Hill (1965, p. 298) reminds us that we should not demand too much of this criteria because 'What is biologically plausible depends upon the biological knowledge of the day'. Determining the mechanisms for the psychological effects of exercise in general, and for depression in particular, is perhaps the greatest challenge to exercise scientists trying to illuminate the relationship between exercise and mental health. It would appear that much of the knowledge has to be developed using animal models until such times when we have technology to study brain function in humans during exercise. Brain imaging is one possible technology that may advance our understanding of the mechanisms. It is clear that the answer to this complex question will not be found in exercise laboratories alone. We must collaborate with colleagues in neuroscience and psychological medicine to expand our knowledge. La Forge (1995, p. 28) provided this sensible guide to future practice:

> The mechanism is likely an extraordinary synergy of biological trans-actions, including genetic, environmental, and acute and adaptive neurobiological processes. Inevitably, the final answers will emerge from a similar synergy of researchers and theoreticians from exercise science, cognitive science and neurobiology.

Coherence

The possible mechanisms should not conflict with what is understood to be the natural history and biology of mental illness. This is Hill's seventh criterion of coherence. While, as with many other aspects of these criteria, the evidence is far from complete, one example might show coherence. More women than men report depression and women report less activity than men. Development of animal models to study inactivity and depression and the use of exercise to combat depression will provide further evidence for coherence.

Experimental evidence

Perhaps the best evidence comes under Hill's eighth criterion of experimental evidence already discussed in the conclusions from the key studies in Table 3.2. The experimental evidence supports a causal link with exercise programmes and depression reduction.

In reviewing the evidence in terms of these criteria it can be seen that the only criterion which the link between inactivity and depression does not fulfil is specificity. Other criteria, such as temporal sequence and dose-response have only modest support, but it does seem reasonable to conclude that there is supportive evidence for a causal link between inactivity and depression although much work remains to be done. There are those who might say that the evidence is still insufficient and therefore we should not recommend the use of exercise in the treatment of depression or consider inactivity to be a factor in the onset of depression. However, as Hill (1965, p. 12) reminded us,

> All scientific work is incomplete – whether it be observational or experimental. All scientific work is liable to be upset or modified by advancing knowledge. That does not confer upon us a freedom to ignore the knowledge we already have, or postpone the action that it appears to demand at a given time.

The potential benefit of advocating the use of exercise as part of a treatment package for depression far outweighs the potential risk that no effect will occur. There are very few possible negative side effects (e.g. injury, exercise dependence) and there have been no negative outcomes reported in the literature. In addition, there are potential physical health benefits such as an increase in fitness, weight reduction, and decreased coronary artery disease risks. Therefore, physical activity/exercise should be advocated as part of the treatment for clinically defined depression. The evidence presented here adds further strength to the arguments used by health promoters for the need to prevent diseases (including mental illness) by increasing the percentage of the population engaged in regular physical activity.

Future practice and research

Having considered the evidence, this section will consider guidelines and future directions for those promoting and researching physical activity and depression.

Guidelines for practice

- Physical activity/exercise should be advocated as part of the treatment of clinically defined depression.
- Health promotion campaigns aimed at increasing the level of physical activity in the population should include the prevention of depression as part of the rationale.
- Exercise leaders, general practitioners and other para-medical staff working with depressed patients need in-service training on how exercise may have an anti-depressant effect.
- Pre-service training for doctors, psychiatrists and clinical psychologists is required on the topic of the anti-depressant effects of exercise.

Guidelines for research

- The exploration of physical activity and depression levels in large population sets should be encouraged.
- Randomised controlled trials of exercise therapy versus standard drug therapy and psychotherapy are required which attempt to overcome the methodological difficulties of earlier studies.
- Qualitative studies of how different patients and medical staff perceive the role of exercise in the treatment of depression should be encouraged.
- Practical and experimental application of exercise is required for both young and old people suffering from depression.
- Exercise scientists must collaborate with medical and neurobiological scientists to explore the mechanisms of the anti-depressant effects of exercise.

What we know

- Epidemiological evidence has demonstrated that physical activity is associated with a decreased risk of developing clinically defined depression.
- Evidence from experimental studies shows that both aerobic exercise and resistance training exercise may be used to treat moderate and more severe depression, usually as an adjunct to standard treatment.

- The anti-depressant effect of exercise is of the same magnitude as that found from psychotherapeutic techniques. However, the range of psychotherapies used in these studies does not perhaps mirror currently available 'best practice' such as cognitive behavioural therapy.
- There is support for a causal link between exercise and decreased depression.
- No negative effects of exercise have been noted in depressed populations.

What we need to know

- Is there an anti-depressant effect from exercise for younger and older adults?
- Are the psychological effects of physical activity the same for different modes of activity (e.g. aerobic, strength-based, flexibility-based)?
- Do different intensities and durations of physical activity make a difference and do fitness levels modulate that effect?
- What is the time course of the effects?
- How do the potential mechanisms of the effects interact?
- How do effects of exercise compare to those of drug treatments and what adjunctive value does exercise have along with drug treatment?
- If drugs are also administered is the interaction of drug and exercise safe?

4 Emotion, mood and physical activity

Stuart J.H. Biddle

This chapter summarises the evidence on exercise and physical activity (PA) and emotional feelings and mood. Appropriate evidence-based conclusions are drawn and implications for guiding future research and practice in health settings provided. Because the areas of mood and emotion are not easy to delimit, studies investigating clinical depression, self-esteem, and cognitive functioning have not been addressed as these are reviewed elsewhere in this volume. Tension-related mood states will be considered, but not the wider literature on anxiety and stress as this also is covered elsewhere. Only studies investigating exercise and 'lifestyle' physical activity, rather than competitive sport, are considered.

Evidence has been drawn from papers located through electronic searches using *Sport Discus*, *PsychLit*, and *Medline*, as well as searching extensive personal files and references cited in other reviews. Preference was given to papers published since 1987, and particularly meta-analyses, epidemiological surveys, and controlled trials.

Given the potentially disparate nature of the topic being addressed, the review is organised around the themes of emotion (affect) and mood but within the overall context of health-related quality of life (HRQL). Research consensus statements are provided in conclusion.

Health-related quality of life

Rejeski, Brawley and Shumaker (1996) suggest that it is typical for HRQL to be defined in terms of participants' perceptions of function. They outline six types of HRQL measures:

- *global indices of HRQL*. These might include general life satisfaction, or self-esteem.
- *physical function*. Perceptions of function; physical self-perceptions; health-related perceptions.
- *physical symptoms*. Fatigue; energy; sleep.
- *emotional function*. Depression, anxiety, mood, affect (emotion).
- *social function*. Social dependency; family/work roles.
- *cognitive function*. Memory; attention; problem-solving.

Rejeski et al. (1996) state that the National Institutes of Health in the US now mandate researchers to include measures of HRQL in most clinical trials. HRQL outcomes are justified in physical activity research for several reasons. First, health-related perceptions of patients are important in their own right. Second, they may act as a motivator of future participation in physical activity. Third, correlations between HRQL and performance measures of dysfunction, such as perceived ability to climb stairs, are usually stronger than between HRQL and changes in physical fitness, such as aerobic capacity. This suggests that performance measures are much more easily detected and are more salient to patients than objective fitness measures.

HRQL measures, however, are usually viewed simply in terms of physical function. This is a narrow view. This chapter, therefore, will review studies that fall primarily into the emotional function category of HRQL. Chapters elsewhere in this volume cover other aspects of HRQL.

Measurement of HRQL

There are many HRQL instruments and these include affective measures, although agreement over measurement is difficult to come by (see Bennett & Murphy, 1997). Key measures are summarised in Table 4.1 and include the SF-36, The Nottingham Health Profile and the EuroQol. The SF-36 is a 36-item questionnaire designed to assess 8 health dimensions covering functional status, well-being, and overall evaluation of health (Dixon, Heaton, Long, & Warburton, 1994). Dixon et al. (1994) conclude that the SF-36 is not designed for specific patient groups, and that it is not directly based on lay views; also there is little evidence that it detects change. Indeed, health changes detected through interview by Hill, Harries and Popay (1996) went undetected by the SF-36 (see also Jenkinson, Layte, Coulter & Wright, 1996). Overall, therefore, an over-reliance on the use of the SF-36 in HRQL studies is not recommended. Where possible, if mood, affect and HRQL are to be assessed in physical activity interventions, more specific measures should be sought.

The Nottingham Health Profile (NHP) (Hunt, McEwan & McKenna, 1986) has been used since the 1970s in intervention and outcome trials and, like the EuroQol (Buxton, O'Hanlon & Rushby, 1990, 1992), assesses six dimensions of HRQL. (See Bowling, 1995, for a review of quality of life measures.)

HRQL and physical activity

Rejeski et al. (1996) provide a comprehensive review of HRQL and physical activity. The present chapter, therefore, will focus on the emotional dimension of HRQL, and specifically mood and affect. Chapters elsewhere

Table 4.1 Common measures of health-related quality of life

Label	Reference(s)	Measures	Comments
SF-36	Dixon et al. (1994)	• general health • physical functioning • mental health • role limitations (physical and emotional) • bodily pain • energy/tiredness • social functioning	Mental health measures include 5 items assessing 'anxiety', depressed mood, happiness. Social functioning subscale assesses whether physical health or emotional problems have interfered with social activities
Nottingham Health Profile	Hunt et al. (1986)	• energy • pain • physical mobility • emotional reactions • social isolation • sleep	
EuroQol	Buxton et al. (1990, 1992)	• mobility • self-care • 'usual activities' • pain/discomfort • anxiety/depression • general health change	

in this volume deal with other aspects of HRQL, such as clinical depression (Mutrie), anxiety (Taylor), self-esteem (Fox), and cognitive functioning (Boutcher). Rejeski et al. (1996) offer the following conclusions from their review of physical activity and HRQL studies:

• HRQL test batteries should include general and condition- or population-specific measures.
• The degree of change observed in HRQL through PA will depend on baseline levels.
• The degree of impact of PA on HRQL will depend on both the physiological stimulus as well as social and behavioural characteristics of the treatment or intervention.
• People vary in the extent to which they value certain health-related outcomes from physical activity, hence this will affect HRQL perceptions of those in intervention studies.

Emotion and mood

The mood states and emotions associated with physical activity have a potentially important role in health promotion. If we believe that physical activity is a positive health behaviour to be encouraged and promoted, how people feel during and after activity may be critical in determining whether they maintain their involvement. Hence, emotion and mood may have motivational properties for an important health-related behaviour. In addition, positive mood and affect are important health outcomes in their own right. For example, Morgan, in the preface to his book on physical activity and mental health stated that 'it is our belief that prevention – not treatment – offers the best solution to the pandemic mental health problems that characterize modern society. This book attempts to demonstrate the extent to which physical activity, a nonpharmacological strategy, can be effective in this regard' (1997, p. xv).

Mood is the global set of affective states we experience on a day-to-day basis. Although mood can be conceptualised in terms of distinct mood states, such as vigour and depression, it differs from emotion, which is normally defined in terms of specific feeling states generated in reaction to certain events or appraisals. However, the distinction between mood and emotion in PA research studies is often not clear.

Measuring emotion and mood

Emotion

Emotion has sometimes been distinguished from 'affect'. Lazarus (1991, p. 6) suggests that emotion is more generic than affect and defines the latter as the subjective experience of emotion, and emotion itself as 'complex, patterned ... reactions to how we think we are doing in our lifelong efforts to survive and flourish and to achieve what we wish for ourselves'. However, the two terms are sometimes not distinguished from each other, and this is often the case in physical activity research. In the present paper the two terms will be used synonymously.

In psychology, there is a debate concerning the nature of emotion. Some prefer to define emotion in terms of discrete emotional reactions, such as pleasure, fear, happiness, and excitement (Clore, Ortony, & Foss, 1987; Lazarus, 1991; Weiner, 1995). Others suggest that emotions are best defined in terms of their common properties, or dimensions, such as positive and negative affect (Watson & Tellegen, 1985).

Lazarus (1991) argues that the distinct qualities of emotional reactions are lost, or blurred, when reduced to a few dimensions. According to his 'cognitive-motivational-relational' theory of emotion, he argues that each emotion is unique because it is created by a different appraisal of the perceived significance of an event. However, it is also logical to see emotions clustered according to common categories. Watson and colleagues (Watson, Clark, & Carey, 1988; Watson, Clark, & Tellegen, 1988; Watson & Tellegen, 1985) have shown that two major factors emerge from an analysis of emotions – positive affect and negative affect. The former refers to feelings such as alertness and activeness, whereas negative affect refers to unpleasant affective states such as anger and fear.

Russell and colleagues have also advocated a dimensional approach to the study of emotions (see Russell, 1980). In their 'circumplex' model, they suggest that emotion can best be defined in terms of the two dimensions of valence (i.e. pleasant–unpleasant) and arousal (i.e. high–low). This gives rise to emotions being classified along these two dimensions, such as tense (high arousal/low pleasure), excited (high arousal/high pleasure), relaxed (low arousal/high pleasure), and depressed (low arousal/low pleasure) (see Warr, 1990).

Mood

Measures of mood have typically involved the Profile of Mood States (POMS) (McNair, Lorr, & Droppleman, 1971), although McDonald and Hodgdon (1991) also located exercise studies using the Multiple Affect Adjective Check List (MAACL) (Zuckerman & Lubin, 1965). The MAACL, however, assesses only anxiety, depression and hostility and is prone to social desirability distortion. Similarly, the POMS is comprised of five negative mood scales and only one positive scale (vigour). Studies using the MAACL, therefore, cannot be considered adequate for the study of psychological well-being (PWB) or mood, and those using the POMS are limited due to the single positive mood subscale. The POMS can also be varied according to the instructions, such as participants describing how they feel/have felt 'right now' or 'over the past few weeks'.

Table 4.2 Summary of mood and affect measures commonly used in physical activity research

Instrument	Reference	Measures	Comments
POMS (Profile of Mood States)	McNair et al. (1971)	65-item scale assessing: • tension • depression • anger • vigour • fatigue • confusion	• only one positive subscale • used extensively in PA research • short and bipolar forms available • time instructions can be varied • can be a state or trait scale • general scale not specific to physical activity
PANAS (Positive and Negative Affect Schedule)	Watson, Clark, & Tellegen (1988)	Two 10-item affect scales assessing: • positive affect: e.g. excited, enthusiastic, inspired • negative affect: e.g. distressed, hostile, irritable	• good psychometric properties • assesses only two general dimensions • time instructions can be varied • can be a state or trait scale • general scale not specific to physical activity
BFS (Befindlichkeitsskalen)	Abele & Brehm (1993)	40-item scale devised in German to assess two-dimensional model of mood: activation (high/low) and evaluation (positive/negative). 8 subscales: • activation (high/positive) • elation (high/positive) • calmness (low/positive) • contemplativeness (low/positive) • excitation (high/negative) • anger (high/negative) • fatigue (low/negative) • depression (low/negative)	• extensive German research supporting validity of scale in sport and exercise settings • state scale

Scale	Author	Description
MAACL (Multiple Affect Adjective Check List)	Zuckerman & Lubin (1965)	• scale comprises 132 adjectives • assesses anxiety, depression and hostility • time instructions can be varied • can be a state or trait scale • general scale not specific to physical activity • some doubts expressed about psychometric properties (see McDonald & Hodgdon (1991)
FS (Feeling Scale)	Hardy & Rejeski (1989)	• single-item scale assessing hedonic tone (pleasure/displeasure) • developed for exercise research • state scale • 11-point scale ranging from −5 to +5

EFI (Exercise-Induced Feeling Inventory)	Gauvin & Rejeski (1993)	• 12-item adjective scale assessing four dimensions:
		  • positive engagement
		  • tranquillity
		  • revitalisation
		  • physical exhaustion
		• developed for exercise research
		• sound psychometric properties
		• state scale

SEES (Subjective Exercise Experiences Scale)	McAuley & Courneya (1994)	• 12-item adjective scale assessing three dimensions:
		  • positive well-being
		  • psychological distress
		  • fatigue
		• developed for exercise research
		• sound psychometric properties
		• state scale

Abele and Brehm (1993) report a number of studies they have conducted in Germany using the 'Befindlichkeitsskalen' (BFS). This scale places mood states along the continua of high/low activation and positive/negative mood. This is similar to Russell's (1980) circumplex model. For example, one can contrast high activation moods that differ in their positive or negative evaluation. A high activation/negative mood might be 'anger' whereas a high activation/positive mood state might be 'elation'.

Measures of mood and affect in physical activity research

The majority of studies investigating exercise, PA and PWB have assessed mood and affect using scales such as the POMS, MAACL and the PANAS (see Table 4.2). The POMS, in particular, has been criticised mainly on the basis that it is restricted to just one positive factor (vigour). Steptoe (1992, pp. 208–9), for example, argues that 'measures like the POMS ... fail to capture the positive feelings of well-being that are more than the mere absence of anxiety, depression or irritation'. The PANAS, while being used increasingly in exercise research, is 'restricted to the assessment of global affect' (Gauvin & Rejeski, 1993, p. 404) and fails to differentiate more specific types of emotion.

Steptoe (1992) reports on his work on mood and exercise by suggesting that 'context-specific' measures might be particularly useful. For example, his research group developed a list of 36 items thought to be associated with exercise and mood. Factor analysis revealed the three factors of 'coping assets', 'coping deficits', and 'physical well-being'. Such a scale (shown in Table 4.3) allows for a more balanced view of PWB in comparison to the POMS. However, Steptoe's scale has not been used by other researchers.

Gauvin and Rejeski (1993) developed the Exercise-induced Feeling Inventory (EFI) in an effort to capture four distinct feeling states in exercise: revitalisation, tranquillity, positive engagement, and physical exhaustion. Psychometric support has been reported for adults (Gauvin & Rejeski, 1993) and children (Vlachopoulos, Biddle, & Fox, 1996).

In a similar vein, McAuley and Courneya (1994) developed the Subjective Exercise Experiences Scale (SEES) comprising three factors of positive well-being, psychological distress, and fatigue and this, too, now has support with children (Markland, Emberton, & Tallon, 1997). Both the SEES and EFI are scales can that easily be used in field assessments of exercise affect. A summary of key measures of mood and affect in physical activity research is shown in Table 4.2 (see also Gauvin & Spence, 1998).

Emotion, mood and physical activity

There are a very large number of studies investigating the relationship between physical activity and affective states. As such, I will draw my

Table 4.3 Factors of psychological well-being for physical activity identified by Moses et al. (1989)

Factor 1 Coping assets	Factor 2 Coping deficits	Factor 3 Physical well-being
self-confident	easily irritated	refreshed
enthusiastic	disappointed with self	healthy
uplifted	calm (−)	strong
proud of self	drained	supple
elated	easily upset	fit
invigorated	distressed	well
coping	bothered	
achieving something	overwhelmed	
overcoming difficulties	under too much pressure	
getting close to goals	run down	
competent		
under control		
attractive		
well-organised		

Nicholas G. Norgan, *Physical Activity and Health*, Steptoe, 1992, Cambridge University Press.

conclusions from three types of studies, as shown in Tables 4.4 and 4.5. Table 4.4 summarises narrative and meta-analytic reviews on PA and mood/affect, as defined for this review. Only two published meta-analyses were located (McDonald & Hodgdon, 1991; Schlicht, 1994), but neither was in a refereed journal. Table 4.5 summarises large epidemiological surveys conducted in Britain on physical activity and psychological well-being.

Studies of mood, affect and PA involve both acute and chronic effects of PA. Acute effects are assessed in terms of state responses to single exercise or PA sessions. Chronic effects are assessed more in terms of generalised traits from involvement in PA over time. Typically, epidemiological surveys assess chronic PA effects whereas experimental trials measure the effects of acute exercise.

Narrative and meta-analytic reviews

Of the 20 reviews listed in Table 4.4, there is cautious support for the proposition that PA is associated with enhanced affect and mood. The caution comes not from the lack of apparent evidence but from the relatively weak research designs utilised. For example, the comprehensive review by Leith (1994) showed that experimental evidence was less convincing than for pre- or quasi-experimental studies. Similarly, reviews by Berger (1996; Berger & McInman, 1993; Wankel & Berger, 1990) conclude that mood effects can be positive after exercise but causal links cannot be supported, and certain conditions, such as non-competitive aerobic exercise, might need to be met for such effects to occur. However,

Table 4.4 Summary of findings from meta-analytic and narrative reviews investigating the relationship between physical activity, mood and affect

Study	Review design and scope	Results and conclusions
Leith & Taylor (1990)	Narrative review of pre-, quasi- and actual experimental studies of exercise and PWB, broadly defined	Pre-experimental: 1 mood study reported. Effect of exercise was positive Quasi-experimental: 10 mood studies; all showed improvement with exercise. 1 affect study; no change detected Experimental: 4 mood studies; 1 showed positive change, 3 no change
Wankel & Berger (1990)	Narrative review of the social psychological benefits of recreational sport. Categories of benefit classified as: personal enjoyment, personal growth, social harmony, and social change	Enjoyment reported as a main reason for sport involvement. '. . . consistency of the accumulated results . . . is impressive' (p. 170) Support for link between PA and psychological well-being but the nature of this relationship remains unclear Sport has potential for developing positive values and social integration, but only if certain conditions are met
Biddle & Mutrie (1991)	Narrative review of psychological effects of exercise in non-clinical populations	Support for positive mood being associated with exercise, but causal and experimental links still to be established
Jex (1991)	Narrative review of psychological benefits of exercise in work settings	The small number of studies reported show a positive effect for exercise, but other factors accounting for this relationship cannot be ruled out
McDonald & Hodgdon (1991)	Meta-analysis of the effects of aerobic fitness training on mood	POMS effect sizes: tension (−0.322), depression (−0.284), anger (−0.182), vigour (−0.399), fatigue (−0.271), confusion (−0.402)

Reference	Description	Findings
Brown (1992)	Narrative review of the relationship between PA and PWB in the elderly	Mood: 3 of 7 studies report positive effect. Life satisfaction: none of 3 studies report effect
Steptoe (1992)	Narrative review of psychological well-being and PA	Exercise has a positive long-term effect on mood and PWB This is not accounted for by selection, group socialisation, expectations or attentional factors. Research indicates that high intensity exercise may confer less benefit than exercise of a more moderate nature
Abele & Brehm (1993)	Narrative review of psychological effects of exercise and sport	Mood effects of aerobic exercise: all 15 studies report positive effect Mood effects of sport competition: studies show increases before a game and decreases after a game in activation and excitation Evidence supports a 'disequilibrium' model of sport mood (i.e. competitors compete to change their mood and seek excitement through sport) and an 'equilibrium' model of exercise mood (i.e. to seek tension reduction and a 'feel better' effect)
Berger & McInman (1993)	Narrative review of the association between exercise and aspects of quality of life	Mood: support for a relationship between exercise and positive mood, but only if certain conditions are met
Fillingim & Blumenthal (1993)	Narrative review of psychological effects of exercise in the elderly	Mood: aerobic exercise studies have yielded less consistent findings than for younger adults
Hutzler & Bar-Eli (1993)	Narrative review of psychological effects of sport for those with disabilities	Mood: 4 of 5 studies showed similar mood profiles for athletes with disabilities compared to those without disabilities

Table 4.4 (continued)

Study	Review design and scope	Results and conclusions
Tuson & Sinyor (1993)	Narrative review of the effects of acute exercise on affect/mood	Anger: 6 of 12 studies showed improved scores after exercise; 1 worsened Anxiety: 21 of 39 showed improvement; 4 worsened Depression: 9 of 28 showed improvement; 0 worsened Vigour: 6 of 15 showed improvement; 0 worsened Fatigue: 3 of 13 showed improvement; 1 worsened Confusion: 3 of 12 showed improvement; 0 worsened
Wykoff (1993)	Narrative review of the psychological effects of exercise for adult women	Non-clinical populations: support for mood enhancing effect of exercise Clinical populations: no studies reported on mood
Leith (1994)	Narrative review of exercise and mood	26 of 34 studies reported showed improvements in mood after exercise: this includes 2 of 2 pre-experimental studies, 19 of 24 quasi-experimental studies, and 5 of 8 experimental studies
Martinsen & Stephens (1994)	Narrative review of exercise and mental health in both clinical and 'free-living' populations	Good population surveys are rare. Studies indicate mental health benefits; only limited support for the mental health benefits of exercise for those initially 'well'
McAuley (1994)	Narrative review of physical activity and psychosocial outcomes	Results of 23 published studies investigating PA and affect (excluding anxiety, depression, stress reactivity, and mood state scales primarily negative in nature) reviewed. 69% showed a positive relationship PA and PWB

Study	Method	Findings
Schlicht (1994)	Meta-analysis of 'sport' and PWB	Overall ES (0.15) was not significantly different from zero, but ranged from −0.31 to 0.81 Studies not listed so quality and appropriateness of selection criteria not possible to check
McAuley & Rudolph (1995)	Narrative review of PA and PWB in older adults	Affect & mood: 25 studies reported of which all but 2 showed positive effects. Positive mood changes generally more evident in men than women Life satisfaction/HRQL: limited evidence for a positive effect
Mutrie & Biddle (1995)	Narrative review of exercise and mental health in non-clinical populations, with an emphasis on European research	Mood: generally positive effects for exercise, but there is a limited amount of experimental research
Berger (1996)	Narrative review of the psychological benefits of an active lifestyle	Mood: support for a relationship between PA and positive mood, but causal links not established

Table 4.5 Summary of findings from British population surveys investigating the relationship between physical activity and psychological well-being

Study	Survey design and scope	Results and conclusions
Sports Council & Health Education Authority (1992)	National Fitness Survey for England of 16–74 year olds (n = 4316). One section of interview assessed perceived well-being	Small but consistent trend showing relationship between PA and well-being. Same trend evident for those in poorest health, reducing the chance that those 'well' choose to exercise, thus reversing the direction of possible influence Association between PA and well-being stronger for those 55 years and over Trends evident for all age groups and both sexes
Thirlaway & Benton (1996)	National Health & Lifestyle Survey data. Representative British sample (n = 6,200) Assessed on PA and General Health Questionnaire. (Unpublished survey data reported in book chapter)	Higher PA associated with better mental health in women over 30 years and men over 50 years No relationship for those under 30 years of age
Steptoe & Butler (1996)	Investigation of the association between emotional well-being and regular sport/vigorous PA in 16-year-olds (n = 5,061). Data from 1986 follow-up to 1970 British Cohort Study	Greater sport/vigorous PA was positively associated with emotional well-being independent of gender, SES or health status Participation in non-vigorous activity was associated with high psychological and somatic symptoms on Malaise Inventory

the cautiously positive conclusions from Table 4.4 are further enhanced by the fact that the reviews span several countries and populations (e.g. workplace, women, people with disabilities) with diverse methods and measuring instruments. Hardly any studies report negative mood effects.

McDonald and Hodgdon (1991) report a meta-analysis on PA and mood. They delimited their review to aerobic fitness training studies and found that researchers used mainly the POMS (tension, depression, anger, fatigue, vigour, and confusion) or MAACL (anxiety, depression, and hostility). Results are shown in Table 4.4 and suggest a clear relationship between exercise and vigour and a lack of negative mood, although the effect sizes are generally small-to-moderate.

Interestingly, Schlicht (1994) reported a brief meta-analytic review of exercise and mental health in which the proposed relationship between physical activity and PWB was not supported. The analyses involved 44 samples from 39 studies and 8,909 research participants. However, the studies selected for the meta-analysis were not listed in his paper and additional information is required on study selection criteria before more can be concluded. Given that the paper was published in German it would be interesting to see how many of the studies included are written in German, and whether many are in English and thus more likely to be included in the North American meta-analyses that have supported a link between physical activity and other indices of mental health (e.g. Petruzzello, Landers, Hatfield, Kubitz, & Salazar, 1991). Nevertheless, Schlicht (1994) reported an overall ES of only 0.15, but with a large range, and the overall ES was not significantly different from zero (see Table 4.4). This may reflect that similar forms of PA are viewed favourably by some individuals but not by others, thus reducing any psychological effect. In other words, the effects of PA on mental health may be quite individual.

Epidemiological surveys

Epidemiological surveys, while often suffering from methodological short-comings such as lacking internal validity and control (see Chapter 8), have the advantage over some other studies in so far as they usually have large samples, are representative of the population, and hence allow good generalisability of findings. Three such studies from Britain are summarised in Table 4.5 and show clear positive relationships between PA and psychological well-being. Confidence in these results is enhanced by noting that the surveys cover both adolescents and adults, use clinical and non-clinical assessment tools, and cover a total sample of 15,577. However, as noted by Thirlaway and Benton (1996), not all groups seemed to benefit from PA.

The three British studies are comparable to Stephens' (1988) secondary analysis of four North American surveys with over 55,000 people. Across several measures, there was a clear association between PA and psychological well-being. For example, positive affect was associated with PA

Table 4.6 Controlled experimental trials from Britain investigating physical activity, exercise and psychological well-being

Study	Participants	Design and treatment	Results and conclusions
Steptoe & Cox (1988)	Female students (n = 32)	Single session experiment testing the effects of exercise intensity and music on mood All participants exercised for four periods: at both low and moderate intensity with music and metronome	Moderate intensity exercise produced more negative mood states (increased tension-anxiety, reduced vigour and exhilaration) Low intensity exercise produced favourable mood state changes Ratings of Perceived Exertion were slightly lower when exercising with music rather than a metronome. No mood effects for music
Steptoe & Bolton (1988)	Female students (n = 40)	Replication and extension of Steptoe & Cox (1988) Exercised for 15 mins at either moderate or low intensity	Immediately after higher intensity exercise, participants reported higher tension-anxiety and mental fatigue than those in the low intensity condition Both groups showed a decline in these states during the exercise recovery period
Moses et al. (1989)	Sedentary adults (n = 109)	An experimental study of the effects of exercise training on mental well-being. Participants assigned to either high intensity aerobic exercise, moderate intensity aerobic exercise, attention-placebo, or wait-list control 10-week training period undertaken	Only the moderate intensity exercise group showed reductions on the tension-anxiety and confusion mood scales and a measure coping deficits

Parfitt et al. (1994)	Students (n = 80)	Experimental test on affective reactions to exercise as a function of exercise intensity and exercise history. High and low active participants reported psychological affect in the last 30 secs and 5 mins after exercising at 60% and 90% of $\dot{V}O_{2max}$	High-active participants reported greater positive affect in the high intensity condition in comparison to the low-active group. No differences at the lower intensity More positive affect reported 5 mins post-exercise compared with last minute of the exercise bout
Parfitt et al. (1996)	High (n = 15) and low active (n = 15) women in mid-20s	Test of affective reactions during and after exercise on cycle ergometer. Exercise took place at 3 different levels of RPE: 9, 13 & 17 Affect assessed with FS (Feeling Scale)	High-active reported more positive affect than low-active Affect was more positive 5 mins post-exercise than in the last 20 secs of the exercise bout Affect was progressively less positive as RPE increased

for both men and women in the two age groups under and over 40 years. Stephens (1988, pp. 41–42) provided the following clear conclusion:

> the inescapable conclusion of this study is that the level of physical activity is positively associated with good mental health in the household populations of the United States and Canada, when mental health is defined as positive mood, general well-being, and relatively infrequent symptoms of anxiety and depression. This relationship is independent of the effects of education and physical health status, and is stronger for women and those age 40 years and over than for men and those age under 40. The robustness of this conclusion derives from the varied sources of evidence: four population samples in two countries over a 10-year period, four different methods of operationalizing physical activity and six different mental health scales.

Evidence from experimental trials

Few studies have investigated the effects of PA on affect and mood through controlled experimental trials. Five British studies are summarised in Table 4.6. These show clearly that the intensity of exercise is important in determining the effects of exercise on mood, something not suggested in other types of studies such as epidemiological surveys. The three studies by Steptoe and his colleagues (Steptoe & Bolton, 1988; Steptoe & Cox, 1988; Moses, Steptoe, Mathews, & Edwards, 1989) show that moderate, but not high intensity exercise, has mood enhancing effects. Similarly, Parfitt, Markland, & Holmes (1994) show that feeling states in exercise are significantly worse at a higher intensity for less active individuals. Moreover, Parfitt, Eston and Connolly (1996) showed that low-active women reported more negative affect at a higher exercise intensity than high-active women.

Raglin has suggested that 'sensations associated with exertion and post-exercise fatigue following high-intensity activity *delay, but do not eliminate*, post-exercise anxiety reductions' (1997, p. 117, emphasis added). The increases in negative mood after high intensity exercise reported in Steptoe's research may be due to the higher exertion required, but studies have shown that positive mood is still enhanced some time later. Indeed, Parfitt et al. (1996) showed that for both high-active and low-active women, positive affect was higher 5 minutes after exercise in comparison to the last 20 seconds of the exercise bout, and this was most pronounced for the highest level of exercise intensity, thus supporting Parfitt et al. (1994).

The temporal nature of changes in mood after different intensities of exercise requires further investigation. However, even if the post-exercise negative mood effect is transitory, it may be enough to affect adherence and reduce physical activity participation.

In a controlled trial of healthy American adults, King, Taylor, Haskell and DeBusk (1989) found that participants assigned to a 6-month PA intervention, in comparison to controls, showed significant improvements in body appearance satisfaction, perceived physical fitness, and satisfaction with weight. No differences, however, were found for depressed mood, tension/anxiety, or confidence/well-being. These results suggest that psychological changes are more likely if they are closely linked to the physical changes associated with an exercise programme.

Exercise and sub-clinical depression

Exercise and clinical depression is covered by Nanette Mutrie in this volume. However, many studies have investigated participants who have not reached clinically defined levels of depression, but may be suffering transitory negative depressive mood. McDonald and Hodgdon (1991) identified five measures of depression in their meta-analysis of aerobic training studies. These were the BDI, the Centre for Epidemiological Studies Depression Scale (CES-D) (Radloff, 1977), Lubin's (1965) Depression Adjective Check List (DACL), the Symptom Check List 90 (SCL-90) (Derogatis, Lipman, & Covi, 1973), and Zung's (1965) Self-Rating Depression Scale (SDS). In addition, the POMS depression subscale has been used (see Leith, 1994) although McDonald and Hodgdon used this as part of their analysis of mood rather than depression per se.

Meta-analytic reviews

Two meta-analyses have been conducted on exercise and depression. McDonald and Hodgdon (1991) have also meta-analysed depression as an outcome variable for their study of aerobic fitness training. In addition, North et al. (1990) reported a meta-analysis of 80 studies yielding 290 effect sizes on exercise and depression. The mean ES was 0.53. Similarly, McDonald and Hodgdon found an overall ES of 0.55 for their 'depression cluster', which included various depression and related mood scales.

Although these meta-analyses probably constitute the best evidence available to date, there are a number of issues that should caution over-confidence. Many of these are argued well by Dunn and Dishman (1991) and Dishman (1995). For example, some studies in the meta-analyses may have included individuals suffering from depression with a primary anxiety component. Dunn and Dishman argue this point on the basis of evidence that shows a large number of people meeting Diagnostic and Statistical Manual (DSM-II-R) criteria for agoraphobia and panic attacks also suffer from depression or have a history of depression, hence exercise may reduce state anxiety and elevate mood which could then produce changes in depression. North et al.'s (1990) meta-analysis is also questioned on the basis of non-uniformity in defining depression, as well as the discrepancy between the results of the meta-analysis and other studies.

Epidemiological surveys

The large-scale survey analysis reported by Stephens (1988) provides evidence at the level of epidemiological data. Concerning depression assessed with the CES-D, results for over 3,000 North American adults from the first National Health and Nutrition Examination Survey (NHANES-I) showed that depression was highest for those reporting 'little/no exercise' in comparison to those classified in the 'moderate' and 'much' exercise categories. Interestingly, this difference is suggestive that only moderate exercise may be sufficient for anti-depressant effects and that additional activity yields no additional benefit. Further support was provided in follow-up data in NHANES-II (Farmer, et al., 1988).

Evidence from experimental trials

Leith (1994) reports 42 studies investigating exercise and depression and 81% show anti-depressant effects. Of these, 25 appear to deal with sub-clinical depression and 84% show positive effects for exercise. Of the 6 sub-clinical studies Leith classifies as experimental, all but one reported positive changes in depression.

Do mood and emotion effects vary across people and settings?

There is some evidence in epidemiological surveys (e.g. Stephens, 1988) that more positive affect results from physical activity for women and those over 40 years of age. However, when specific aspects of affect are studied, such as depression, the picture is not clear. Similarly, it is not known whether specific forms of exercise, such as aerobic exercise, are more beneficial than others when affect is considered. Some might argue that we will never resolve this issue since people will 'feel good' after exercise they prefer, and feel 'less good' after exercise that is not to their liking. Such individual differences will mask any population trends linking PA and affect. However, this has yet to be shown.

Nevertheless, one area of research in sport psychology may shed some light on contextual factors influencing exercise affect. The approach people have in some physical activities (their goals), and the environment perceived by the participants (climate) may be important. We have studied two main achievement goals in PA. A task goal orientation is held when success is defined primarily in terms of self-improvement and task mastery. It is highly correlated with the belief that effort will bring success. An ego goal orientation is held when success is defined in terms of winning and demonstrating superiority over others. This correlates highly with the belief that ability is necessary for success (see Duda, 1993).

We conducted a meta-analysis of 37 studies, with a total of 41 independent samples (n = 7,950), investigating the relationship between task

and ego goals and positive (PA) and negative affect (NA) (Ntoumanis &
Biddle, 1999a). After correcting for measurement and sampling error, the
correlation between task orientation and positive affect was moderate-
to-high (0.55). The other correlations were generally small: task – NA =
−0.18; ego – PA = 0.10; ego – NA = 0.04. These results suggest that
adopting a task goal orientation in exercise will lead to more positive
affective reactions. This may be due to greater perceptions of control and
higher intrinsic motivation.

In another review, we calculated effect sizes for the relationship between
task and ego climates in PA and positive and negative affect (Ntoumanis
& Biddle, 1999b). Climates refer to the perception of contextual cues in
a situation (e.g. exercise class) that may emphasise more of a task climate
or an ego climate. In the former, group members perceive they have
greater decision-making involvement, success is defined and evaluated in
terms of individual effort and improvement, and new learning strategies
are encouraged. An ego climate, on the other hand, emphasises inter-
personal comparison, and evaluation is based on normative standards.

Calculations from 14 studies (n= 4,484) revealed that a task climate
was associated quite strongly with positive affective and motivational
outcomes, such as satisfaction and intrinsic motivation (Effect Size [ES]
= 0.71). Conversely, an ego climate was associated with positive outcomes
in a negative direction (ES =−0.30). Negative outcomes, such as worry,
were negatively associated with a task climate (ES =−0.26) and positively
with an ego climate (ES = 0.46). These results suggest that a task climate
is associated with greater positive and less negative affect. Of course we
cannot conclude whether those in a task climate, or those with a task goal,
are better off than non-participants, but given the evidence presented elsewhere in this review, it seems highly likely that they will be.

A brief overview of possible mechanisms

The review so far suggests that physical activity is associated with positive mood and affect. However, this is not enough. We also need to know
more about *why* and *how* such effects occur. This necessitates a brief
discussion on the mechanisms of the links between PA and PWB, although
a more generic discussion is provided in the final chapter.

Mechanisms for the effects of PA on mood and affect have not been
clearly identified. Several proposed mechanisms are plausible, including
biochemical, physiological, and psychological (see Biddle & Mutrie, 1991;
Boutcher, 1993; Morgan, 1997). Possible biochemical and physiological
mechanisms include changes associated with an increase in core body
temperature with exercise (thermogenic hypothesis; see Koltyn, 1997),
increase in endorphin production following exercise (endorphin hypothesis; see Hoffmann, 1997), changes in central serotonergic systems from
exercise (serotonin hypothesis; see Chaouloff, 1997), and the effects of

exercise on neurotransmitters (e.g. norepinephrine hypothesis; see Dishman, 1997). In addition, the 'feel better' effect from PA may result from changes in self-esteem from mastering new tasks, or from time away from negative or more stressful aspects of our lives.

In an elegant analysis of possible mechanisms and their interaction with exercise experience, Boutcher (1993) proposes that for those just starting exercise (i.e. in the 'adoption phase'), greater emphasis should be placed on psychological mechanisms since the exerciser had not adapted, physiologically, to the PA stimulus. In the maintenance phase, Boutcher suggests that both psychological and physiological mechanisms are likely to be important, and in the final habituation phase, he suggests that emphasis should be placed on physiological mechanisms and the influence of behavioural conditioning.

Guidelines for research and practice in health settings

It is clear from this review that physical activity is associated, in a positive way, with emotion, mood and psychological well-being. Despite methodological difficulties in this area, health professionals should have some confidence in the promotion of physical activity for the purposes of enhancing psychological well-being, however defined.

Guidelines for research

This review has drawn evidence from numerous narrative reviews, two meta-analytic reviews, several large-scale surveys, and a few well-designed experimental trials. Despite this, research into emotion, mood and PWB and physical activity is fraught with difficulties. First, the measurement of PWB has been inconsistent or restrictive in nature. Affect and mood are difficult to define, at least in operational terms, and when they have been assessed, many different instruments have been used. In the assessment of mood, the POMS has been the dominant instrument, yet, as already alluded to, this is narrow and allows for the assessment of only one positive factor. In short, generalised measures of affect and mood are in need of development to be suitable for physical activity research.

To this end, two recent measures of exercise-related affect have been developed (EFI and SEES). These allow for the acute effects of exercise to be assessed and should be tested further in this country during exercise trials. However, they present difficulties when assessing the effects of alternative treatments and do not solve the problem of using a consistent measurement technology for assessing the chronic effects of physical activity and exercise.

The work of Steptoe and his colleagues (see Steptoe, 1992) has demonstrated that moderate rather than high intensity exercise is associated with positive well-being. This requires further testing with more varied intensities and activities, as well as investigating whether high intensity exercise is associated with PWB but only after some delay.

It is not possible, at this stage, to draw clear conclusions concerning the characteristics of participants or exercise modalities. Some surveys have suggested that women and older individuals gain most from physical activity, and that aerobic over anaerobic exercise produces superior psychological effects. However, these trends have not always been confirmed and further work is required.

Guidelines for practice

It has been concluded that physical activity is consistently associated with positive affect and mood. Although we are unable to state with confidence that physical activity *causes* positive affect, it is clear that an association exists for both acute and chronic involvement. Health professionals can, with confidence, promote moderate physical activity in the knowledge that 'good mental health' will be correlated with such behaviours. The current message associated with the *Active for Life* campaign in England is wholly consistent with this approach. Advocating more vigorous exercise appears to be less easy to justify, except in fitter individuals.

If positive affect is a desired outcome of physical activity promotion by health professionals, evidence supports the use of moderate aerobic PA and the adoption of a task goal orientation. Moderate PA, such as walking and cycling, are currently promoted as key activities in *Active for Life*. These types of activities have the added advantage of being possible to fit into a typical daily schedule with minimal disruption and thus aid adherence.

As far a task orientation is concerned, this means that individuals playing sport or taking part in a physical activity where some form of 'achievement' is salient, should adopt reference standards that are internally focused. In other words, success should be judged in terms of personal progress and effort. Similarly, a mastery (task-oriented) motivational climate is associated with greater PWB. Promotion of this group environment entails promoting individual challenges, involving group members in decision making, recognising individual progress, having evaluation based on individual progress, and providing opportunities for practice and improvement (Ames, 1992).

Although there will be a wide variety of types of physical activities that are associated with PWB, the promotion of moderate aerobic PA, emphasising personal effort, progress and participation, seems an appropriate strategy at this point in our knowledge.

What we know

Based on the evidence reviewed, the following statements are offered for what we currently know about the relationship between affect, mood and physical activity:

- Physical activity is consistently associated with positive affect and mood.
- Where quantified trends have been identified, aerobic exercise has a small-to-moderate effect on tension (–), depression (–), vigour (+), fatigue (–), and confusion (–), and a small effect on anger (–).
- A positive relationship between physical activity and psychological well-being has been confirmed in several large epidemiological surveys, including in the UK, using different measures of activity and well-being.
- Experimental trials support a positive effect for moderate intensity exercise on psychological well-being.
- Meta-analytic evidence shows that adopting a goal in exercise that is focused on personal improvement, effort, and mastery has a moderate-to-high association with positive affect.
- Meta-analytic evidence shows that a group climate in exercise settings focused on personal improvement and effort has a moderate-to-high association with positive affect.

What we need to know

Our knowledge is far from complete. The following questions address key concerns and represent what we need to know:

- Are the associations between physical activity and psychological well-being causal?
- Do different types of physical activity produce different affective responses?
- Is physical activity likely to produce superior psychological effects for some groups, such as women?
- When might high intensity exercise produce positive affective responses?
- Are current psychometric measures of HRQL and exercise-related affect adequate for capturing the range of affective responses in physical activity?

- Are current psychometric measures of HRQL and exercise-related affect adequate for assessing change over time?
- What mechanisms explain the link between PA, affect and mood?

5 The effects of exercise on self-perceptions and self-esteem

Kenneth R. Fox

Background

Volumes of research have been generated on the topic of self-esteem and self-concept to the point where it is difficult to find a psychological construct that has attracted more academic attention. Self-esteem is also one of the few psychological terms that has acquired a meaning among the general public. It regularly crops up in informal conversations, usually in the context of explaining particular mental states and behaviours. Reference to self-esteem also features in formal policy documents of a range of organisations and institutions. The National Curriculum for schools in England and Wales, for example, places enhancement of self-esteem as a major curricular goal. Corporations include improvement in mental well-being and self-esteem as an important target for the welfare of their workforce. Health interventions, particularly programmes to facilitate rehabilitation from substance abuse, acute and chronic injury and disease, often focus on improved self-esteem as a primary objective. More recently, self-esteem has been considered as an important aspect of quality of life and mental well-being and as such has been considered as a possible target for public health campaigns.

Why is so much significance attached to a phenomenon that merely exists in the mind of the individual as a mental abstraction? Several features make self-esteem and other self-perception constructs very relevant to health.

- Self-esteem is widely accepted as a key indicator of emotional stability and adjustment to life demands. High self-esteem has been related to a range of positive qualities such as life satisfaction, positive social adjustment, independence, adaptability, leadership, resilience to stress, and high level of achievement in education and work. Self-esteem has emerged therefore as one of the strongest predictors of *subjective* well-being (Diener, 1984) and is consequently an important element of mental well-being and quality of life.
- Self-esteem and related self-perceptions are closely implicated with choice and persistence in a range of achievement and health behaviours.

Many contemporary theories of human motivation feature elements of the self. Needless to say, we enjoy feeling good about ourselves and it is clear that we tend to gravitate to those settings in life which provide opportunities for high self-ratings. High self-esteem is associated with healthy behaviours (particularly in adolescents) such as not smoking, lower suicide risk, greater involvement in sport and exercise, and healthier eating patterns (Torres & Fernandez, 1995). Self-esteem and self-perceptions of ability are therefore critical to understanding determinants of health behaviours and this is evident in patients in the primary care setting (Hurst, Boswell, Boogard, & Watson, 1997).

• Low self-esteem is closely related to mental illness and absence of mental well-being. It frequently accompanies depression, trait anxiety, neuroses, suicidal ideation, sense of hopelessness, lack of assertiveness and low perceived personal control. Improved self-esteem has therefore been used frequently as a target for change and also as a success marker for psychotherapy (Wylie, 1979).

In essence, beyond the satisfaction of basic physiological needs such as food and warmth, there is little of more importance to an individual than maintaining a high degree of self-esteem. The search for self-esteem is considered so strong that it has been termed by Campbell (1984) as the First Law of Human Nature and many theorists believe that sense of self is central to the possession of mental and even physical health.

Self-esteem and the self-system

In order to meaningfully overview the literature on exercise and its impact on self-esteem, it is necessary to first unravel the tangle of constructs involved. The self is best described as a complex system of constructs. Theorists believe that these may be organised by a *self director* who acts as an information processor and decision maker. Information relevant to the self is gathered and organised to form a self-description, termed *self-concept*, *identity,* or *set of identities* based on its abilities, qualities, traits and the roles it performs. Murphy (1947, p. 996) describes the self-concept as 'the individual as known to the individual'. Roles in several life domains may contribute to the self-concept and might include perceptions of self at work, in social relationships, in the family, and also the physical self which is dictated by qualities related to our appearance and physical prowess.

The self director will invest time in directing choice and persistence in activities and use a range of self-promotion and self-presentation strategies (including self-serving biases and defensiveness) to achieve the best results for self. The bank balance at the end of the day constitutes *self-esteem* or *self-worth*. Whereas self-concept is a self-description, *self-esteem is a self-rating of how well the self is doing*. Campbell (1984) defines it as 'an awareness of good possessed by self'. The criteria and content used to determine worth are dictated both by the individual and the primary culture in which he/she operates. Additionally, individuals might ascribe to subcultures that value other aspects of life such as athletic ability, higher spiritual or moral ground, or even criminal behaviour. Within these constraints, each person will draw upon a personal menu of attributes and achievements, dependent on exposure and experience, placing greater value on some elements than others. Some personal menus may closely conform to cultural norms and expectations, while others might be more individualised. However, the criteria on which self-esteem is based are ultimately set by the individual. Self-esteem is therefore essentially phenomenological and based on being an 'OK person' dependent on what the individual considers as 'OK'. This is an important principle as it suggests that the effect of exercise on self-esteem cannot be explained in the absence of consideration of the past experiences and values of the individual.

Measuring self-esteem and self-perceptions

A great deal of research was generated on self-esteem in the 1970s and 80s. Instruments consisted of banks of items, each calling for a response on perceived possession of some personal quality or competence such as having attractive facial features, academic ability, or lots of friends. These responses were simply totalled to produce a self-esteem score, a technique that has since been widely criticised as it does not take into account the multidimensionality of the self (Marsh, 1997; Wylie, 1979, 1989). More recently, a profile approach has been adopted where instruments are made up of several subscales each assessing self-ratings in different aspects of life or domains of competence such as work, family and friendships. Overall or global self-esteem or self-worth is best measured by a separate subscale using items which avoid specific domain content and refer to pride in self, general competence, and equal worth to others. Rosenberg's 10-item Global Self-Esteem Scale (Rosenberg, 1965) has been widely used and validated for adolescents onward. Harter's self-perception profiles for adolescents and adults include a General Self-Worth subscale of this nature (Harter, 1988; Messer & Harter, 1986), as does Marsh's Self-Description Questionnaire series (Marsh, 1992a, 1992b)

Following the use of self-perception profiles and separate global or self-esteem scales, models depicting how dimensions are related to self-esteem have been offered and in some cases tested. Some support has been provided for a hierarchical structure like the roots of a tree, with self-esteem forming the stable apex or tree trunk. Domains of life form the main roots, with increasingly finer roots that search out closer contact with life experiences and represent more specific content (see Figure 5.1).

Of particular significance to exercise and mental health is the physical self. This is consistently featured as a strong root in the self system with an overall physical self-worth underpinned by a range of physical attributes

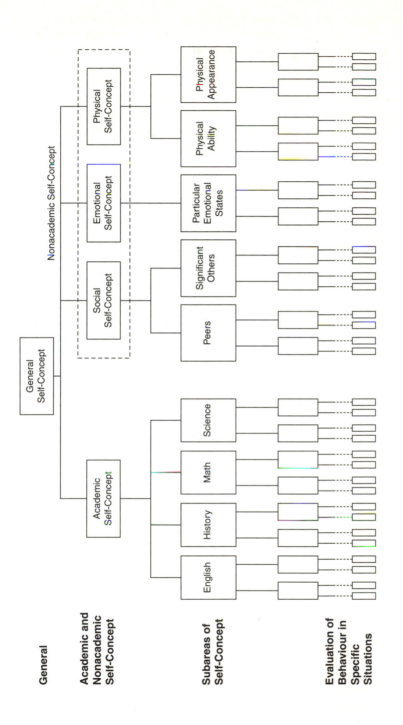

Figure 5.1 A hierarchical model of self-concept.

From R.J. Shavelson, J.J. Hubner, and G.C. Stanton. (1976). 'Self-concept: Validation of Construct Interpretations.' *Review of Educational Research*, 46, p.413. Copyright by the American Educational Research Association, reprinted by permission of the publisher.

and competencies. With the development and validation of hierarchical models, it has become possible to locate measures of self-perception according to the specificity of their content (see Figure 5.2).

The Tennessee Self-Concept Scale (TSCS) was one of the first instruments to utilise a multidimensional structure and the review featured later, in this chapter will identify it as the instrument of choice in many of the earlier exercise/self-esteem studies. It consists of a physical self subscale as well as subscales to assess moral/ethical, personal, family and social dimensions in addition to a lie scale. Unfortunately, the physical self subscale totals diverse items, many of which have little relevance to exercise. Marsh and Richards (1988) through confirmatory factor analysis, criticised the instrument for poor psychometric qualities. Results using the TSCS are likely to be less convincing than they might be, although the instrument has recently been upgraded and may be particularly useful for clinical settings with patients with psychiatric disorders (Byrne, 1996).

Two well-validated comprehensive instruments have been developed in recent years to assess self-ratings at two levels of the physical domain. The Physical Self-Perception Profile (Fox & Corbin, 1989) measures perceptions of sport competence, physical strength, physical condition, body attractiveness and overall self-worth. The Physical Self-Description Questionnaire measures nine elements of the physical self (Marsh, Richards, Johnson, Roche, & Tremayne, 1994), general physical self and general self-esteem. In addition to profiles, there are also instruments to measure singular aspects of the physical self. Aspects of body appearance have been assessed for many years such as body image, body satisfaction (with whole and parts), body acceptance, and more recently social physique anxiety (anxiety associated with displaying the body in public settings).

Figure 5.2 Self-perception constructs measurable at different levels of specificity.

From K.R. Fox (1998). 'Advances in the Measurement of the Physical Self'. In J.L. Duda, *Advances in Sport and Exercise Psychology Measurement*. Morgantown, WV: Fitness Information Technology.

It is also possible to assess quite specific aspects of the physical self that have particular relevance to an intervention. *Self-efficacy* measures fall into this category and represent an individual's perceived confidence in their ability to successfully complete a task such as climbing stairs, visiting a swimming pool, maintaining a three-times-a-week exercise programme. Although these self-ratings do not represent self-esteem change, they may help identify possible mechanisms through which self-esteem might be enhanced. These measures are of particular significance to interventions with older people and those in rehabilitation where confidence in movement ability may initially be low.

What is clear is that an array of measures to assess self-perceptions and self-esteem is available to the health professional or researcher who wishes to document possible change due to participation in an exercise programme. It is not within the scope of this chapter to review all available instruments. The interested reader should see Byrne (1996) for the whole range of self-concept instruments. For the assessment of physical self-perceptions, see Fox (1998), for body image, see Bane and McAuley (1998) and for self-efficacy and exercise-related confidence, see McAuley and Mihalko (1998).

Unfortunately, it is only recently that the more theoretically grounded and comprehensive instrumentation has appeared in the exercise/self-esteem intervention literature so that much of the evidence is based on poorly validated assessments. Furthermore, there has not been a systematic approach adopted. The general view is that specific elements are more accessible to change, and Sonstroem and Morgan (1989) have presented a testable model indicating how experiences with exercise might improve self-efficacy and eventually affect physical self-worth and self-esteem (Figure 5.3). Models such as this could offer a consistent framework for furthering exercise and self-esteem research but to date published studies are not in evidence.

Recently, Sonstroem, Harlow and Josephs (1994) modified the original model of Sonstroem and Morgan (1989) in conjunction with the Physical Self-Perception Profile (Figure 5.4). The relationships in the model were supported through structural equation modelling. This provides an example of how improved instrumentation in combination can offer a more comprehensive and systematic framework for the study of self-perception change through exercise.

The potential for exercise in the promotion of self-esteem

However, the focus of interventions has been the simple description of change and little research has been conducted on the identification of mechanisms of change. There are many potential candidates. High value is attached in the dominant western culture to physical attractiveness (particularly for women), and a range of competencies and status indicators such as educational attainment, success at work, physical and artistic

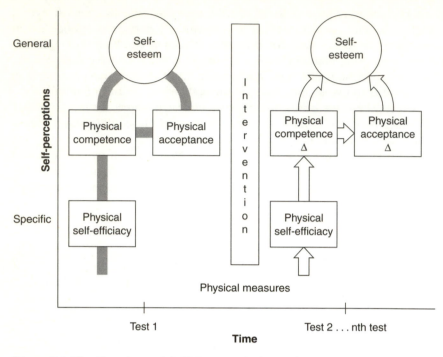

Figure 5.3 The Exercise and Self-Esteem Model for intervention studies.

W.P. Morgan, and R.J. Sonstroem (1989). 'Exercise and self-esteem: Rationale and model.' *Medicine and Science in Sports and Exercise*, 21, 329–337.

skills, sporting ability, and to some extent wealth and material possessions. With improved competence comes a sense of *effectiveness*, feelings of *self-determination* and *personal control*. These are tied to self-esteem. Furthermore, *self-acceptance* – the degree to which we accept our strengths and weaknesses, may also influence self-esteem, based on the assumption that we cannot all excel at everything. These are important considerations in the design of interventions to promote self-esteem. It is possible, for example, that self-esteem can be lowered through experiences in the physical domain if the conditions raise awareness and self-criticism without increasing perceived competence. In addition, several theorists argue that humans have a need to sense social significance as reflected by feelings of power, importance, relatedness, belonging, love worthiness, and unconditional worth. This social need may offer a further route to self-esteem enhancement.

The physical domain features strongly in the value system of the western culture and as a result is consistently included in models of self-esteem. Elements of physical self are particularly significant as the body functions as the *public interface* of the self with the social world and is used to project characteristics such as status, sexuality, youthfulness,

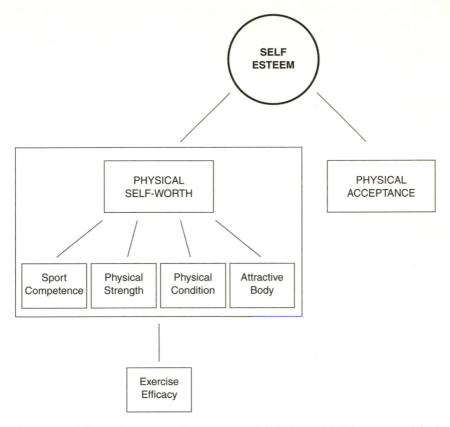

Figure 5.4 Adaptation of the Exercise and Self-Esteem Model for use with the
Physical Self-Perception Profile (after Sonstroem, Harlow, & Josephs,
1994).

From K. R.Fox (1998). 'Advances in the Measurement of the Physical Self.' In J.L. Duda,
Advances in Sport and Exercise Psychology Measurement. Morgantown, WV: Fitness
Information Technology.

and prowess. For this reason, the physical self may be particularly important in the development of self-esteem. Cross-sectional research has
indicated that body image provides the strongest correlation with self-
esteem (r = 0.6–0.8) throughout the lifespan. Physical skills, fitness, and
sport competencies are also important to many, especially youngsters
as they grow and learn to make comparisons, but the strengths of
these correlations vary among populations. The potential mechanisms by
which involvement in exercise or sport might promote self-esteem therefore are broadly:

• An undetermined psychophysiological mechanism that enhances mood
  and positive self-regard.

- Enhanced body image, body satisfaction or body acceptance through weight loss or improved muscle tone.
- Enhanced perceived physical competence through improved abilities, prowess, and aspects of fitness such as strength and cardiorespiratory function.
- Enhanced sense of autonomy and personal control over the body, its appearance, and functioning.
- Improved sense of belonging and significance through relationships with exercise leaders or others in the exercise group.

For further discussion of potential mechanisms some of which have yet to be adequately researched, see Fox (1997) and Sonstroem (1997a, 1997b).

It is in the context of these recent developments in theory and instrumentation that the literature investigating the influence of exercise on self-esteem should be examined. This is particularly the case for the physical self which has emerged as a strong correlate of global self-esteem and a likely location for the operation of the main mechanisms of its change.

Evidence of the effect of exercise on self-esteem

Against this background, the second section of this paper will provide an update and overview of existing research that is relevant to the effect of exercise on self-esteem and self-perceptions. The following sources were used:

- electronic data bases including Medline, Psychinfo, PsychLit, Sport Discus, with follow up using BIDS;
- previous reviews with at a least a section on self-esteem/self-concept including Berger and McInman (1993), Calfas and Taylor (1994), Doan and Scherman (1987), Gleser and Mendelberg (1990), Leith (1994), Leith and Taylor (1990), Sonstroem, (1984), Sonstroem (1997a, 1997b), and Spence (unpublished);
- personal records of papers and abstracts.

Cross-sectional research

The early descriptive literature related to self-esteem, physical activity, exercise and sport is vast, with much of it lacking theoretical grounding and generated with poor instrumentation. Studies generally fall into three categories:

- those comparing groups who take part in specific sports or exercise activities with similar groups who are not involved;
- those comparing groups who are fit or low in body fat with those who are unfit or overweight; and

- those involving larger population samples where level of leisure activity has been related through correlation analyses to aspects of well-being including self-esteem.

In many studies, measures were composite self-esteem scales or assessments of body cathexis or body image. More recent research has used perception profiles that have provided a richer documentation of relationships. The following general conclusions can be drawn from this literature:

- Taking part in regular sport or exercise is moderately associated with more positive physical self-perceptions, including body image, from late adolescence onwards (e.g. Fox & Corbin, 1989; Sonstroem, Speliotis, & Fava, 1992).
- Being fit and slim are weakly associated with positive physical self-perceptions, body image and in some populations body satisfaction (e.g. Balogun, 1987; Fox, Page, Armstrong, & Kirby, 1994; Tucker, 1987).
- Sport and exercise participation are weakly associated with global self-esteem in many studies but this relationship is inconsistent and is probably dependent on population, environmental, and individual characteristics.

There are several anomalies to these patterns, particularly among females who exercise heavily (Davis, 1997; Sonstroem, 1997a, 1997b), and athletes involved in activities where maintenance of low weight or a slim body is required for elite performance. Here, the benefits of activity appear not quite so apparent. Participation of this kind may heighten awareness, body centrality, and self-criticism. Also, some females seem susceptible to a 'shifting goal posts' phenomenon whereby their body satisfaction, body acceptance and self-esteem does not improve when they exercise, even though they acknowledge some success with weight loss or improved fitness. This demonstrates that confounding and mediating factors are often present to weaken self-esteem-exercise associations.

For the vast majority of the public who are the likely targets of exercise-based interventions in health care, the positive relationships seem to hold firm, particularly with increasing age. Those who are involved in sport or exercise generally have a higher level of physical self-perceptions, including physical self-worth and body image and there is a tendency for them also to have higher self-esteem than their age-group peers.

However, cross-sectional research tells us little about causality. Although participation in sport and exercise is associated with a higher degree of well-being, it is impossible to determine the degree to which positive self-perceptions are the *determinants* or *outcomes* of sport and physical activity participation. There is likely to be a high degree of simultaneous processing as self-perception benefits are experienced and this increases motivation to participate. It is also likely that associations are strengthened by previous drop-out from sport and exercise of those who have experienced failure, embarrassment and whose physical self-perceptions and self-esteem have been under threat. Also those suffering mental disorders such as depression are more likely to avoid structured physical activity.

Intervention research

In comparison to other aspects of exercise and mental well-being, surprisingly few reviews of exercise and self-esteem research have been published. Sonstroem conducted a narrative review in 1984 and reported the findings of 16 intervention studies. He concluded 'Exercise programs are associated with significant increases in self-esteem scores of participants' (p. 138). However, only ten studies had control groups, only four were randomised, and half the studies had 20 or fewer subjects in the experimental treatment. Nine studies employed physical self as well as self-esteem measures. Sonstroem went on to state, 'At this time it is not known why or in what manner exercise programs affect self-esteem, or which people are responsive' (p. 150).

Although several reviews have included sections on self-concept, and Gruber (1985) conducted a meta-analysis of studies with children, the only other comprehensive review has been Leith (1994). He reported 16 experimental, 21 quasi-experimental, and 10 pre-experimental studies and concluded 'Approximately one-half of the studies reviewed reported significant changes in self-concept/self-esteem following participation in an exercise programme. These results appear quite inconsistent'. However, he also went on to make several interesting summary statements and observations, several of which are taken on board in the remaining section of this paper.

In the context of evidence-based health initiatives, this paper prioritises randomised controlled studies (RCSs) and these are summarised in Table 5.1. RCSs are particularly important given the special difficulties encountered in self-esteem research which include effects from socially desirable responding, expectancy, self-presentation strategies, pleasing the leader/researcher, and temporary versus lasting effects. In addition, a further 44 non-randomised controlled studies were considered.

General conclusions

Table 5.1 shows that only 36 RCSs were identified in the literature since 1970, and these included nine unpublished masters and doctoral dissertations. This represents little more than a study per year and contrasts vividly with the many hundreds of studies in some areas of health services research. These investigations involved a wide range of populations, exercise modes and instrumentation, making comparisons and generalisations difficult and in some instances meaningless.

Of the 36 studies, 28 (78%) indicated positive changes in some aspects of physical self-esteem or self-concept. This is a robust and significant finding that gives clear evidence that exercise helps people see themselves more positively. The results appear stronger for aspects of the physical self (particularly aspects of body image). This is important as they are consistently related to global self-esteem throughout the lifespan. Furthermore, an important recent study has indicated that *physical self-worth* (from the PSPP) which is the global summary of all perceptions in the physical domain carries important emotional adjustment qualities. This has been established independently of self-esteem and socially desirable responding on questionnaires (Sonstroem & Potts, 1996). This suggests that physical self-worth and related constructs should be regarded as key mental health indicators in their own right and should be assessed systematically in interventions. As physical self-perception profiles featuring global physical self-worth subscales have only appeared in the last 10 years, a critical construct has not been assessed in most of the studies.

Where *global self-esteem* was assessed, there were mixed findings with about half the studies showing generalised improvement. This is similar to the conclusions of Leith (1994) and also Berger and McInman (1993) who found that 44% of reviewed studies indicated positive change. It is also supported by conclusions from a recent meta-analysis by Spence and Poon (1997) that has yet to be published as a full paper. They conclude that a small (0.22) but significant effect size emerges for the effect of exercise on self-concept or self-esteem. The inconsistency or weakness in findings across studies may be partly due to differences in instrumentation. Where the Rosenberg scale was used, which is one of the better validated scales, significant change beyond controls was rarely reported. Significant improvements were more likely to be recorded with TSCS (which does not contain a true global self-esteem scale) or the summed-item composite self-concept measures which have been highly criticised.

Certainly the evidence suggests that increases in self-esteem (a) do not automatically arise through exercise involvement, and (b) may not always accompany positive changes in physical self-perceptions. However, this is entirely in line with theoretical projections which suggest that the self-esteem construct is the stable outcome from a wide array of life events. Exercise would have to be a particularly powerful experience to instigate a group change in a matter of a few weeks (especially if sense of mastery is the key mechanism), although it may occur with particularly receptive individuals.

Another explanation for the discrepant findings with self-esteem is the likely interaction between the nature of the population studied and the type and setting of exercise. What works for some may not be effective for others and mediating or confounding factors have rarely been assessed in studies.

Table 5.1 Randomised control trials addressing the effect of exercise on self-esteem and physical self-perceptions

(i) Children

Author(s)	Date	Subjects	Groups	Treatment	Instruments	Results
McGowan et al.	1974	37 grade 7 boys with low self-esteem	1. endurance training and team sport (with winning enhanced) 2. Control	18 weeks 3–4 × per week	TSCS	Greater increase in exercise group
Neal[a]	1977	60 grade 9 boys (15 per group)	1. CV fitness 2. Counselling (goals) 3. CV fitness + counselling 4. Control	10 weeks Exercise program not outlined	CSEI	No change
Martinek et al.	1978	344 boys and girls from grades 1–5	1. Motor activities and gymnastics 2. Control	45 minutes 1 × per week	MZ	Increase in the treatment group
Percy et al.	1981	30 grades 5 and 6 girls and boys	1. Running 2. Control	7 weeks 3 × per week	CSEI	Marked increase in treatment group
Schempp et al.	1983	208 boys and girls from grades 1–5	1. Shared decision 2. Teacher dominated 3. Control	Movement ed./gym 8 weeks 1 × 45 mins per week	MZ	Greater increases in both treatment groups. Effect size 0.59
Smith[a]	1984	49 boys and girls grades 4 and 5	1. Running 2. Yoga 3. Control (PE class)	10 weeks 3 × per week	PHSCS	No significant change

Study	Year	Sample	Conditions	Duration	Instrument	Results
Marsh & Peart	1988	137 grade 8 girls	1. Competitive exercise 2. Cooperative exercise 3. Volleyball control	6 weeks 14 sessions of 35 mins aerobic exercise	SDQ II	Increases in physical self in cooperative group and decline in competitive group. No change in global self.
Calfas & Cooper (Abs.)	1996	44 adolescent girls	1. CV exercise + computer classes 2. Computer classes	5 weeks at summer school 10 hours CV exercise/week	SPPA	Athletic competence increased in Group 1 and self-esteem in both groups
(ii) Adults						
Johnston[a]	1970	73 male college students of low–average fitness	1. Physical condition 2. Sport skills 3. Control	Not stated	Q-Sort technique	No change in self-concept or movement concept
Davis[a]	1971	39 male college students	1. CV exercise I 2. CV exercise II 3. Control	Not stated	TSCS	No change
White[a]	1974	152 college students enrolled in PE classes	1. Individualised circuit training 2. Normal PE classes	10 weeks (frequency and time not stated)	TSCS	Increased self-esteem and subscales beyond controls

Table 5.1 (continued)

Author(s)	Date	Subjects	Groups	Treatment	Instruments	Results
Hilyer & Mitchell	1979	120 college students	1. Running & stretching 2. Same + counselling 3. Controls	10 weeks 3 × per week	TSCS	Increased self-concept in Group 2
Trujillo	1983	35 female college students	1. Weight training 2. Running 3. Active controls	16 weeks typical college activity classes?	TSCS	Groups 1 & 2 increased self-concept. Group 1 improved significantly greater than active control
Brown & Harrison	1986	85 mature and young women	1. Weight training 2. Inactive control	12 weeks 3 × per week for 60 minutes	TSCS	Increases in physical self-concept and self-satisfaction for both young and mature groups
Ben Shlomo & Short	1986	sedentary females	1. Arm training 2. Leg training 3. Control	6 weeks 3 × per week of leg or arm ergometry at 60–80% max HR	TSCS BCS	No change in self-concept, physical self-concept or body cathexis
O'Neill[a]	1989	53 non-athlete female college students	1. Aerobic exercise sessions 2. Aerobics lectures	4 weeks (frequency & time not stated)	TSCS	Physical self-concept increased in Group 1.

Author	Year	Sample	Intervention/Groups	Design	Measures	Results
Cocklin[a]	1989	69 women aged 20–50	1. Exercise (mod. int.) 2. Exercise (light int.) 3. Inactive controls	8 weeks × 3 per week 1. To improve CV fitness 2. As placebo	IAV BCS	Self-acceptance increase in both exercise groups but body cathexis unrelated
Cusumano & Robinson	1992	95 female college students	1. Hatha yoga 2. Progressive relaxation	3 weeks 3×80 mins session	RSES PSES	PSES decreased while self-esteem increased in both groups. No group differences
Desharnais et al.	1993	male and female adults	Running		RSES	Positive changes
Brown et al.	1995	135 middle-aged sedentary men and women	1. Mod. int. walking 2. Low int. walking 3. low int walking + relaxation response 4. Group t'ai chi 5. Control	16 weeks 3 × per week (must have completed at least 42 sessions). All sessions at indoor facility	RSES SPES BCS Success expectancies	Positive changes in exercise groups for body cathexis and physical competence, time effect for self-esteem but not group differences

Table 5.1 (continued)

Author(s)	Date	Subjects	Groups	Treatment	Instruments	Results
King et al.	1989	120 middle-aged mainly sedentary men and women	1. Home-based exercise 2. Inactive controls	6 months of walk/jog at 65–77% max HR. 5 sessions per week prescribed	Perceptions of satisfaction with appearance, fitness, weight and ratings of health behaviours	Increase in satisfaction levels and health ratings in exercise group
King et al.	1993	357 50–65 year-old sedentary men and women	1. High int. ex. group 2. High int. home ex. 3. Low int. home ex. 4. Inactive controls	12 months programme High int. – 3 × 40 mins per week at 73–83% max. Low int. – 5 × 30 mins	Self-perception of change in health, appearance, fitness, and weight	Higher rating of change in all 3 exercise groups than controls
Tucker & Mortell	1993	60 early middle-aged women	1. Walking 2. Weight training	12 weeks 3 × per week home-based weights or walking	BCS ratings of fitness and fitness improvement	Improvements in both groups but greater in weight weight training
Alferman & Stoll	1995	Sedentary middle-aged adults	1. Exercise 2. Waiting list control	6 months 1–2 sessions per week for 60 mins	Not stated	Increase in physical concept but not self-esteem

	Year	Population	Conditions	Exercise protocol	Measures	Results
Alferman & Stoll	1995	Sedentary middle-aged adults	1. Fitness 2. Jogging 3. Relaxation 4. Back exercises	6 months 1–2 sessions per week for 60 mins	Not stated	All groups increase in physical self-concept and self-esteem but exercise groups significantly greater improvement in physical self-concept
Palmer	1995	27, nonclinical, premenopausal women	1. Supervised walking 2. Non-walking control	8 weeks building from 20 mins per session. Frequency not stated	RSES	Increase in self-esteem in walking group only
Talbot & Taylor (Abs.)	1998	142 middle-aged patients with risk of CHD	1. Exercise prescription scheme 2. Non-referred controls	CV exercise + weights (shortened) 10 weeks 2 × per week	PSPP PIP	Increase in physical self-worth, condition, appearance, and health

(iii) Special populations

	Year	Population	Conditions	Exercise protocol	Measures	Results
Collingwood	1972	50 male adult rehabilitation patients	1. Physical training 2. Control	4 weeks, 5 × per week for 60 mins of general fitness work	Body attitude scales IAV	Improvements in body attitude, self-concept and self-acceptance in exercise group
Whiting[a]	1981	80 alcoholics	1. Therapy 2. Therapy + exercise	Exercise 5 days per week incl. 2 miles walk, gym activity and swim	TSCS	Increases in both groups but no additional effect due to exercise

Table 5.1 (continued)

Author(s)	Date	Subjects	Groups	Treatment	Instruments	Results
Hilyer et al.	1982	60 males, 15–18 years, 55% black youth offenders	1. Fitness group + counsellor support 2. Team sports	Strength, CV exercise and flexibility 20 weeks 3 × 90 mins	Self-esteem Inv Form A	Increase (but impact of counselling not known)
Hannaford[a]	1984	25 depressed males	1. Exercise 2. Corrective therapy 3. Waiting list controls	Jogging 3 days per week × 30 mins (length not stated)	RSES	No increase in self-esteem even with increase in CV fitness and reduced depression
Short et al.	1984	45 overweight/obese policemen 29–52 years old	1. Instruction + conditioning 2. Instruction alone	8 weeks of 90 mins lifestyle instruction and 3 × 45 mins walk/jog.	TSCS	Greater increases (2–3 times) in exercise group in physical self, personal self and self-satisfiction
MacMahon & Gross	1988	54 learning disabled boys	1. High int. exercise and sports 2. Low int. exercise and sports	20 weeks 1. HR >160. 2. Intermittent with HR < 160	PH with assistance	Increase in both groups with high intensity greatest.

Study	Year	Sample	Conditions	Protocol	Measures	Results
Ossip-Klein et al.	1989	32 depressed female adults	1. Running 2. Weights 3. Delayed control	8 weeks 3–4 × per week 20 mins running or weights + warmup & cool down	Beck Self-Concept Test Osgood's Semantic Differential	Increase in self-concept, perceptions of energy and fitness in both exercise groups
Mactavish & Searle	1992	26 middle-aged males and females with mental retardation	1. Physical activity 2. No activity	5 weeks of subject selected activity and sports	Perceived Leisure Competence Scale RSES	Greater increases in perceived competence and self-esteem in treatment group
Donaghy & Mutrie	1998	117 men and women in alcohol rehabilitation	1. Group and home exercise 2. Control	3 weeks formal exercise followed by 12 weeks home-based activity	PSPP	Change in physical self-worth, perceived condition and strength at 4 weeks month and condition and strength at 8 weeks in exercise group. NS at 5 months

Notes:
[a] = PhD Abstract only.
BCS (Body Cathexis Scale: Secord & Jourard, 1953) CSEI (Coopersmith Self-Esteem Inventory: Coopersmith, 1967) IAV (Index of Adjustment and Values: Bills, Vance, & McLean, 1951) MZ (Martinek-Zaichowsky Self-Concept Scale for Children: Martinek & Zaichowsky, 1977) PHSCS (Piers-Harris Self-Concept Scale for Children: Piers, 1984) PSES (Physical Self-Efficacy Scale: Ryckman, Robbins, Thornton & Cantrell, 1982) PSPP (Physical Self-Perception Profile: Fox, 1990; Fox & Corbin, 1989) PIP (Perceived Importance Profile: Fox, 1990) PSDQ (Physical Self-Description Questionnaire: Marsh et al, 1994) RSES (Rosenberg Self-Esteem Scale: Rosenberg, 1965) SDQ II (Self-Description Questionnaire for Adolescents: Marsh, 1992a) SPES (Sonstroem's Physical Estimation Scale: Sonstroem, 1978) SPPA (Self-Perception Profile for Adolescents: Harter, 1988) TSCS (Tennesse Self-Concept Scale: Fitts, 1965)

Which populations can benefit?

Children and adolescents

Gruber (1986) conducted a meta analysis of studies with children and in 1994, Calfas and Taylor reviewed the impact of physical activity on the psychological well-being of adolescents, and included a section on self-concept. Gruber concluded that the effect of activity programmes was positive, particularly for those already low in self-esteem. Physical fitness and aerobics programmes produced superior results to motor skill and sport programmes. There is also some evidence (Marsh & Peart, 1988; Schempp, Cheffers, & Zaichowsky, 1983) that cooperative and more democratic exercise settings produce stronger effects and this is supported by recent literature on motivational climate in sport, exercise and physical education. Calfas and Taylor (1994) when comparing the effects on the range of mental benefits found that the strongest changes were for self-esteem, self-concept or self-efficacy with nine out of ten studies revealing positive results. Of the eight RCSs conducted with children in Table 5.1 (which include two reported by Calfas & Taylor) five report self-concept or self-esteem changes and a sixth found changes in physical self-concept accompanying exercise. One trial (Hilyer et al., 1982) reported self-esteem improvements with youth offenders when exercise was combined with counsellor support. Although exercise/self-esteem studies have been conducted with obese children, it is not possible to single out the effects of exercise from weight loss (French, Story, & Perry, 1995)

The evidence is sufficient to conclude that exercise is an effective medium for developing a positive self in children, is particularly effective for those with low self-esteem, and has greatest potential when presented in a style that will encourage mastery and self-development. It must also be kept in mind that school-based programmes have potential to lower self-esteem, as youngsters are not in the same position as adults to drop out if experiences are negative.

Young adults

Seven RCTs were located with young adults who were mainly US college males and females. Six of the studies used the Tennessee Self-Concept Scale. Six showed positive change with one restricted to change in the physical self and another in the group where exercise was combined with exercise counselling (Hilyer & Mitchell, 1979). A range of exercise modes was used with the majority being aerobics or running, circuit training, and weight training. A further 20 controlled studies with intact groups were identified, 13 being unpublished theses or dissertations. Fifteen of these studies involved students across a range of college activity classes, with the majority focusing on aerobic dance, cardiovascular fitness and weight training. Most studies used the TSCS and the Body Cathexis Scale. Half the studies reported non-significant results and some of the remaining studies showed only weak gains.

This literature is biased towards US college students, the majority already having average to high self-esteem and being involved in regular physical activity. It is unlikely therefore that young adults as a group will experience the greatest mental benefits from exercise. They are also a low health risk population and therefore unlikely to receive priority attention for mental health service provision.

Middle-aged adults

Middle-age appears a particularly crucial time for exercise interventions as the population becomes less active, increases in weight and symptoms of ageing become more apparent and yet there seems to remain some potential for lifestyle change. This is a population therefore that is of particular interest to health service providers. Seven of the best designed and most recent RCSs were with large groups of previously sedentary populations in this age range (Alferman & Stoll, 1995 [two studies]; Brown et al., 1995; King, Taylor, & Haskell, 1993; King, Taylor, Haskell, & DeBusk, 1989; Talbot & Taylor, 1998; Tucker & Mortell, 1993). Studies ranged in length from 10 weeks to a year with four studies lasting at least 6 months. Programmes included moderate versus low intensity walking, home-based versus group exercise, walking versus weight training, and fitness and jogging versus relaxation. All studies indicated positive improvement in physical self-perceptions. These included ratings of fitness, appearance, physical health, body cathexis, and physical self-worth. However, only three studies assessed global self-esteem and this did not indicate significant improvement. Even in the absence of global self-esteem change, this produces a robust picture of psychological improvement in these groups and warrants further consideration for health service investment. These studies are also backed up by a growing literature on self-efficacy and physique anxiety in middle-aged individuals which reveals potential exercise benefits (McAuley, Courneya, & Lettunich, 1991; McAuley, Mihalko, & Bane, 1995). It is well established that this population can benefit a great deal in reduced incidence of morbidity and mortality through heart disease, obesity, diabetes and some cancers. Improvements in mental well-being may increase motivation so that the full array of benefits is experienced.

Older adults

No RCSs were located for elderly adults. This is surprising given the potential of exercise to increase functionality, independence, and life quality. Studies have tended to address other constructs such as life satisfaction, subjective well-being and quality of life. Four unpublished controlled studies involving exercising groups were identified. Flexibility programmes were ineffective (Bozoian & McAuley, 1994; Yeagle, 1982) but strength and fitness programmes indicated positive self-concept changes (Bozoian & McAuley, 1994; Olfman, 1987). Recently, Mutrie and Davison (1994) recruited 83 adults with a mean age of 61 years who self-selected into either a home-based or class-based exercise programme lasting 3 months. Measures using the PSPP were applied pre- and post-programme and 6 months after the programme. Positive changes in physical self worth were found for both groups and these were greatest for the class-based exercisers. Further trials with this population are required that combine self-efficacy, physical self-perception and self-esteem measures.

Special populations

Several groups fall into this category including those with mental disorders, those who are in rehabilitation from substance abuse, ill-health or injury, those who have physically disability, and those who are obese. In reviewing the effect of exercise on self-esteem of special groups, Leith (1994) pointed out that only 3 of 13 studies did not produce significant change. This was attributed in part to these groups initially being low in self-esteem. However, there are few well-designed studies with special groups, possibly because of recruitment and randomisation difficulties. There are RCSs to support change due to exercise in adults with mental retardation (Mactavish & Searle, 1992), depressed females (Ossip-Klein et al., 1989), youth offenders (Hilyer et al., 1982), obese males (Short, DiCarlo, Steffee, & Pavlou, 1984), male rehabilitation patients (Collingwood, 1972) and problem drinkers (Donaghy & Mutrie, 1998). There is a body of literature on disability and sport participation indicating that there is great potential for involvement to improve mental well-being in people with disabilities (Sherrill, 1997). However, as yet there are no well-controlled studies with this population. Clearly, the potential benefits for a range of special populations is high and much further research is required.

Gender differences

There is evidence that exercise has a beneficial effect for males and females. There may be greatest potential for females as they consistently score lower initially on self-confidence in physical activity and also body image, physical self-worth and self-esteem (Lirgg, 1991).

What are the characteristics of effective exercise?

Type of activity

The effect of a wide range of physical activities and sports has been investigated. Various forms of cardiovascular exercise including running, walking, aerobic dance, and circuit training are most common in studies. All of these activities have indicated that they can be effective in improving self-perceptions, although there is a reflection of the general finding that only approximately 50% produce significant change. Studies with other activities such as swimming, flexibility training, martial arts, and expressive dance have generally failed to indicate significant change, however they are too few in number to make firm conclusions. Many of these studies have been conducted on college-age males and females, a population prone to non-significant results. Where endurance exercise and walking has been used with middle-aged adults, there is more conclusive evidence of success than with younger adults.

Weight training has attracted increasing attention and ten studies including two RCSs have recorded improvements in body image and other physical self-perceptions in men and both young and middle-aged women. Some RCSs have made comparisons between resistance exercise and other activities including running (Trujillo, 1983), walking (Tucker & Mortell, 1993) and also swimming, aerobics, and PE classes. There is some indication that resistance training is superior to endurance exercise in improving body image and physical self-esteem.

Exercise frequency, intensity and duration

There is insufficient variance in the studies to assess the impact of frequency of exercise with the vast majority of programmes opting for three sessions per week. This is in contrast to current recommendations for health-related activity which is five or six occasions of moderate intensity activity per week. Intensity is rarely reported and only two RCSs compared low with high intensity exercise. King et al. (1993) found that both treatments were effective in stimulating psychological improvement in adults with no differences in degree of change. MacMahon and Gross (1988) found that higher intensity sports were more successful with learning disabled boys. Most studies report the length of the exercise session and programmes that last longer than 60 minutes are more likely to produce positive change. This may reflect an increasing level of commitment in the participants.

Programme duration

Programmes have varied in length from a single session to 12 months. Leith (1994) recently divided studies into those lasting 8 weeks or less, 9 to 12 weeks, and more than 12 weeks. He concluded that although there was evidence of change in some studies in all of these groups, there was a higher likelihood of self-esteem change in longer programmes. The RCSs reported here support this observation. However, the longer well-controlled studies have not assessed global self-esteem and the time required for lasting change; also, how long change lasts is still not known.

What are the mechanisms?

Although there is sound evidence that exercise can produce positive changes in well-being through improved physical self-perceptions and sometimes self-esteem, the question still remains as to the main mechanisms underpinning such change. For the fine tuning of intervention design, it is important not only for mechanisms to be determined but also for the conditions under which they optimally function to be identified.

Returning to possible mechanisms outlined earlier in this paper:

1   *An undetermined psychophysiological mechanism.* The cross sectional and longitudinal evidence fail to show a *consistent* relationship between global self-esteem and exercise participation. This suggests the absence of a generic or generalised psychophysiological or psychobiochemical effect. The variance among studies both for populations and characteristics of the exercise setting suggests that mechanisms are more likely to be psychosocial in origin.

2   *Improvements in fitness or weight loss.* There is evidence from several studies that fitness change (as measured by standard laboratory or field tests of fitness) is not necessary for enhanced self-esteem or improved physical self-perceptions (Ben-Shlomo & Short, 1986; King et al. 1989; Ossip-Klein et al., 1989; Palmer, 1995). This parallels the obesity treatment literature where amount of weight lost is not consistently reflected in the psychological benefits (French, Story & Perry, 1995). Perceptions of health, physical competence, fitness and body image may arise simply because there is a *feeling* that the body is improving through exercise. There is some indication that muscular fitness reflected in improved tone or strength can have a more rapid and powerful sensory effect than cardiovascular or flexibility change.

3   *Autonomy and personal control.* There is no direct evidence to establish sense of control over the body, its appearance and functioning as the main route to self-esteem change. Instrumentation has not been systematically used to test this hypothesis. Furthermore, because autonomy is tied to identity change, it is unlikely that many studies have been conducted for long enough for any effect to be adequately documented. However, the cross-sectional evidence that changes in self-efficacy for exercise is associated with adherence in middle-aged

and older people (see McAuley et al., 1995) suggests a promising line for intervention research.

4   *Sense of belonging and significance.* Group or individual social support can produce mental benefits and this may be possible in the exercise setting. However, the effect of exercising regularly in a group or regular contact with an exercise counsellor on social well-being has not been adequately tested. Two studies have included some form of counselling with the exercise programme and reported positive effects. To date, there is insufficient evidence to show that group exercise produces greater improvements in self-esteem or self-perceptions than home-based or individual exercise. It is likely to vary with the individual, and the population, and there may be gender differences in preference. Leisure-centre based exercise prescription schemes, for example, attract mainly middle-aged females who report social benefits (Fox, Biddle, Edmunds, Bowler, & Killoran, 1997). Exercise groups for the older middle-aged and elderly held in community and leisure centre settings seem to rely on social interaction as a key component to successful attendance patterns.

In summary, we still do not know what it is about exercise that helps people feel better about themselves. It is likely that there are several mechanisms operating, some tied to improvements in the body, others linked to social significance and the exercise setting. Firmer conclusions cannot be drawn at this time. The greater use of multidimensional self-perception instruments that are capable of more comprehensive documentation of the nature of change may be more revealing in future studies.

Cross-sectional research has already indicated that there may be several *mediating* variables involved in exercise/self-esteem links. These probably include factors such as the degree of autonomy experienced by the exerciser, the centrality or importance of exercise to the individual, and the nature of the exercise leadership. It is conceivable that some factors are *necessary* conditions under which self-esteem enhancement can take place. There are also factors attached to the exercise setting that may work against self-esteem development and this is particularly crucial for captive audiences such as schoolchildren.

Possibly more than any other element of well-being, self-esteem, because of its essentially subjective nature, is likely to be more consistently explained with a 'horses for courses' explanation. It is unlikely that a group mean approach will be sufficiently sensitive to individual differences in response to the many different characteristics of the exercise environment and motivational climate in which it is conducted.

It must also be realised that almost all studies report results of those who remain in the programme. Those who choose to drop-out may form an interesting group to study as they may reveal elements of the programme that are potentially negative in their effect such as increasing social physique anxiety or initiating feelings of incompetence and failure.

Implications for research

- Given the importance of the self to human functioning and health outlined at the beginning of this document, there has been a pitiful amount of well-designed research conducted, particularly in the form of true experiments (one trial per year). The reasons for this are not clear but this has been an underfunded area that has been seen to have little more than academic appeal and consequently has been ascribed low priority for health services funding.
- Research has largely been conducted by physical educators and sport and exercise scientists whose interests and needs are often quite different from those of health services professionals. This is reflected in an absence of evidence-based health principles underpinning research. For example, intention to treat statistics are not included in any of the studies reported in this paper and there is little evidence that cost-effectiveness has been considered.
- Randomised controlled trials are important but will not tell us all we need to know. Individual responses to the conditions of exercise and exercise settings will vary and it will be necessary to use time series case studies and a range of qualitative techniques to adequately unravel the mechanisms at work.
- Generally, studies have been too short to fully test out the influence of exercise on self-esteem. It is likely that a construct so critical to mental functioning as self-esteem will take some time for lasting change to occur. Unfortunately, where studies have lasted for 6 or 12 months, they have not assessed self-esteem (see Sonstroem, 1997a). Longer studies are required which utilise comprehensive self-perception measures and evidence-based health principles.
- Studies are required that investigate degree of well-being change (such as emotional adjustment, reductions in depression, and life satisfaction) alongside self-perception change. As yet, clinical criteria attached to self-esteem or physical self-perception levels have not been developed, so it remains difficult to attach practical significance to self-esteem change scores.

Implications for practice

- Greatest self-perception/self-esteem improvements are likely to occur in those groups who have the most to gain physically from exercise participation. This includes those who are in poor physical condition such as the middle-aged, the elderly and the overweight and obese.
- Greatest improvements are also likely to occur in those who are initially low in self-confidence, self-esteem, physical self-worth, and body image, including women in general, those with mild depression,

physically disabled children and adults, overweight and obese adults and children, and perhaps offenders.

- Currently there is greatest support for the effectiveness of cardiovascular exercise and weight training programmes.
- Not enough is known about the effectiveness of specific exercise characteristics but it seems wise to focus on exercise that is moderately demanding for the population, with sessions optimally lasting in the region of 60 minutes.
- Programmes should last at least 12 weeks with some form of contact continuing for 6 months or more. Limited evidence presented here suggests that global changes in self-esteem and identity are more likely given longer intervention.
- Adherence factors cannot be separated from those which promote self-esteem. On the one hand, the programme cannot be effective without participation and on the other, mental benefits are associated with sustained adherence. In this sense, conditions which affect the attractiveness of the exercise programme, such as the qualities of the leader or the exercise setting, may be critical to changes in self-esteem.

Final comments

Exercise and sports participation are associated with more positive self-perceptions but this does not allow us to determine whether participation causes enhanced well-being or helps prevent mental disorders and ill-health. The evidence from intervention studies shows clearly that exercise helps people feel better about themselves and this contributes to their mental well-being and presumably their quality of life. This in itself suggests that health professionals should consider physical activity as an important element of health promotion. In addition, improved self-esteem is an important marker of recovery from clinical symptoms of depression and anxiety and should be systematically assessed. Similarly, physical self-worth has been shown to be independently associated with elements of well-being and should provide an important benchmark for success. Finally, self-esteem and physical self-perceptions are inextricably linked to motivation through choice and persistence in health behaviours, including exercise. For this reason alone, it has to be given serious consideration in any intervention. A problem facing recognition of the importance of self-esteem is that it is often seen by health professionals as an outcome rather than a cause of either well-being or ill-health. Its centrality to human functioning demands that it be given serious consideration as a determinant.

What we know

- Exercise can be used as a medium to promote physical self-worth and other important physical self-perceptions such as body image. In some situations, this improvement is accompanied by improved self-esteem.
- Physical self-worth carries mental well-being properties in its own right and should be considered as a valuable end-point of exercise programmes.
- Positive effects can be experienced by all age groups but there is greater evidence of change in children and middle-aged adults.
- These effects can be experienced by men and women.
- Effects are likely to be greater for those with low self-esteem but these individuals may be difficult to attract into programmes.
- Several types of exercise are effective in changing self-perceptions but there is most evidence to support aerobic exercise and weight training, with weight training indicating greatest effectiveness in the short term.

What we need to know

- The degree to which self-perception and self-esteem change is accompanied by reductions in clinical symptoms, indicators of emotional adjustment and general well-being.
- More about the mechanisms of change.
- More about the optimal conditions under which mechanisms might operate.
- More about which populations are responsive to which mechanisms.
- More about which individual characteristics increase responsiveness to mechanisms of change.
- More about some populations that might particularly benefit from exercise including the elderly, the obese, those with mental disorders, and those with physical disability.
- More about the dynamics of change. Little is known about how long it takes to produce changes, and how long they last.
- More about the conditions under which improvements in self-esteem and self-perceptions are inhibited.
- More about those who do not volunteer for studies or who drop out and do not feature in the results.

- How much change in self-esteem scores is necessary for a meaningful impact on functioning, behaviours and well-being. To date, insufficient evidence has become available to develop clinical criteria and targets of change.

Acknowledgements

Appreciation is extended to Emma Stratton M.Sc. and Dave Carless M.Sc. for their assistance in preparing this review.

6 Cognitive performance, fitness, and ageing

Stephen H. Boutcher

It is well established that a decrease in cognitive performance is an inevitable consequence of growing old (Botwinick, 1973; Dustman, Emmerson, & Shearer, 1990). Behavioural slowing is the most significant aspect of the reduced cognitive performance that accompanies ageing. Almost all studies that have examined speed task performance have found older adults to be slower than their younger counterparts (Salthouse, 1985). This increased slowness of response is of major consequence for older individuals. For example, behavioural slowing affects the ability to drive a car, thus older adults are prone to higher accident rates and, as a result, pay higher insurance premiums. Slower movement speeds also contribute to higher accident rates at home and at work. Also, Hertzog (1989) has demonstrated that behavioural slowing in older adults is the major cause of their decline in intelligence. He has shown that the deterioration in mental abilities, typically found in older adults, may not reflect a loss of thinking but more a slowing of the rate of intelligent thought.

If age-related degradation in cognitive performance could be prevented then health care costs and suffering could be significantly reduced and functional ability and quality of life improved. Physical fitness is one of the few non-pharmacological interventions that could offset the cognitive decline accompanying ageing. However, the relationship between fitness, ageing, and cognitive performance is extremely complex and the methodological barriers are daunting. Also the mechanisms underlying the effects of fitness on the cognitive performance of older adults are unclear and those that have been proposed have little empirical support.

This review draws evidence from a number of narrative reviews, cross-sectional and intervention studies, and two meta-analyses. Papers were located through electronic searches using Sport Discus, Medline, and PsychLit. The major emphasis of the review is on the effect of aerobic fitness on cognitive performance of older adults from non-clinical populations. The ability of physical exercise to improve the cognitive performance of older adults has important health implications and consequently has attracted the greatest research interest. Firstly, the concepts of ageing, cognitive performance, and physical fitness will be discussed. Then the cross-sectional and intervention research results in this area will be sum-marised, after which possible mechanisms underlying the fitness and enhanced cognitive performance of older adults will be outlined.

Concepts

Ageing

Ageing concerns processes in humans that occur with the passing of time. Chronological age refers to the number of years a person has existed, whereas functional age is the age at which a person functions. Biological age is to do with biological rather than chronological processes. Researchers in the fitness, ageing, cognitive performance area focus on both chronological and biological ageing as they assume that fit older adults are biologically younger than unfit older adults (Chodzko-Zajko & Moore, 1994). Age categories used in this review are: 'young-old' between 65–74 years, 'old' between 75–84 years, and 'old-old' between 85–99 years. Gerontologists also disassociate the ageing process (Busse, 1969) that occurs in the absence of disease (primary ageing) from physiological and mental decline caused by poor health (secondary ageing).

Cognitive performance

Spirduso (1994) suggests that cognition can be viewed as functions of the brain that include memory, association, abstract reasoning, and spatial ability. She further suggests that attention, information-processing speed, and perception are some of the processes of cognition that support the cognitive functions. These processes interact and allow humans to process information and make decisions. Tests used to assess these different cognitive functions and processes are extensive. One of the most used tests in the fitness and cognitive research area is the reaction time (RT) task that mainly assesses attention and speed of response. In this task participants attend to a stimulus, usually a light, and depress a button as quickly as possible when the stimulus light goes off or the colour of the light changes. Examples of other tests that have been used to assess cognitive perfor-mance in ageing are listed in Table 6.1.

Physical fitness

Fitness is a multifactorial concept that includes flexibility, strength, stamina, and anaerobic and aerobic fitness. Individuals who are aerobically fit possess high maximal oxygen uptake ($\dot{V}O_{2max}$). Thus, $\dot{V}O_{2max}$ represents the maximal amount of aerobic work an individual can accomplish. It is represented as millilitres of oxygen consumed per kilogram of body mass per minute of exercise. The great majority of studies in this area have

Table 6.1 Examples of cognitive tests used in fitness, cognitive performance and ageing research

Test	Aspect of cognition that test measures
Reaction time	Speed and attention
Choice reaction time	Speed and attention
Wechsler Adult Intelligence Scale (WAIS)	Intelligence
Recall and recognition	Memory
Dual-time attention task	Attention
Culture Fair Intelligence Scale	Fluid intelligence
Digit Symbol WAIS subtest	Fluid intelligence
Dots Estimation	Memory
Stroop Colour Test	Attention
Line matching tests	Memory
Verbal comparison tests	Verbal fluency
Stanford-Binet Intelligence Quotient	Intelligence
Wechsler Memory Scale	Memory
Sternberg Number task	Memory
Raven's Progressive Matrices Test	Memory

examined the relationship between aerobic fitness and cognitive performance. Aerobic fitness has been assessed directly and indirectly by $\dot{V}O_{2max}$, sub maximal tests, field tests, resting cardiovascular parameters, and self-report of physical activity levels. This review will primarily focus on the relationship between chronic aerobic exercise (e.g. regular walking, jogging, swimming), ageing, and cognitive performance.

Ageing and cognition

As people age not all aspects of cognitive performance decline. Chodzko-Zajko and Moore (1994) have suggested that cognitive decline with ageing is more likely to occur in processes that require attention. Using the concepts of Hasher and Zacks (1988) and others (see Chodzko-Zajko & Moore, 1994) they view cognitive processes as being distributed along an automatic-to-effortful processing continuum. Thus, tasks that require effort, such as attention and speed, are likely to be performed less well by older adults. The literature on ageing supports this view as behavioural slowing is a typical characteristic of advancing age (Dustman et al., 1990; Salthouse, 1985; Stelmach, 1994). Although the mechanisms underlying these slowing of behaviours have not been determined, the prevalent view is that reduced speed of performance occurs because of central processing limitations rather than peripheral factors (Chodzko-Zajko & Moore, 1994).

Another factor that influences ageing and cognitive performance is health status or secondary ageing. As people age the incidence of disease increases and disease has been linked to cognitive decline (Milligan,

Powell, Harley, & Furchtgott, 1984). Because people who exercise generally possess less disease (e.g., cardiovascular disease, adult onset diabetes) fitness may positively influence cognitive performance by keeping people healthy. Thus, the effect of fitness on both primary and secondary ageing are important issues for this research area.

The effects of fitness on cognitive performance of older adults

Cross-sectional studies

Researchers using cross-sectional designs have typically been interested in comparing the cognitive response of physically fit to unfit older adults. They have usually compared the cognitive performance of groups of older athletes or adults engaged in physical activity with older adults who are inactive (Hart, 1981; Sherwood & Selder, 1979; Spirduso, 1975; Spirduso & Clifford, 1978). Other cross-sectional studies conducted into the effects of fitness on cognitive performance of older individuals include Abourez and Toole (1995), Arito and Oguri (1990), Baylor and Spirduso (1988), Clarkson-Smith and Hartley (1989), Del Rey (1982), Dustman, et al. (1990), Era (1988), Hart and Shay (1964), Hoyer, Labouvie and Baltes (1973), Ismail and El-Naggar (1981), Milligan et al. (1984), Molloy, Beerschoten, Borrie, Crilly and Cape (1988), Offenbach, Chodko-Zajko and Ringel (1990), Perlmutter and Nyquist (1990), Rikli and Busch (1986), Roberts (1990), Stacey, Kozma and Stones (1985), Stones and Kozma (1989), Suominen, Heikkinen, Parkatti, Forsberg and Kiiskinen (1980) and Szafran (1966).

The first study to use this approach was conducted by Spirduso (1975). Both young (20 year olds) and older males (above 60 years) who regularly exercised (racquetball) for three years were compared to young and old non-exercising controls. Findings were positive and reflect the results of the majority of cross-sectional studies conducted in this area. Older males who regularly exercised possessed significantly quicker RTs than older inactive males. It is significant that the RTs of the exercising old were similar to those of the exercising young who were more than 40 years younger.

Other studies using differing exercise modalities such as walking (Arito & Oguri, 1990), jogging (Baylor & Spirduso, 1988), and swimming (Hawkins, Kramer, & Capaldi, 1992) have also found similar results. These effects have also been found using varying methods of fitness assessment. Studies examining other aspects of cognitive functioning, such as memory and fluid and crystallised intelligence, have generally not found consistent differences between fit and unfit older adults (Chodzko-Zajko & Moore, 1994).

The meta-analysis by Thomas, Landers, Salazar and Etnier (1994) indicates that the effect size for cross-sectional studies examining the relationship between fitness and cognitive performance in older adults was significant but moderate (effect size [ES] = 0.31; standard deviation [SD] = 0.54). The most reliable effects were found for RT, maths, and acuity tasks. Also the analysis revealed that exercising women (ES = 0.47; SD = 0.59) showed greater levels of cognitive performance than exercising men (ES = 0.15; SD = 0.68). These large standard deviations reflect the inherent variability of the results of studies in this area.

Because of the limitations of the cross-sectional design the relationships described may not be causal and thus results should be viewed with caution. For example, there are a number of problems concerning physical activity that pose problems for the cross-sectional design (see Chapter 8 for discussion on methodological issues regarding physical activity). Also the use of valid measures of cognition is another issue for both cross-sectional and intervention research (Spirduso, 1994). Measures of cognitive performance in the exercise gerontology research area have included a range of tests and tasks that are described in Table 6.1. Most cognitive measures have involved speed such as simple and choice RT tasks. The attainment of maximum speed on these tasks is influenced by a range of factors such as the motivation of the individual. Also it may take considerable practice on the task before people can perform at their fastest. Few researchers have allowed participants to practice long enough to produce well-learned performances. Thus, these studies are limited by the amount of practice received (Spirduso, 1994).

Summary

Results of the majority of cross-sectional studies suggest that physically fit or active older adults typically process information more efficiently than their less fit counterparts. These effects are most pronounced in tasks that are attention demanding and rapid (e.g., RT tasks).

Intervention studies

As described in Chapter 8 there are numerous internal validity threats to the cross-sectional design. Furthermore, this design does not allow causal relationships to be inferred. The pre- to post-study design circumvents many of the problems that besiege cross-sectional research. Intervention studies typically administer an aerobic fitness programme to older subjects and assess cognitive performance and fitness before and after the programme. Fourteen published intervention studies in this area were located and these are shown in Table 6.2.

One of the first intervention studies was carried out by Dustman et al. (1984). Authors used adults between the ages of 55 and 70 years (non-exercise control, strength-and-flexibility exercise control, and an aerobic exercise group) with similar socio-economic and intelligence levels. Cognitive performance was assessed though a battery of tests (see Figure

6.1). After 4 months of exercise training the cognitive performance of the aerobic exercise group was significantly improved. In contrast, the cognitive performance of the sedentary group did not change. This study provides strong support for the relationship between fitness and cognitive performance because authors used appropriate control groups and trained subjects significantly improved their aerobic power (a 27% increase).

In another intervention study both RT and choice RT improved after a one-year exercise programme and then remained at that level with two more years of exercising (Rikli & Edwards, 1991). Three years after the start of the exercise programme RTs of the non-exercising subjects were significantly slower suggesting that the exercise programme may have delayed age-related slowing in RT.

A number of investigations have attempted to replicate Dustman et al.'s findings. For example, in a series of experiments Blumenthal and colleagues (1988, 1989) administered aerobic exercise, strength training, yoga or sedentary living and examined pre-to-post changes in a number of cognitive parameters. Results indicated that increases in aerobic power did not result in enhanced cognitive performance. Chodzko-Zajko and Moore (1994) have raised a number of criticisms about this study that have included the young age of participants, lack of a control group, and the high fitness levels of participants before the exercise intervention.

Blumenthal et al. (1991) attempted to control for some of these factors in a further study. Although exercisers increased aerobic power by 11.6% their cognitive performance did not improve. These non-significant findings are similar to the results of another training study by Panton, Graves, Pollock, Hayhery and Chen (1990). In contrast, a study by Hawkins et al. (1992), of similar design to that of Blumenthal et al. (1991), did find significant improvements in dual-task performance after a ten-week aerobic exercise programme. However, fitness change in this study was measured by changes in resting heart rate and not by direct fitness assessment.

As can be seen from Table 6.2, five of the intervention studies did find an increase in cognitive performance after aerobic training, whereas the others did not. Interestingly, the biggest increase in cognitive performance was found in participants who showed the biggest increase in aerobic fitness (Dustman et al., 1984). Spirduso (1994) has pointed out, however, that these participants' initial level of aerobic power was unusually low. Nevertheless, it is feasible that older individuals may have to record large increases in aerobic power before cognitive performance is enhanced. The meta-analysis by Etnier et al. (1997) indicates that the overall effect size for intervention studies examining the relationship between fitness and cognitive performance was significant and large for adults aged between 45 and 60 years (ES = 1.02; SD = 1.15) and significant but small for adults aged between 60 and 90 years (ES = 0.19; SD = 0.37). Methodological issues concerning physical activity and the intervention design are discussed in Chapter 8.

Table 6.2 Intervention studies examining the effect of fitness on cognitive performance of older adults

Authors	Participants	Design	Treatment	Cognitive measures	Cognitive results	Fitness results
Barry et al. (1966)	n = 13 males and females (71 yrs)	3 months training	aerobic exercises	RT, Raven's Matrices	no change	increase in agility muscular endurance
Elsayed et al. (1980)	n = 36 old and young males (24–64 yrs)	4 months training	jogging, calisthenics	fluid and crystallised intelligence tests	increases in fluid intelligence	increase in a composite fitness score
Dustman et al. (1984)	n = 43 individuals (55–70 yrs)	4 months training	aerobic, strength training	a battery of tests	increased performance	27% increase in $\dot{V}O_{2max}$
Blumenthal et al. (1988)	n = 28 males (43 yrs)	3 months training	jogging, strength training	RT in a memory-search task	no change	15% increase in $\dot{V}O_{2max}$
Blumenthal et al. (1989)	n = 101 males and females (67 yrs)	4 months training	aerobic, flexibility, control	a battery of tests	no change	11.6% increase in $\dot{V}O_{2max}$
Madden et al. (1989)	n = 85 males and females (60–80 yrs)	4 months training	aerobic, anaerobic,	RT, memory retrieval	no change control	11% increase in $\dot{V}O_{2max}$
Stones & Kozma (1989)	n = 200 males and females	12 months training	aerobic exercises	RT, digit symbol subtest	increased performance	increase in an aggregated fitness score

Study	Sample	Training	Conditions	Measures	Cognitive result	Fitness result
Emery & Gatz (1990)	n = 48 males and females (61–86 yrs)	3 months training	aerobic exercise, social activity, control waiting	digit span subtest, digit symbol subtest	no change	unclear
Panton et al. (1990) USA	n = 49 males and females	6 months training	walk/jog, strength training, control	RT, PMT, MT	no change	20% increase in $\dot{V}O_{2max}$
Blumenthal et al. (1991)	n = 101 males and females (60–83 yrs)	14 months training	aerobic exercise, yoga, waiting list	a battery of tests	no change	10–15% increase in $\dot{V}O_{2max}$
Hawkins et al. (1992)	n = 37 males and females (63–82 yrs)	10 weeks training	swimming, control	time-sharing, dual-task performance	increase in dual-task performance	not measured
Hill et al. (1993)	n = 87 adults	12 months training	endurance, exercise control	Wechsler memory scale	no change	increase in fitness
Paas et al. (1994)	n = 58 adults	10 months training	running, control	RT, CRT, letter recognition	no change	20% increase in fitness
Moul et al. (1995)	n = 30 males and females	4 months training	walking, weights, control	Ross Information Processing Assessment	increased performance	15.8 % increase in $\dot{V}O_{2max}$

Notes:
RT = reaction time, MT = movement time, PMT = pre-motor time, CRT = choice reaction time.

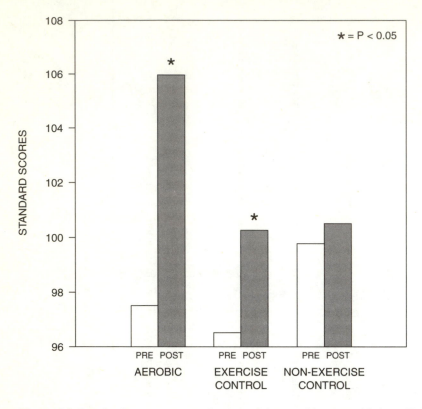

Figure 6.1 Standard scores averaged across eight cognitive tests (Culture Fair IQ, Digit Span, Digit Symbol, Dots, RT, Stroop Interference and Stroop Total) for aerobically trained, strength trained, and control subjects.

Adapted from R.E. Dustman, R.O. Ruhling, E.M. Russell, D.E. Shearer, H.W. Bonekat, J.W. Shigeoka, J.S. Wood, & D.C. Bradford (1984). 'Aerobic exercise training and improved neuropsychological function of older individuals.' *Neurobiology of Aging*, 5, 35–42, with permission from Elsevier Science.

Summary

Results of intervention studies examining the effect of exercise on cognitive functioning in older individuals are equivocal. Five intervention studies demonstrate improvement in cognitive performance following aerobic training whereas a number of well-controlled experiments have not (Table 6.2). The meta-analysis by Etnier et al. (1997) indicates that the overall effect size for intervention studies examining the relationship between fitness and cognitive performance in older adults is significant but small.

Mechanisms underlying the fitness/cognitive performance relationship

Although the mechanisms underlying the fitness/cognitive relationship have not been identified, several lines of evidence provide preliminary support for a number of hypotheses (see Chodzo-Zajko & Moore, 1994; Spirduso, 1980; Spirduso, 1994). These include cerebral circulation, neurotrophic stimulation, neural efficiency, secondary ageing, and psychosocial mechanisms.

Cerebral circulation

Evidence suggests that impaired cerebral circulation is associated with reduced cognitive performance (see Chodzo-Zaiko & Moore, 1994; Speith, 1965). For instance, induced hypoxia has resulted in cognitive decline on a number of cognitive tasks (Kennedy, Dunlap, Bandert, Smith, & Houston, 1989; McFarland, 1963). Significantly, cognitive decline was similar to that seen in non-hypoxic elderly subjects. In contrast, oxygen supplementation has been found to result in improved cognitive performance (Ben-Yashai & Diller, 1973). Thus, chronic exercise could maintain cerebrovascular integrity by enhancing oxygen transportation to the brain and the enhanced blood flow may positively influence cognitive performance (Chodzo-Zaiko & Moore, 1994).

Neurotrophic stimulation

Reduced neurotransmitter synthesis, structural alterations to neurones, and a general degradation of the central nervous system are associated with ageing (Chodzo-Zajko & Moore, 1994; Cottman & Holets, 1985). It is possible that participation in physical activity may offset these changes associated with advancing age (Chodzo-Zaiko & Moore, 1994). For example, chronic exercise is associated with increased brain weight in both primates (Floeter & Greenough, 1979) and rats (Pysh & Weiss, 1979). Thus, regular exercise may improve cognitive functioning by offsetting the general degradation of the central nervous system.

Neural efficiency

Whereas cerebral circulation and neurotrophic adaptations are direct mechanisms, other explanations are indirect, and focus on the information processing efficiency of the central nervous system (Chodzo-Zaiko & Moore, 1994). For example, electroencephalographic (EEG) responses have been examined to determine if fitness improves cognitive processing in old age (Spirduso, 1994). It has been found that old age is associated with changes in EEG responses (Dustman, Emmerson et al., 1990).

Dustman, Emmerson et al. (1990) recorded the EEG response of fit and unfit young (20–31 years) and older (50–62 years) adults and found that both the young and older fit adults possessed faster components to their visual evoked potentials than those who did not exercise. Thus, there is preliminary evidence to indicate that participation in regular aerobic exercise by older adults is associated with enhanced central nervous system processing.

Secondary ageing mechanisms

Regular exercise may also have a secondary effect on the cognitive performance of older individuals by preventing disease. Cardiovascular disease, adult onset diabetes, and hypertension are thought to impair cognitive function (Birren, Woods, & Williams, 1980; Hertzog, Schaie, & Gribbin, 1978). As people age the incidence of these diseases increases significantly (Birren et al., 1980). In contrast, regular exercise has been associated with reduced incidence of cardiovascular disease and hypertension and is important in helping to control adult onset diabetes by enhancing glucose tolerance and insulin sensitivity.

Psychosocial mechanisms

Chronic exercisers differ in a number of ways from inactive individuals. For example, people who exercise regularly have generally higher incomes, educational levels, and cognitive abilities (Stones & Kozma, 1989), and typically have more positive attitudes (Clarkson-Smith & Hartley, 1989). Thus, the development of more positive attitudes accompanying participation in a fitness programme could result in greater motivation to try harder on the cognitive tasks during the post-programme test.

Summary

A number of direct and indirect mechanisms could underpin the relationship between fitness and the cognitive performance of older adults. These include enhanced cerebral blood-flow, increased neurotrophic stimulation, increased neural efficiency, improved health, and greater motivation. Research into these mechanisms is preliminary at this stage and has not produced conclusive findings.

Future research

There is a need for exercise scientists to collaborate with medical and gerontological researchers to identify the mechanisms underlying the cognitive performance enhancement effects of exercise. In addition, randomised controlled trials need to be long enough to bring about physiological adaptation and need to use valid measures of cognitive performance and valid measurement of aerobic fitness. Finally, cross-sectional studies comparing highly trained and untrained older adults' cognitive performance whilst controlling for subject differences are required.

What we know

- The majority of cross-sectional studies show that fit older adults display better cognitive performance than less fit older adults.
- The association between fitness and cognitive performance is task-dependent with most pronounced effects in tasks that are attention-demanding and rapid (e.g. RT tasks).
- Results of intervention studies are equivocal but meta-analytic findings indicate a small but significant improvement in cognitive performance of older adults who experience an increase in aerobic fitness.
- Research into possible mechanisms underlying the effects of fitness on cognitive performance in older adults is preliminary at this stage and has not produced conclusive findings.

What we need to know

- What are the mechanisms underlying the effects of fitness on the enhanced cognitive performance of older adults?
- What is the dose-response relationship? In other words how much of a fitness improvement needs to occur before an increase in cognitive performance is demonstrated?
- Is it necessary to develop physiological adaptations to an exercise regimen before cognitive performance increases occur?
- What aspect of cognitive functioning of older adults is most greatly affected by increases in fitness? For instance, is speed in contrast to memory recall most likely to be improved with increases in fitness?
- If regular exercise results in enhanced cognitive performance does it do so at all ages or are the effects more significant in older adults?
- What happens to the cognitive performance of those individuals who stop exercising?
- Do older females record greater increases in cognitive performance after exercise training than older males?

7 Physical activity as a source of psychological dysfunction

Attila Szabo

The mental and physiological benefits of physical activity are almost undisputed. There is a strong consensus in scientific circles with regard to the value of integrating physical activity in one's regular lifestyle (Bouchard, Shephard, & Stephens, 1994). However, in isolated cases (a key term throughout this article is *isolated cases*) physical activity can lead to undesirable or harmful psychological states. Although these states are mostly transient, their impact may have irreversible damage on the life of the individual. The aim of this chapter is by no means to take a stand against physical activity, but simply to discuss the relatively rare circumstances in which exercise or physical activity may inflict substantial or even permanent damage on physically active people. The aim of the chapter is to help the reader become aware of exercise related factors that are associated with psychological dysfunction. It is hoped that knowledge and timely recognition of these factors may prevent the development of 'unhealthy' exercise behaviours and their negative consequences.

The dark side of physical activity

Negative consequences of physical activity

Negative psychological experiences associated with exercise participation may occur early in the adoption phase or later in the exercise maintenance phase. They may be classified as having *acute* (transient) and *chronic* (persistent) effects. In the adoption phase, psychological hardship is mostly transient and it may lead to drop-out from the exercise programme (Dishman, 1988, 1993; Gauvin, 1990). In the exercise maintenance phase, more severe psychological dysfunction is associated with one's attitude towards physical activity and, therefore, it may persist for a relatively long period.

During the adoption phase

At the early phases of adoption of physical activity there are two general outcomes. The person will either like the activity and continue exercising, or dislike it – for a number of reasons – and discontinue the activity. In the case of exercise maintenance the early experiences may often be stressful. Levels of physical effort exerted by the novice exerciser may be high which in turn may lead to negative affect (Raglin, 1993). Further, if socially undesirable physical appearance was among the motives for the adoption of physical activity, a possible anxiety associated with one's appearance – 'social physique anxiety' – may have aversive psychological effects (Hart, Leary, & Rejeski, 1989). Social physique anxiety is relatively common and it results from the comparison of the self with the appearance of co-exercisers. Therefore, this exercise-related anxiety is most prevalent in physical activities practised in social settings.

Physical activity can also induce anxiety in 'exercise sensitive' individuals. Cameron and Hudson (1986) reported that 20% of 66 patients diagnosed with anxiety disorders, on the basis of the Diagnostic and Statistical Manual (DSM-III), as well as 22% of 37 controls reported experiencing anxiety during exercise. Whilst the patients responded with greater anxiety in general, both groups experienced increasingly greater anxiety when exercise intensity was increased sequentially from 'very mild' to 'very vigorous' levels through five stages. The findings of Cameron and Hudson (1986) were expanded to healthy individuals in a recent inquiry that demonstrated that a 20-minute bout of high intensity resistance exercise increased state anxiety whereas low intensity exercise had the opposite effect (Bartholomew & Linder, 1998). High intensity exercise training, especially in competitive athletes, was also associated with negative changes in mood states (Raglin, 1993; Raglin, Eksten, & Garl, 1995; Raglin, Koceja, Stager, & Harms, 1996). Consequently, high intensity exercise may lead to anxiety and negative mood which than can lead to the abandonment of the exercise regimen (see also Biddle, this volume).

Often the early phases of adoption of physical activity will end with non-adherence to exercise. There may be many reasons for this including inappropriate physical challenge, unpleasant social and/or environmental settings, or an inability to handle other life commitments effectively. Non-adherence is extremely common. In fact about 60% of those who intend to adopt an exercise activity will discontinue the selected activity within the first six months (Dishman, 1988, 1993). Non-adherence may have a significant negative impact on the mental health of the individual (Brewer, 1993). For example, feelings of guilt, inadequacy, lack of determination, and social critique can trigger decrements in one's self-concept and/or self-esteem, predisposing the person to a number of psychological dysfunctions such as depression and anxiety. Regrettably, no scientific inquiries have been undertaken to identify the psychological consequences of abandoning exercise regimens.

After the adoption phase

Once physical activity has been adopted as a regular part of the individual's lifestyle the most critical issue is the pattern or habit of practising the activity. As with all behaviours, moderation is important. Overdoing the adopted physical activity can lead to both injuries and to the neglect of other important responsibilities in life. In fact, for various reasons, exercisers may lose control over their exercise and travel a 'path of self-destruction' (Morgan, 1979). The most common psychological dysfunction associated with over-exercising, is exercise dependence. This disorder is classified as 'primary exercise dependence' when it manifests itself in the form of behavioural addiction, and as 'secondary exercise dependence' when it appears in conjunction with eating disorders (De Coverley Veale, 1987). The remainder of the text will examine primary and secondary exercise dependence.

Primary exercise dependence

An abnormal reliance on physical activity is frequently termed *exercise addiction* (e.g. Thaxton, 1982), *exercise dependence* (e.g. Cockerill & Riddington, 1996), or *obligatory exercising* (Pasman & Thompson, 1988). The term *exercise* is often replaced by the term *physical activity* or the name of the activity, such as running (e.g. Chapman & De Castro, 1990). In some instances the concept is referred to as *negative addiction* (e.g. Rudy & Estok, 1989) to contrast the idea of *positive addiction* (Glasser, 1976) that was introduced as a more favourable perspective. Unfortunately, the use of the latter terminology yielded confusion in the scientific literature and will be discussed later. The currently preferred terminology is *exercise dependence* (Cockerill & Riddington, 1996; De Coverley Veale, 1987). The prevalence of exercise dependence is not well known, but it is speculated that only a very small percentage of regular exercisers are affected (De Coverley Veale, 1987; Morris, 1989).

The conceptual meaning of exercise dependence

In 1976, Glasser introduced the term *positive addiction* to denote the personally and socially beneficial aspects of a regular physical activity regimen in contrast to some self-destructive behaviours. The 'positive' perception and subsequent adoption of the terminology led to its widespread but loose usage within both athletic and scientific circles. Morgan (1979) was first to realise the dilemma. To discuss some rare but existing compulsive exercise behaviours, he introduced the term *negative addiction* as a counter-term to positive addiction. The fact is, however, that all addicted behaviours are pathological and they are *always* negative (Rozin & Stoess, 1993).

Glasser's (1976) 'positive' prefix referred to the benefits of commitment to physical activity (a healthy behaviour) as opposed to the negative effects of 'unhealthy' addictions, such as smoking, drinking, or drug abuse. In fact, positive addiction can be viewed as a synonym for *commitment to physical activity* (Carmack & Martens, 1979; Pierce, 1994). However, when commitment to physical activity is equated to *addiction* or to *dependence* on exercise (Conboy, 1994; Sachs, 1981; Thornton & Scott, 1995) a conceptual confusion is created. For example, Thornton and Scott (1995) found that they could classify 77% of a sample of 40 runners as moderately or highly addicted to running. Since any addiction is a serious psychopathological condition, this figure is certainly exaggerated. Some researchers have realised this problem and attempted to draw a fine line between *commitment* and *addiction* to physical activity (Chapman & De Castro, 1990; Summers & Hinton, 1986; Szabo, Frenkl, & Caputo, 1997). Most recent evidence indicates that addiction to exercise and commitment to exercise are independent concepts (Szabo et al., 1997).

Drawing a fine line between commitment and addiction to physical activity

Commitment to physical activity

This is a reflection of how dedicated or devoted a person is to her/his physical activity. It is a measure of the strength of adherence to an adopted physical activity regimen. For the committed exerciser, satisfaction, enjoyment, and achievement derived from exercise are incentives that motivate the continuity of the behaviour (Chapman & De Castro, 1990). Sachs (1981) viewed commitment to exercise as a result of intellectual analysis of the rewards gained from exercise, including social relationships, health benefits, status, prestige, or monetary advantages. Committed exercisers, in light of Sachs' (1981) description (a) often exercise for extrinsic rewards, (b) view their exercise as an important, but not central, part of their lives, and (c) may not suffer severe withdrawal symptoms when they cannot exercise for some reason (Summers & Hinton, 1986). The committed exerciser controls her/his physical activity (Johnson, 1995).

Addiction to physical activity

In contrast to committed exercisers, addicted exercisers, according to Sachs (1981) are more likely to (a) exercise for internal satisfaction, (b) view exercise as the chief part of their lives, and (c) experience strong deprivation sensations when they are unable to exercise (Summers & Hinton, 1986). Motivation for exercise is another distinguishing feature between commitment and addiction to exercise. Exercise-dependent individuals may be motivated by negative (avoiding withdrawal symptoms) and/or positive ('runners' high') reinforcements (Pierce, 1994; Szabo, 1995). However, negative reinforcement, or avoidance behaviour, is not a usual motivating factor for the committed exerciser (Szabo, 1995). Finally, in contrast to the committed exerciser, the exercise dependent person loses control over her/his physical activity (Johnson, 1995).

Definition and symptoms of exercise dependence

An *abnormal* or *unhealthy* exercise pattern is a pre-requisite in the classification of exercise dependence (Cockerill & Riddington, 1996). A commonly used definition for exercise dependence stems from Sachs (1981, p. 118) who described addiction to running as 'addiction of a psychological and/or physiological nature, upon a regular regimen of running, characterized by withdrawal symptoms after 24 to 36 hours without participation'. This definition is well accepted in the literature (Furst & Germone, 1993; Morris, 1989; Sachs & Pargman, 1984). However, there is a problem with this definition because withdrawal symptoms are only one of the many characteristics of addictive behaviours (Brown, 1993; Griffiths, 1997). Further, many empirical studies have simply assessed the mere presence, rather than the type, frequency, and intensity of withdrawal symptoms (Szabo, 1995; Szabo et al., 1997). Yet negative psychological symptoms are reported by all committed, not necessarily addicted, exercisers for the times when exercise is prevented for an involuntary reason (Szabo, 1997; Szabo, Frenkl, & Caputo, 1996). Even participants in physically less strenuous leisure activities, such as bowlers, report deprivation sensations when bowling is not possible. However, the *intensity* of the symptoms reported by this group is less than that reported by aerobic dancers, weight-trainers, cross-trainers, or fencers (Szabo et al., 1996).

Consequently, it is clear that the presence of withdrawal symptoms in itself is insufficient for the diagnosis of exercise dependence. Cockerill and Riddington (1996) do not even mention withdrawal symptoms in their listing of characteristics associated with exercise dependence. In fact the presence of withdrawal symptoms, in many forms of physical activity, suggests that exercise has a positive effect on people's psychological well-being. This effect is missed when an interruption of the habitual activity is commanded by unforeseen circumstances.

A close analysis of the literature reveals that there is a lack of a sound definition of exercise dependence. Johnson's (1995) point, that the exercise-dependent individual is controlled by her/his physical activity, may be a starting point in the quest for a more appealing conceptual definition. The joint presence of a number of commonly reported symptoms should then be closely observed in the classification of genuine exercise dependence (see Table 7.1). These symptoms, unfortunately, were either ignored or only loosely attended to (i.e. the degree of their severity was overlooked) in empirical research.

Assessment of exercise dependence

There are major limitations in the assessment of exercise dependence. The available 'addiction' scales (see Table 7.2) are embedded, at least in part, with questions pertaining to commitment rather than to dependence on

Table 7.1 Components or symptoms of exercise dependence

Components of addiction	Description
1 Salience (Brown, 1993; De Coverley Veale, 1987; Griffiths, 1997)	The physical activity assumes a primary role in the person's life and there is an obsessive preoccupation with the practiced activity many times a day, and even during other activities
2 Euphoria/satisfaction (Brown, 1993; Cockerill & Riddington, 1996; Griffiths, 1997)	A psychological and/or physical experience that may be identified as the main driving force (i.e. the key source of motivation) for the chosen physical activity and its pattern
3 Tolerance (Brown, 1993; De Coverley Veale 1987; Griffiths, 1997)	The 'dose-dependent' aspect of exercise addiction. The person needs to progressively increase the frequency, duration, and/or the intensity of the adopted physical activity to derive the level of satisfaction previously attained with lesser exercise
4 Withdrawal symptoms (Brown, 1993; De Coverley Veale 1987; Griffiths, 1997)	Severe negative physical or psychological feelings experienced when the adopted physical activity cannot be performed for an involuntary reason (i.e. injury or other commitments)
5 Conflict (Brown, 1993; Griffiths, 1997)	Interpersonal problems arising from over-exercising and intrapersonal (intrapsychic) conflict arising from feelings of guilt and dissatisfaction associated with the neglect of other (than exercise) life obligations
6 Relapse (Brown, 1993; De Coverley Veale 1987; Griffiths, 1997)	A predisposition to re-establishment of the previously 'unhealthy' pattern of exercise behaviour after a period of abstinence or 'normal' exercising. (Due to the effort involved in most physical activities, this component is argued to be weak in exercise addiction (Cockerill & Riddington, 1996))
7 Loss of control over life-activities (Griffiths, 1997)	The urge for exercising becomes so intense that it interferes with other activities and the need for exercise often becomes immediate. Until that need is satisfied, the other life-activities are deficiently performed
8 Loss of control over one's exercise behaviour (Cockerill & Riddington, 1996; Johnson, 1995)	The exerciser cannot resist the urge to exercise. While the exercise dependent person may try to set limits in her/his exercise patterns, she/he is unable to respect those self-set limits. In short, a lack of ability to exercise with moderation
9 Negative consequences (Griffiths, 1997)	The negative outcomes directly associated with over-exercising. It may involve the loss of employment, poor academic performance, break-up in marriage or other relationship(s) and other consequences generally considered to have an undesirable effect on a person's life

Table 7.1 (continued)

Components of addiction	Description
10 Risk of self-injury (De Coverley Veale, 1987; Wichmann & Martin, 1992)	At times of mild injuries the addicted exerciser cannot abstain from exercise and, thus, assumes the risk of self-injury by maintaining her/his physical activity
11 Social withdrawal (Cockerill & Riddington, 1996)	A search for approval from other exercisers, and avoidance of the company of those who criticise the physical activity pattern of the exercise-dependent person
12 Lack of compromise (Wichmann & Martin, 1992)	Signs of neglecting family or work responsibilities to spend more time exercising. Other life-commitments are ignored even though this carries significant negative consequences
13 Denial of a problem or self-justification (Wichmann & Martin, 1992)	The rationalisation of the problem via conscious search for reasons why exercise should take priority over all other life commitments
14 Full awareness of the problem (De Coverley Veale,1987)	The exercise dependent person knows well that there is a problem with her/his exercise behaviour through feedback from other people or from the negative life-events directly resulting from over-exercising

exercise. Furthermore, like most Likert scales, they were developed to measure the *degree of addiction*, rather than to positively diagnose exercise dependence. Then there is confusion between the distinct concepts of addiction and commitment. For example, Conboy (1994) used the Commitment to Running Scale (Carmack & Martens, 1979) to measure addiction. Such confusion hinders the valid assessment of exercise dependence. In-depth interviews, structured around the classic symptoms of addiction (Table 7.1), conducted with both the exercisers and her/his relatives and/or colleagues may be the most appropriate technique for the positive identification of exercise dependence.

Possible causes of addiction to physical activity

Physiological explanations

While the symptoms of exercise addiction may be recognised, the causes of exercise dependence are far from clear. A number of hypotheses have been put forward. One of them is the popular endorphin hypothesis. According to this model, exercise stimulates the release of beta-endorphins, a natural opiate in the brain, that induces feelings of euphoria such as the well known 'runners' high' (Pierce, 1994). This hypothesis views exercisers as 'opiate junkies' and is highly challenged. Indeed, there is psychopharmacological counter-evidence for this explanation (De Coverley Veale, 1987; Pierce, 1994). Further, there is a lack of correlation between exercise dependence scores and beta-endorphin immunoreactivity (Pierce, 1994). Finally, the biological obstacle presented by the blood brain barrier in the transport of the peripheral beta-endorphins to the brain also argues against the endorphin hypothesis (De Coverley Veale, 1987; Pierce, 1994).

A more plausible physiological explanation, known as the 'sympathetic arousal hypothesis', was proposed by Thompson and Blanton (1987). According to this model, regular exercise leads to decreased sympathetic arousal at rest. This adaptation leads to a lethargic state with lack of exercise. To maintain an optimal level of arousal, and to overcome the lethargic state at rest, the habituated exerciser needs to exercise to increase her/his level of arousal. The associated symptoms match the symptoms of exercise dependence. Therefore, on physiological grounds this explanation may be plausible.

Psychological explanations

Some runners try to run away from their psychological problems (Morris, 1989). They are very few in number and use exercise as a means of coping or escape from serious distress. Like others, who turn to drugs and alcohol in cases of severe distress, exercisers may abuse their exercise so that behavioural addiction becomes evident (Griffiths, 1997). Since exercise, in contrast to alcohol or drugs, requires substantial physical effort (Cockerill & Riddington, 1996), it is a less 'convenient' coping mechanism that requires strong self-determination and self-discipline. Therefore, the cases of exercise addiction or dependence are very rare in contrast to other forms of escape behaviours.

Correlates of exercise dependence

Researchers have looked at the correlates of exercise dependence (see Table 7.2), but have been unable to identify when or why a transition takes place from 'healthy' to 'unhealthy' exercise behaviour (Johnson, 1995). Exercise dependence appears to be positively related to anxiety (Morgan, 1979; Rudy & Estok, 1989) and negatively related to self-esteem (Estok & Rudy, 1986; Rudy & Estok, 1989). Further, the length of experience with a particular physical activity appears to be positively associated with exercise dependence (Furst & Germone, 1993; Hailey & Bailey, 1982; Thaxton, 1982). If experience is associated with exercise dependence, it is reasonable to speculate that a major life event change (or stress) may trigger addiction that is exhibited through 'revolutionary' rather than evolutionary changes in the habitual physical activity pattern of the individual. The affected individual may see this form of coping as healthy on the

Table 7.2 Summary table of research into exercise dependence

Author(s)	Participants and type of physical activity	Measure(s) of exercise dependence/addiction	Correlates of addiction to physical activity	Main findings and/or conclusions
Anshel (1991)	60 exercisers in health and fitness centre (30 males & 30 females)	amount (frequency and hours) or participation in exercise sessions	restlessness, withdrawal symptoms, positive mood after exercise, ignorance of physical discomfort (i.e., injuries)	differences observed between the addicted and non-addicted exercisers as well as between males and females
Carmack & Martens (1979)	315 runners (250 males & 65 females)	subjectively perceived levels of addiction ('very much', 'somewhat', & 'not at all')	examined as a secondary variable; subjective conceptualisation by the participants	perceived addiction was found to be a predictor of commitment to running
Chapman & De Castro (1990)	47 runner (32 males & 17 females)	Running Addiction Scale (RAS – self-developed)	addiction scores were related to high frequency of running and positive psychological characteristics	(1) large gender differences observed; (2) duration of run, but not addiction, was related to mood enhancement
Conboy (1994)	61 runners (51 males & 10 females)	Commitment to Running Scale (CR – Carmack & Martens, 1979)	withdrawal symptoms on non-running days	withdrawal effects can only be seen when commitment and dependence are jointly tested

Study	Sample	Measure	Findings	
Crossman, Jamieson, & Henderson (1987)	31 runners (15 males & 16 females – study 1) and 20 swimmers (12 females & 8 males – study 2)	self-perceived addiction rated on a 9-point Likert scale ranging from 'not at all' to 'extremely'	exercise withdrawal was unrelated to the scores of subjectively reported addiction	postulates the existence of two opposing processes; one negative due to exercise withdrawal and one positive due to rest during periods of exercise withdrawal
Estok & Rudy (1986)	57 marathon and 38 non-marathon runner females	Running Addiction Scale (RAS – self-developed)	higher addiction scores were related to lower self-esteem	higher addiction scores were not related to more physical injuries and no differences were seen between the groups
Furst & Germone (1993)	98 runners (72 males & 26 females) and 90 other exercisers (60 males & 30 females)	Negative Addiction Scale (Hailey & Bailey, 1982)	duration of involvement in physical activity was related to higher addiction scores	no gender or physical activity (type) differences were seen in relation to the addiction scores
Griffiths (1997)	1 female jiu-jitsu practitioner	interview modelled on Brown's (1993) addictive components	salience, tolerance, withdrawal, euphoria, conflict, loss of control, relapse	exercise has taken over a person's life which argues against the concept of 'positive addiction'
Hailey & Bailey (1982)	60 male runners placed in groups on the basis of their running history	Negative Addiction Scale	duration of involvement in running was related to higher negative addiction scores	with a few exceptions negative addiction is linearly related to length of running experience

Table 7.2 (continued)

Author(s)	Participants and type of physical activity	Measure(s) of exercise dependence/addiction	Correlates of addiction to physical activity	Main findings and/or conclusions
Morgan (1979)	8 case studies (6 runners, 1 swimmer and 1 wrestler)	self-reported compulsive patterns of exercising and withdrawal symptoms in lack of exercise	withdrawal symptoms, exercise in spite of injuries, ignorance of major life-commitments, multiple exercise sessions on the same days	runners (exercisers) may lose perspective and the control over their exercise and finally undergo the path of self-destruction
Pasman & Thompson, (1988)	90 participants (45 males & 45 females who were represented equally in three groups: runners, weightlifters and controls)	Obligatory Exercise Questionnaire (modified from the Obligatory Running Questionnaire (Blumenthal et al., 1985))	withdrawal symptoms and the maintenance of exercise in spite of injuries	related obligatory exercising to eating disturbances
Pierce, Daleng, & McGowan (1993)	102 females (47 dancers, 39 runners, and 16 field-hockey athletes	Negative Addiction Scale (Hailey & Bailey, 1982)	type of activity may be related to exercise addiction	dancers showed greater addiction to their physical activity than runners, but only speculative explanations are provided
Rudy & Estok (1989)	202 marathon runners (104 females & 98 males)	Running Addiction Scale (Estok & Rudy, 1986) that was further improved here	addiction was positively related to anxiety and it was negatively related to self-esteem	proposes that the Running Addiction Scale is a useful tool for gauging negative addiction in runners

Study	Sample	Measure	Findings	Conclusions
Rudy & Estok (1990)	35 runners (22 females & 13 males and their spouses)	Running Addiction Scale (Rudy & Estok, 1989)	addiction to running was unrelated to dyadic adjustment, but spouses' rating of addiction was negatively related to their own adjustment	speculates that intense running jeopardises family relationships and dyadic adjustments
Sachs & Pargman (1979)	12 runners (all males)	in-depth interview	related running addiction to the high life-priority of running and feelings of accomplishment and relaxation after running	health reasons play an important role in running addiction and the withdrawal symptoms (when not running) are key signs of addiction
Thaxton (1982)	33 runners (24 males & 9 females)	self-reported on a 10-point rating scale (ranging from 'non-addicted' to 'extremely addicted')	related running addiction to running experience (years of running) and weekly frequency of running	concludes that even slight variation from the running schedule can have negative effects on habitual runners
Thornton & Scott (1995)	40 male runners	Running Addiction Scale (Rudy & Estok, 1989) and Negative Addiction Scale (Hailey & Bailey, 1982)	related running addiction to the frequency and the distance of running, rather than to running experience	stresses the individual differences in the examination of running addiction

basis of popular knowledge and the media-spread information about the positive aspects of exercise.

Indeed, the media plays an important role in what people believe about and expect from their exercise. The media-propagated positive image of the exercising individual provides a mask behind which some exercisers with severe emotional distress can hide. Thus the media-projected positive information about physical activity can be used to deny the existence of the problem (a characteristic of addictive behaviours) and to delay its detection to the advanced stages when all symptoms of addiction are vividly present. Because of such a possible delay, it is likely that only case studies, presented in the literature, reflect genuine cases of exercise dependence. Indeed, a random sample of habitual exercisers may contain very few cases, if any (!), of exercise addicts (Morris, 1989).

Recommendations for the individual

Physically active people should keep their physical activity in perspective. The person who feels that she/he is at risk may wish to evaluate the statements in Table 7.3(a). The statements are based on some critical addictive components presented in Table 7.1 and Zaitz's (1989) opinion. If most of the statements are 'true' there is a need to acknowledge the possibility of a problem and to take immediate action. For the rebuilding of a healthy exercise pattern, Zaitz (1989) proposes some self-help strategies (see Table 7.3(b)). However, if no self-set changes in exercise habits seem to be viable, the person should consider seeking professional help. At this stage it is important to remember that over-exercising may have serious detrimental and irreversible effects and the root of the problem (i.e. the reason(s) for over-exercise) can and must be identified. The mere self-acknowledgement of the problem is already a significant step towards the rectification of the problem.

Recommendations for health practitioners

Exercise-dependent people (Wichmann & Martin, 1992) frequently visit orthopaedic clinics because they continue exercising even at times of minor injuries. These injuries then become more severe and force the individual to seek medical help. Therefore, orthopaedic surgeons, physiotherapists, and occupational therapists should be familiar with the symptoms of exercise dependence. When recognising the symptoms in a patient, they should refer the affected individual to their colleagues specialised in the area of behavioural addictions. Exercise dependence, like other behavioural addictions, should be considered to be a serious condition. Once a positive diagnosis has emerged, the principal concern should be to find the main causes of the dependence. The treatment should be geared toward the cause, not the symptom, of over-exercising.

Table 7.3(a) Exercise dependence self-evaluation check list

1 Exercise has the highest priority in my life.
2 I have experienced major losses due to exercise.
3 I cannot miss a scheduled exercise no matter what.
4 I will exercise against medical advice or when injured.
5 I am irritated and intolerable when I miss my exercise.
6 I will make no compromises when it comes to exercise.

Table 7.3(b) Self-help strategies for the modification of exercise habits (based on Zaitz (1989)

1 Fulfil the urge of exercising with different modalities of exercise (i.e. cross-training).
2 Consciously schedule a 'reasonable' rest period between two bouts of exercise to prevent mental and physical fatigue.
3 Exercise your mind by getting involved in mental and social activities that can lower anxiety and give a burst to the self-esteem.
4 Learn stress-management techniques, relaxation. and/or meditation.

Recommendations for research

Future research should treat exercise dependence as a potentially serious disorder that may be part of a class of disorders often referred to as *behavioural addictions*. Since most likely only a very small portion of the exercising population is exercise dependent (Morris, 1989; Pierce, 1994), clinical case studies should form the infrastructure of research on exercise dependence. Excessive exercise, whether conceptualised in terms of high frequency, intensity, duration, or history, should not be used as the only criterion in the diagnosis of exercise dependence. If the physically active individual has not experienced major negative life-events directly traceable to her or his exercising behaviour and she/he is not jeopardising personal health and social relationships, the presence of exercise dependence is unlikely. Further, because existing tools for gauging exercise dependence are mostly Likert scales, they always yield a score of dependence that ranges from low to high. Graded scales are perhaps effective in the evaluation of tendencies for exercise dependence, but not in the diagnosis of dependence. People scoring in the upper end of these scales should be followed-up over time. This method will allow researchers to identify the life-event(s) that trigger dependence.

Secondary exercise dependence

De Coverley Veale (1987) differentiated between primary and secondary exercise dependence. In the previous section primary dependence was examined. Secondary exercise dependence is a common characteristic of eating disorders such as anorexia nervosa and bulimia nervosa (De Coverley Veale, 1987). In these disorders, excessive exercise is considered to be an auxiliary feature used in caloric control and weight loss. Secondary exercise dependence occurs in different 'doses' in people affected by eating disorders. It has been estimated that one third of anorectics might be affected (Crisp, Hsu, Harding, & Hartshorn, 1980).

The relationship between exercise and eating disorders

A team of long-distance runners and scholars specialised in eating disorders (Yates, Leehey, & Shisslak, 1983) observed a striking resemblance between the psychology of anorectic patients and the very committed runners whom they named obligatory runners. They interviewed sixty marathoners and closely examined the traits of a subgroup of male athletes who corresponded to the 'obligatory' category. They reported that male obligatory runners resembled anorexic women in some personality traits, such as expression of anger, high self-expectation, tolerance of pain, and depression as well as in some demographic details. Yates et al. (1983) related these observations to a unique and hazardous way of establishment of self-identity. This work has marked the foundation of research into the relationship between exercise and eating disorders.

The analogy between anorexia and excessive exercising

Since Yates et al. (1983) published their article, a large number of studies have examined the relationship between exercise and eating disorders. A close examination of these studies (Table 7.4) reveals some opposing findings to the original report. For example, three studies that compared anorectic patients with high level, or obligatory, exercisers (Blumenthal, O'Toole & Chang, 1984; Davis et al., 1995; Knight, Schocken, Powers, Feld, & Smith, 1987) failed to demonstrate an analogy between anorexia and excessive exercising. The differences in methodology between these inquiries are, however, significant. They all looked for an analogy between excessive exercise and anorexia, but from a different perspective. Blumenthal et al. (1984) and Knight et al. (1987) examined a mixed gender sample's scores on a popular personality test (the Minnesota Multiphasic Personality Inventory – MMPI). Davis et al. (1995) tested a female sample using specific questionnaires aimed at assessing compulsiveness, commitment to exercise, and eating disorders. Finally, Yates et al. (1983) looked to some demographic and personality parallels between obligatory runners and anorectic patients. Further, the classification of the exercise behaviour may have differed in these studies. Therefore, these studies are not easily comparable.

The controversy between the above studies may be partly solved by considering the results of a more recent study. Wolf and Akamatsu (1994)

Table 7.4 Summary table of published papers on physical activity and eating disorders relationships

Author(s)	Participants	Objectives	Measurements	Conclusion about the relationship between exercise and eating disorders
Blumenthal, O'Toole, & Chang (1984)	compared 24 anorectics to 43 obligatory runners	to assess the similarity between anorexia nervosa and obligatory running	Minnesota Multiphasic Personality Inventory (MMPI); Clinical diagnosis based on the DSM II and the DSM III (Diagnostic and Statistical Manual of Mental Disorders)	Runners and anorectics are different. The relationship is superficial on the basis of the ten subscales of the MMPI
Brewerton, Stellefson, Hibbs, Hodges, & Cochrane (1995)	110 anorexic, bulimic or both females grouped into compulsive (n = 31) and non-compulsive exercise (n = 79) groups	to compare compulsively exercising and non-exercising patients suffering from eating disorders	Diagnostic Survey of the Eating Disorders; Clinical diagnosis based on the DSM III for anorexia nervosa and bulimia nervosa	Compulsive exercising was related to elevated body dissatisfaction in patients with eating disorders and it was more prevalent (39%) in anorectics than in bulimics (23%)
Davis (1990a)	86 exercising and 72 non-exercising women	to compare body image and weight preoccupation between exercising and non-exercising women	Eysenk Personality Inventory; Body Image Questionnaire; and Subjective Body Shape; Eating Disorder Inventory (EDI)	Body-dissatisfaction was related to poorer emotional well-being in the exercise group only. EDI scores did not differ between the groups
Davis (1990b)	53 exercising and 43 non-exercising women	to study addictiveness, weight preoccupation, and	Addictiveness with the Eysenk Personality Questionnaire	Addictiveness was related to weight and dieting

Table 7.4 (continued)

Author(s)	Participants	Objectives	Measurements	Conclusion about the relationship between exercise and eating disorders
		exercise patterns in a non-clinical population	(EPQ); Body Focus; Eating Disorder Inventory (EDI)	variables in both groups and to perfectionism in the exercise group. EDI scores did not differ between the groups
Davis, Brewer, & Ratusny (1993)	88 men and 97 women	to present a new 'Commitment to Exercise' questionnaire and to study the relationship between exercising and obsessive compulsiveness, weight preoccupation and addictiveness	Addictiveness; Commitment to Obsessive compulsiveness; Eating Disorder Inventory (EDI), 'Drive for Thinness' subscale	Presents validity and reliability data for the two factor (obligatory exercising and pathological exercising) 'Commitment to Exercise Questionnaire'. Excessive exercising was found to be distinct from eating disorders
Davis et al. (1995)	46 anorexic patients, 76 high-level exercisers, 55 moderate exercisers, all females	to test the relationship between obsessive compulsiveness and exercise in anorectics in contrast to moderate and high-level exercising controls	Commitment to exercise, Obsessive compulsiveness; Eating Disorder Inventory (EDI), 'Drive for Thinness' subscale	Weight preoccupation and excessive exercising were related in both high-level exercisers and anorectics

Study	Sample	Aim	Measures	Results
French, Perry, Leon, & Fulkerson (1995)	852 female students	to observe changes, over a three-year period, in psychological and health variables in dieting and non-dieting women	Negative emotionality; Self-concept; Eating Disorders Symptom Scores (based on DSM III), Restrained Eating Scale, Eating Disorder Inventory	Dieting habits were not related to physical activity levels over three years, but dieters reported greater decreases in physical activity than non-dieters
French, Perry, Leon, & Fulkerson (1994)	1494 adolescents	to examine correlates of symptoms of eating disorders, including food preferences, eating patterns, and physical activity	Food preference and eating patterns questionnaires and Eating Disorders Symptoms	High-performance sport participation was found to be a predictor of eating disorders symptoms
Levine, Marcus, & Moulton (1996)	77 females (44 assigned to regular walking & 33 control) suffering from binge-eating disorder	to examine the effects of an exercise intervention in the treatment of obese women with binge-eating disorder	Beck Depression Inventory; Eating Disorder examination (a semi-structured clinical interview)	Binge-eating disorder was successfully managed through a 24-week (aimed to burn 1000 calories per week) walking programme
Pasman & Thompson (1988)	90 participants (45 males & 45 females) equal in three groups: obligatory runners, obligatory weight-lifters and sedentary controls	to examine body image and eating disturbance in obligatory runners and weight-lifters and in sedentary controls	Obligatory Exercise Questionnaire; Eating Disorders Inventory (EDI); Body Self-relations Questionnaire (BSRQ)	Runners and weightlifters reported greater eating disturbance than controls. Females also reported greater eating disturbance than males
Richert & Hummers (1986)	345 students	to examine the relationship between exercise pattern risk for eating disorders	Eating Attitude Test (EAT)	Exercise was positively correlated with EAT scores and participants with relatively high EAT scores showed a preference for jogging

Table 7.4 (continued)

Author(s)	Participants	Objectives	Measurements	Conclusion about the relationship between exercise and eating disorders
Szymanski & Chrisler (1990)	66 female athletes and 20 non-athletes	to examine the relationships between eating disorders, gender roles, and athletic activity	Bem Sex-Role Inventory; Eating Disorder Inventory (EDI)	Athletes scored higher on most subscales of the EDI than non-athletes
Thiel, Gottfried, & Hesse (1993)	84 low-weight male athletes (25 wrestlers & 59 rowers)	to study the prevalence of eating disorders in male athletes who, by the nature of their sport, are pressured to maintain low weight	Eating Disorder Inventory (EDI)	52% of the athletes reported binging and 11% of the respondents evinced subclinical eating disorders. Concludes that low-weight wrestlers and rowers should be considered at risk for eating disorders
Williamson et al. (1995)	98 female college athletes	to study the risk factors involved in the development of eating disorders in female college athletes	Social Influence; Sports Competition Anxiety Test (SCAT); Athletic self-appraisal; Interview for Diagnosis of Eating Disorders	Validated a psychosocial model of risk factors for the development of eating disorders in female college athletes. The model suggests that social influence, performance anxiety and self-appraisal together influence body-size concern which in turn is a strong

				determinant of eating disorder symptoms
Wolf & Akamatsu (1994)	120 male and 168 female students classified as 159 exercisers and 129 non-exercisers	to study the relationship between exercise and eating disorders in college students	Eating Disorder Inventory (EDI); Eating Attitude Test (EAT)	Women involved in athletics demonstrated more anorectic/bulimic attitudes and greater weight preoccupation than non-exercising women but they did not manifest the same personality characteristics as female non-exercisers with the same level of eating disorder
Yates, Leehey, & Shissiak (1983)	60 male long-distance or trail runners	to study the similarity between obligatory running and anorexia nervosa	Interview	Found a strong resemblance between the characteristics of obligatory running and anorexia nervosa and, thus, marked the interest in further exploration of the relationship

studied female athletes who exhibited tendencies for eating disorders. These females, however, did not manifest the personality characteristics associated with eating disorders. Thus, in agreement with Blumenthal et al.'s (1984) and Knight et al.'s (1987) explanation, differences between obligatory exercisers and anorectic patients may outweigh substantially the similarities reported by Yates et al. (1983). In a more recent theoretical article, Yates, Shisslak, Crago and Allender (1994) also admit that the comparison of excessive exercisers with eating-disordered patients is erroneous because the two populations are significantly different.

Prevalence of eating disorder symptoms in exercisers and non-exercisers

Davis (1990a, 1990b) and Davis, Brewer and Ratusny (1993) conducted a series of studies (see Table 7.4) in which they examined exercising and non-exercising individuals and their tendency for eating disorders. In none of these studies was exercise behaviour clearly related to eating disorders. Opposing these conclusions are the results reported by French, Perry, Leon and Fulkerson (1994), Pasman and Thompson (1988), Richert and Hummers (1986), Szymanski and Chrisler (1990), and Wolf and Akamatsu (1994). Because similar measurements were used in general, the discrepancy between the two sets of studies may be most closely related to the definition of exercise. In the latter set of studies either excessive exercisers or athletes were tested in contrast to those tested in the first set. However, the definition of 'excessive exercise' needs to be standardised in research. Four factors, including mode, frequency, intensity, and duration, must be reported otherwise it is unclear what 'excessive exercise' or 'athlete' means. Reporting only one or two exercise parameter(s) is often insufficient, especially in studies dealing with eating disorders because the latter is suspected to occur only in a very limited segment of the physically active population.

The majority of the reviewed studies (Table 7.4) suggest that high level of exercise or athleticism is associated with symptoms of eating disorders. The determinants of this relationship are not well known. Recently, Williamson et al. (1995) proposed a psychosocial model for the development of eating disorder symptoms in female athletes (see Figure 7.1). The authors revealed that over-concern with body size, that was mediated by social influence for thinness, anxiety about athletic performance, and negative appraisal of athletic achievement, was a primary and strong determinant of the aetiology of eating disorder symptoms. This model should be given serious consideration in the future and tested in several segments of the exercising population.

Although women are at higher risk for developing eating disorders (Yates et al., 1994), male athletes may be at risk too. For example, Thiel, Gottfried and Hesse (1993) reported a high frequency of eating-disorder

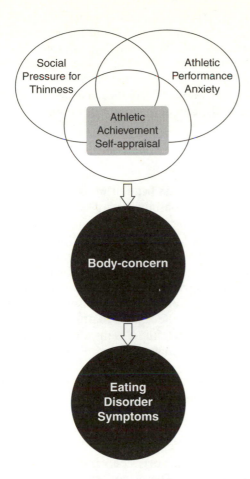

Figure 7.1 A psychosocial model for the development of eating disorder symptoms in athletes (based on Williamson et al., 1995).

symptoms and even subclinical incidences of eating disorders in low weight male wrestlers and rowers (Table 7.4). This report attracts attention to the fact that in some sports (i.e. gymnastics, boxing, and wrestling), in which weight maintenance is critical, athletes may be at high risk for developing eating disorders. Athletes in these sports may turn to often 'unhealthy' weight control methods (Enns, Drewnowski, & Grinker, 1987). This high-risk population, however, has received little attention in the literature. In the future more research should be aimed at this segment of the athletic population.

The relationship between physical activity and eating disorders is not always negative. It is wrong to assume that exercise is directly related to eating disorders. Only a very small segment of the physically active population is affected negatively. One study, purposefully included in Table 7.4, has used physical activity successfully as a means of treatment for eating disorders. Levine, Marcus and Moulton (1996) have shown that a simple walking regimen, performed three to five times a week and aimed to expend 1,000 kcal, was efficient in managing binge-eating disorders in a clinically diagnosed sample of obese women. In fact, about 71% of the experimental group was abstinent from binge eating by the end of the 6-month study.

Is excessive physical activity the cause or the consequence of eating disorders?

In view of De Coverley Veale's (1987) classification of 'secondary exercise dependence' excessive exercise is a consequence of eating disorders. In these conditions exercise is used as a means for decreasing body weight (Blumenthal, Rose, & Chang, 1985; De Coverley Veale, 1987). However, Davis (1990a) argues that exercise may foster a higher degree of body narcissism and a distorted perception of one's body size which, in turn, may trigger eating disturbances. She suggests that it may be inappropriate to perceive exercise simply as the consequence of eating disorders. Indeed some exercisers may resort to dieting for the sake of better performance (De Coverley Veale, 1987). However, to date there is insufficient evidence to claim that exercise may be a contributing factor to eating disorders. Therefore, the hypothesis that was proposed by Davis (1990a) needs further scrutiny. The model proposed by Williamson et al. (1995) might be a valuable starting point in future studies.

Recommendations for future research

The majority of studies on the relationship between exercise and eating disorders have no conceptual foundation. Therefore, future studies need to use psychosocial models, such as that proposed by Williamson et al. (1995), to test the relationship and causality between physical activity and eating disorders. A clear definition of what is meant by *excessive exercise* or *high-level exercise* or *athlete* must be presented to allow for comparability with other studies. Longitudinal studies that monitor both exercise behaviour and eating habits, along with psychological factors such as anxiety, self-concept, body-image or body-concern, may be the most promising in the quest for a clearer understanding of the relationship between exercise and eating disorders.

General conclusions

Physical exercise in moderation seldom carries negative consequences. In most cases of psychological dysfunction associated with exercise behaviour, physical activity is a means of coping with emotional problems. The coping mechanism, whether exercise, alcohol, or medication can be abused. The abuse of the former is rare because there is physical effort involved, in contrast to the latter two (Cockerill & Riddington, 1996). Thus genuine exercise dependence is extremely rare in the exercising population (Morris, 1989). People affected by eating disorders often use exercise as a means of weight control. Some correlates of excessive exercise are anxiety, low self-esteem, and long-term fidelity to the activity, as well as distorted body image in some cases of eating disorders. Generally, excessive physical activity is not a cause of psychological dysfunction, but rather a symptom of the latter.

What we know

- Exercise dependence should not be equated with commitment to exercise.
- Exercise dependence is best understood in runners since other exercisers have seldom been examined.
- Exercise dependence is very rare.
- A significant proportion of people suffering from eating disorders resort to high levels of physical activity to lose weight.
- The personality characteristics of anorectics and highly committed exercisers are significantly different.
- A relationship between exercise and eating disorders is evident in athletic populations, particularly high-level exercisers and professional athletes.
- Female athletes, and those in sports participated in within weight categories, are at greater risk than other athletes of developing eating disorders.

What we need to know

- What factors cause exercise dependence?
- What is the role of exercise history, anxiety, and self-esteem in exercise dependence?
- To what extent is excessive exercising a consequence of eating disorders?
- Could exercise have a positive effect on some eating disorders?
- What are the relationships between aspects of athleticism, body image/concern, exercise and eating disorders?
- What is the risk of male athletes developing eating disorders?

8 The way forward for physical activity and the promotion of psychological well-being

Stuart J.H. Biddle, Kenneth R. Fox, Stephen H. Boutcher and Guy E. Faulkner

This volume has covered key aspects of the literature on physical activity and psychological well-being – anxiety, depression, affect and mood, self-esteem, cognitive functioning, and psychological dysfunction. Space and time limitations have precluded coverage of sleep, wider aspects of quality of life, or certain mental illnesses.

The purpose of the review was to draw evidence-based conclusions for health professionals and to inform the development of health policy. This final chapter will summarise the evidence in each of the areas addressed, consider some limitations of the existing literature, summarise what we need to know, and finally, address key issues for the design and delivery of physical activity for the promotion of psychological well-being.

Summary of research findings

In this section, we summarise the key findings from each research area examined in the book. Much of this will be based on the statements in each chapter that represent 'what we know' about the field. These have been arrived at either through clear existing evidence or are based on our best judgement at this time.

Anxiety and stress

The importance of tackling anxiety and stress-related disorders is best highlighted by the huge cost to industry and the NHS, as well as to the quality of life of individuals. In addition, stress can be linked to many of the current political priorities in health, such as coronary heart disease (CHD), mental illness and accidents.

The area of anxiety and stress is complex. Physical activity interventions might affect immediate anxiety feelings (state anxiety), relatively stable anxiety characteristics of the individual (trait anxiety), or psychophysiological markers of anxiety, such as blood pressure or heart rate. When taking into account such complexity, some might argue that the consistency of findings is impressive, providing convincing evidence of an important effect for physical activity. This said, the evidence shows rather low effects in terms of strength when viewed overall. Meta-analytic effect sizes typically are in the low-to-moderate range (about 0.25–0.50). However, this is achieved across diverse methods using different measures of anxiety and physical activity. In addition, stronger effects appear in what are considered superior research designs, such as experimental trials. These observations help strengthen the case for the anxiety-reduction effects of activity. The key findings on physical activity, anxiety and stress are summarised below.

Anxiety and stress: what we know
- Exercise has a low-to-moderate anxiety-reducing effect.
- Exercise training can reduce trait anxiety and single exercise sessions can result in reductions in state anxiety.
- The strongest anxiety-reduction effects are shown in randomised controlled trials.
- Single sessions of moderate exercise can reduce short-term physiological reactivity to and enhance recovery from brief psychosocial stressors.

Depression

As with stress-related disorders, depression is a major health problem in the UK and other Western countries. It represents a major economic cost to the NHS and industry and leads to considerable human misery and suffering (see Chapter 1). Common day-to-day depressive moods are addressed in the section on mood and affect (see Chapter 4), while depression in this text has been delimited to clinically defined depression (see Chapter 3).

Overall, the evidence is strong enough for us to conclude that there is support for a *causal* link between physical activity and reduced clinically defined depression. This is the first time such a statement has been made. It is worth recalling that the first published statement on the causal link between physical activity and CHD was only in 1987 (Powell, Thompson, Caspersen, & Kendrick, 1987). We arrive at our conclusion by judging the evidence against eight standard criteria in epidemiological research. Summarising, it is clear that the criteria of strength of association, consistency of evidence from different populations and settings, the temporal sequencing (of inactivity preceding depression), biological plausibility, and experimental evidence support the view that (a) inactivity produces higher risk of subsequent depression, and (b) physical activity can be an effective medium for its treatment. Summary findings are shown below.

Clinically defined depression: what we know
- There is support for a causal link between exercise and decreased depression.
- Epidemiological evidence has demonstrated that physical activity is associated with a decreased risk of developing clinically defined depression.
- Evidence from experimental studies shows that both aerobic and resistance exercise may be used to treat moderate and more severe depression, usually as an adjunct to standard treatment.
- The anti-depressant effect of exercise can be of the same magnitude as that found for other psychotherapeutic interventions.
- No negative effects of exercise have been noted in depressed populations.

Emotion and mood

Although day-to-day moods and emotions may not be seen as a high priority in some clinical settings, we should not underestimate their importance in public health promotion. First, if people 'feel good' through exercise, they are more likely to adhere to a physical activity programme or active lifestyle; that is, enhanced mood acts as a positive reinforcer of activity. This enables them to receive important protective physical health benefits from exercise. Second, enhanced mood is an important part of overall quality of life – something seen as increasingly important in health promotion. Third, an emotionally satisfied individual is less likely to become one of the 'worried well' who frequently present in primary care.

Evidence from diverse mood-related studies in physical activity is fairly consistent. Whether we draw on meta-analytic or narrative reviews, experimental studies, or large-scale epidemiological surveys, evidence points to a convincing relationship between physical activity and improved positive mood. Key findings are summarised below.

Emotion and mood: what we know
- Physical activity and exercise have consistently been associated with positive mood and affect.
- Meta-analytic evidence shows that aerobic exercise has a small-to-moderate effect on vigour (+), tension (−), depression (−), fatigue (−) and confusion (−), and a small effect on anger (−).
- A positive relationship between physical activity and psychological well-being has been confirmed in several large-scale

epidemiological surveys, including in the UK, using different measures of activity and well-being.
- Experimental trials support a positive effect for moderate intensity exercise on psychological well-being.
- Meta-analytic evidence shows that adopting a goal in exercise that is focused on personal improvement, effort, and mastery has a moderate-to-high association with positive affect.
- Meta-analytic evidence shows that a group climate in exercise and sport settings that is focused on personal improvement and effort has a moderate-to-high association with positive affect.

Self-esteem

Self-esteem – itself widely recognised as a critical indicator of mental health – is important in many contexts. An individual with high self-esteem is more likely to be emotionally stable, and to cope better with life demands, and is likely to be less dependent on support services. In addition, self-esteem and more specific self-perceptions can determine motivation and drive individuals towards positive health behaviours.

Although the number of randomised controlled trials (RCTs) in this area is small, the evidence does point to an effect for physical activity on self-esteem, particularly in terms of physical self-perceptions. This is an important finding in the light that physical self-perceptions, such as body image and perceived physical self-worth, may carry important mental health properties in their own right. Effects on generalised self-esteem tend to be mixed, which is not surprising given the large array of life opportunities for affecting the relatively stable quality of self-esteem. Summary evidence is shown below.

Self-esteem: what we know
- Exercise can be used as a medium to promote physical self-worth and other important physical self-perceptions such as body image. In some situations, this improvement is accompanied by improved self-esteem.
- Physical self-worth carries mental well-being properties in its own right and should be considered as a valuable end-point of exercise programmes.
- Positive effects of exercise on self-perceptions can be experienced by all age groups but there is strongest evidence for change for children and middle-aged adults.

- Positive effects of exercise on self-perceptions can be experienced by men and women.
- Positive effects of exercise on self-perceptions are likely to be greater for those with initially low self-esteem.
- Several types of exercise are effective in changing self-perceptions but there is most evidence to support aerobic exercise and resistance training, with the latter indicating greatest effectiveness in the short term.

Cognitive functioning

The population distribution progressively includes a higher percentage of older people and the consequences of this trend are profound. If evidence can demonstrate that physical activity affects the functional capacity and quality of life of older adults, this will have important implications for the way we promote health-enhancing activities and environments for older people. Although there are several ways in which physical activity might benefit the older adult, this issue has largely been approached through the effect of activity on the slowing or prevention of age-related decline in cognitive functioning. Research in this area has remained rather constrained in its approach and the evidence for a broad-based causal effect from physical activity is weak. Summary findings are shown below.

Cognitive functioning: what we know
- The majority of cross-sectional studies show that fit older adults display better cognitive performance than less fit older adults.
- The association between fitness and cognitive performance is task-dependent, with most pronounced effects in tasks that are attention-demanding and rapid (e.g. reaction time tasks).
- Results of intervention studies are equivocal but meta-analytic findings indicate a small but significant improvement in cognitive functioning of older adults who experience an increase in aerobic fitness.

Psychological dysfunction

Although the benefits of physical activity are becoming increasingly well documented, all sides of the argument must be addressed to arrive at a credible evidence base. For this reason, it is important to investigate whether exercise can have negative psychological effects in some individuals.

Indeed, the media have shown great interest over the past decade in the issue of exercise 'addiction' ('dependence'), and researchers have debated whether exercise addiction and eating disorders are related. Summary evidence is shown below and highlights that the negative effects of exercise that have been shown in some individuals are rare and need not be seen as an issue of concern for public health.

Psychological dysfunction: what we know
- Exercise dependence is extremely rare.
- Many people suffering from eating disorders undertake high levels of physical activity.
- The personality characteristics of anorectics are significantly different from highly committed exercisers.

Limitations of research on physical activity and psychological well-being

In arriving at a summary of the evidence linking physical activity and psychological well-being, all authors have drawn on a variety of sources and methods, including narrative reviews, meta-analyses, experimental designs, and large-scale surveys. Despite this, a common theme running through all of the literature in this field is that strong research designs are in the minority. Much of the research is in the form of small-scale cross-sectional studies, or experiments without controls and/or randomisation, the weaknesses of which are well known. The reasons for this are not fully obvious, but it is probably due to the emergent status of the field of exercise science where much of the work has been conducted, and the paucity of research funding. It is not our intention to dwell on the methodological weaknesses of this literature, however we consider it important to provide some summary remarks regarding the general nature of research in this area.

Measurement

It is clear from the studies reviewed that there is little consensus concerning the measurement of physical activity and domains of psychological well-being. For example, studies often adopt differing methods for assessing physical activity, such as different self-report scales, or different 'objective' measures such as heart rate monitors or movement sensors. In addition, each area of psychological well-being calls on many different scales to assess the construct of interest. For example, in self-esteem research, some researchers assess generalised self-esteem only, others assess physical domains of self-perceptions. Even within the latter approach, several instruments have been used. In addition, the best method of assessing physical fitness in the area of physical activity and psychological well-being is undetermined.

Research designs

A number of authors have highlighted the methodological inadequacy of the cross-sectional approach (Boutcher, 1990; Folkins & Sime, 1981; Spirduso, 1994). Often non-equivalent groups have been studied and the temporal effects of physical activity cannot be established. These types of data are not likely to be accepted as admissable evidence of the effect of exercise on aspects of psychological well-being by health authorities and fortunately is now rarely found in refereed literature.

However, even when an intervention approach is adopted, many studies do not randomise to treatment and control groups. This is undoubtedly due to the convenience of studying intact exercising groups. Clearly, however, the results of such studies are likely to be influenced by self-selecting variables such as personality disposition, attitudes, and socio-economic background (Boutcher, 1990). No less important is a problem facing many field trials, even if there is randomisation. Those who finally accept participation in a trial will have signed a consent form and may well be more inclined towards exercise than those who refuse. Almost all findings are based on the effect of exercise on those who volunteered for an exercise study.

Attrition

Unfortunately, attrition often occurs for non-exercisers starting a training programme for the first time. Attrition itself may not be uniform among types of individuals within each group or between treatment and control groups, often leading to non-equivalence by the end of the study. Such effects are rarely reported or corrected through statistical treatment. Conclusions are usually drawn upon those who have volunteered for the study and who have remained in the study and results are usually not presented on an intention-to-treat basis. The characteristics of drop-outs are also rarely considered.

Exercise dose-response

The issue of intensity and duration of exercise has important public health implications yet remains poorly controlled in many studies. With the adoption of the 'moderate' message for physical activity (see Killoran, Fentem, & Caspersen, 1994), we need to identify the psychological effects of more moderate forms of physical activity and also the effect of intermittent versus continuous exercise bouts. For example, Murphy and Hardman

(1998) have found similar improvements in fitness for previously sedentary women between those undertaking a brisk walking programme involving one 30-minute walk per day and those doing a 10-minute walk three times per day. Currently, because many reports have not clearly stated the exercise mode and dosage, the effect of different regimes on psychological well-being is not possible to determine.

Cost-effectiveness

Research to date has focused on the efficacy of physical activity to improve aspects of psychological well-being. The use of field trials to test the cost-effectiveness of delivery of physical activity programmes within health service settings is rare. The language of economic analysis is notably absent in the literature. For example, numbers-needed-to-treat statistics have not been calculated. The use of physical activity either in the treatment of mental disorders or the promotion of general well-being has rarely been compared with alternative interventions. This is undoubtedly due to the emergent state of the field of study, but is perhaps also due to its roots. With the exception of the literature on clinically diagnosed populations, the research has been conducted by exercise and sport scientists whose main objective until recently has been academic progress rather than health service design and delivery.

When judged against the rigours of the evidence-based health movement, where the randomised controlled trial is treated as the gold standard and less credence is offered to other approaches, some areas of the literature appear weak or at best in their infancy. The body of knowledge on clinical depression offers a clear exception to this. In addition, for an area of research that has received relatively little government or commercial sponsorship, the body of knowledge could be considered surprisingly convincing. Finally, the study of exercise and psychological well-being may not lend itself quite so well to the randomised controlled trial design. It is not possible to offer a placebo, ethical clearance requires the control group to be offered some form of intervention, and the public nature of exercise (versus medication, for example) means there is a strong chance of contamination across groups. Furthermore, with clinically diagnosed populations where there is limited access to limited subject numbers, RCTs may not be feasible at all. This suggests a more flexible and forgiving approach to the interpretation of the existing literature and the planning for future research.

Following our consideration of a number of different issues and methodological difficulties, we have summarised points requiring research attention in the future. These are shown below and are grouped according to measurement, different populations, exercise and physical activity programming, economic issues and mechanisms of the relationship between physical activity and psychological well-being.

What we need to know

Measurement

- Are current psychometric measures adequate for capturing the range of affective responses in physical activity and for assessing change over time?
- How much change in scores is necessary for a meaningful impact on functioning, behaviours and well-being? To date, insufficient evidence is available in many areas to develop clinical criteria and targets of change.

Populations

- How do special groups (e.g. the obese with social physique anxiety; asthmatics and chronic obstructive pulmonary disease (COPD) patients who experience fears about breathing; older people with a fear of falling) differ in the benefits of a programme of exercise?
- Is the mental health effect from exercise the same across all ages and both genders?
- More information is needed on those who do not volunteer for studies or who drop out and do not feature in the results.

Exercise and physical activity programming

- What are the long-term effects of accumulated doses of activity (in line with current recommendations for physical activity for cardiovascular disease prevention)?
- What are the longer term effects (i.e. over 4 months) of physical activity? We need to know, for example, whether a 10-week exercise programme will have lasting effects, and if not what is necessary to maintain the effects?
- What are the effects of short bouts (< 15 minutes) of free-living, unsupervised aerobic physical activity, which can be most easily integrated into an active lifestyle, as a low-cost intervention?
- What are the social effects of exercise on mental well-being?
- We need to know whether exercise practitioner manipulations of self-efficacy, outcome expectancy, perceived competence, goal setting, feedback, attentional focus and perceived exertion and enjoyment can have effects, particularly among inactive and inexperienced exercisers.
- Adherence to exercise training appears to be greater when it is of moderate intensity (e.g. walking), and integrated into an active lifestyle. What are the determinants of adherence to free-living and facility-based exercise programmes?

- What are the competencies and skills required by exercise professionals to most effectively promote physical activity for psychological well-being? What is the role of other mental health professionals?
- Are the psychological effects of physical activity the same for different modes of activity (e.g. aerobic, strength-based, flexibility-based)?
- Do different intensities and durations of physical activity make a difference and do fitness levels modulate that effect?
- When might high intensity exercise produce positive affective responses?

Economic issues
- The cost-effectiveness of physical activity as a treatment for mental health has not been considered. More studies need to compare activity with other interventions, not only in terms of mental health but also cost. Related to this would be careful consideration of adherence to the respective interventions.

Mechanisms
- How do the potential mechanisms underlying the effects interact?
- How do effects of exercise compare to those of drug treatments and what adjunctive value does exercise have along with drug treatment?
- If drugs are also administered is the interaction of drug and exercise safe?
- Under what conditions are the associations between physical activity and psychological well-being causal?
- What mechanisms explain the link between activity and psychological well-being?
- We need information on the dynamics of change. Little is known about how long it takes to produce changes and how long they last.
- Is it necessary to develop physiological adaptations to an exercise regimen before psychological well-being increases occur?

A key theme emerging from this review of 'what we need to know' concerns the mechanisms explaining the relationship between physical activity and psychological well-being. Given that the identification of underlying mechanisms for the explanation for why physical activity may have beneficial effects is so important, some brief expansion of these points is made here.

Explanatory mechanisms

Table 8.1 illustrates some psychological and physiological mechanisms that have the potential to influence psychological well-being (see Boutcher, 1993). This is an important issue and crucial for physical activity promotion, exercise prescription and intervention. For example, the mechanisms underlying emotional change caused by a bout of physical activity may be very different for the neophyte and the experienced jogger. The beginning jogger may be more likely to be influenced by cognitive factors during exercise whereas the experienced jogger is more likely to be influenced by physiological factors, particularly as they may operate at different exercise intensities by choice. The rationale here is that greater exposure to an exercise stimulus will cause greater physiological adaptation that in turn will bring about a greater physiological influence on well-being. Initially cognitive factors may influence affect but with greater physiological adaptation to the exercise stimulus and increased activity at higher percentages of maximum capacity, physiological mechanisms may also become influential.

In the initial phase of starting to exercise, cognitive processes in the form of attributions and self-efficacy may be especially important influences on psychological well-being. Consequently, key determinants of mental health status for the unfit, neophyte exerciser may be their expectations, level of self-efficacy, and the type of attributions and appraisals they make. This

Table 8.1 Psychological and physiological mechanisms that could underlie the relationship between physical activity and mental health

Psychological	*Physiological*
Time-out	Endorphins
Mastery	Biochemical changes
Confidence	(e.g. catecholamines)
Fellow exercisers' characteristics	Hyperthermic change
Exercise leader characteristics	Autonomic changes
Exercise facilities	Visceral feedback
Exercise environment	
Self esteem	
Social support	

suggestion is supported by research that has indicated that self-efficacy is most influential during the adoption phase of exercise.

When the individual starts to physiologically adapt to exercise or is exposed to repeated exercise, physiological mechanisms developed through adaptation to regular exercise may play a more prominent role. This suggestion is supported indirectly by past research that has indicated that trained and untrained participants can possess different patterns of emotional response to exercise stimuli. It is also feasible, however, that individuals may exercise repeatedly but exercise intensity may not be great enough to bring about significant physiological adaptations. For these individuals repeated exposure to light exercise may bring about little physiological change but may result in behavioural conditioning to the characteristics of the exercise stimulus. For instance, a recreational runner's positive post-exercise psychological state may be generated by the conditioning of pleasant cognitions by jogging in an attractive park.

Throughout the 1990s, research into physical activity and psychological well-being has expanded, quite often producing better quality research than before. We also have a number of large-scale surveys to consult, as well as meta-analytic reviews of specific topics in this field. However, despite this impressive research effort, we seem no closer to identifying a clear set of mechanisms explaining why physical activity might have effects on psychological well-being. Researchers must continue to attempt to identify the mechanisms underlying this relationship. As authors in this review have stated, the mechanisms explaining why physical activity might be associated with different parameters of mental health require a great deal of consideration. Readers are referred to Morgan (1997) for comprehensive coverage of this area.

Key issues in the promotion of physical activity for psychological well-being

One purpose of this text is to provide a consensus on the evidence linking physical activity and psychological well-being with a view to reaching health professionals. With the growing evidence of the psychological benefits of physical activity, as presented here, the increasing recognition of the importance of addressing the *mental* health of the nation, as developed at length in the latest British government policy documents (DoH, 1999), it is opportune to consider the issue of physical activity interventions through health services. While there might be some acceptance of the role of physical activity in psychological well-being by health professionals, such as through self-reports of enhanced mood from patients on primary-care exercise schemes (Fox, Biddle, Edmunds, Bowler, & Killoran, 1997; Riddoch, Puig-Ribera, & Cooper, 1998), some real difficulties have yet to be overcome.

Difficulties facing health professionals

Physical activity promotion for mental health is a new area for health service professionals to consider. As with any new venture, barriers may impede its progress. Firstly, there are attitudinal barriers that are related to the status of physical activity and beliefs as to its efficacy in promoting psychological well-being. On consideration of their review of the evidence in the US, Tkachuk and Martin (1999) were surprised that 'exercise' had not become a more popular treatment for certain mental health conditions. Similarly, in the UK there are likely to be factors that constrain the development of physical activity as an accepted element of interventions to promote psychological well-being.

One key factor concerns dualistic tendencies to treat the mind and body as separate entities. For example, McEntee and Halgin (1996, pp. 55, 58), in their survey of psychotherapists' use of exercise, concluded that 'many therapists simply do not see their work as pertaining to the body' and that 'topics such as exercise are viewed as unimportant by some mental health workers who fail to appreciate the relationship between physical and psychological health'. This may be exacerbated by the increasingly narrow scope of specialisation developing within health services that encourages differential diagnosis and treatment along physical or psychological lines.

Another subtle barrier concerns the nature of 'exercise' itself. Martinsen and Stephens (1994) first suggested that the status of exercise interventions was low in the field of psychiatry. Specifically, if one spent years learning sophisticated techniques for treating clinical conditions then some reluctance could be predicted if something as 'simple' as exercise was suggested as having comparable treatment effects. This 'simplicity' also invokes notions of a common sense approach to health. Intuitively, being physically active is good for psychological well-being. However, becoming more active may be something that individuals can attempt themselves without the help of mental health professionals. Exercise then becomes a non-professional type of intervention and consequently may not be considered.

Such barriers may be more relevant when developing the role of physical activity in alleviating clinical conditions and less relevant in the general promotion of psychological well-being. In relation to clinical conditions, physical activity should not be seen as competing with other strategies for promoting psychological well-being and rather as being an important addition to a range of therapeutic options. Given the highlighted weaknesses in the research such positioning is deserved. Further experimental studies and the cost-effectiveness of physical activity interventions are undoubtedly needed but more importantly, future research findings must be effectively disseminated outside the traditional boundaries of sport and exercise research fields.

In general, some of the systemic barriers faced by primary care professionals in promoting physical activity will certainly be applicable to the current context. For example, McKenna, Naylor and McDowell (1998) suggested time constraints, lack of incentive or reimbursement, lack of standard protocols, lack of success in the counselling role, lack of appropriate training, and the absence of a coordinated and systematic daily approach in practice operations were all influential.

These barriers may only exacerbate the relative absence of exercise specialists in health care settings which limits the likelihood that physical activity promotion for mental health will be comprehensively adopted as part of health improvement plans or activities of primary care groups. Given the short protocols that are now being developed for exercise counselling, the shift to lifestyle physical activity as the promotional message in addition to the growth of subsidised exercise referral schemes and other leisure opportunities, such barriers can be reduced further through the creative efforts of health care professionals. Specifically, greater partnership will be essential between health and leisure services. Exercise specialists, in particular, can play a more proactive role in creating links with health care professionals in developing physical activity opportunities.

It must be reiterated that physical activity should be promoted regardless of its impact on psychological well-being due to the associated physical health benefits. However, this book highlights that there is *sufficient* evidence to consider physical activity in promoting psychological well-being. Further justification is now available for health professionals in developing physical activity promotion schemes. Health professionals can evaluate such efforts to not only strengthen the evidence but also inform as to how physical activity is best promoted for psychological well-being, of which little is presently known. We may have an emerging evidence base, but not necessarily the evidence-based practice. To further this aim, research must also continue to develop accepted and standardised measures of physical activity, and reach consensus on the most effective types of instruments and indicators to measure mental health outcomes, in order to assist the practitioner in implementing and evaluating practice.

Pointers for interventions

Interventions can be focused on mental health and psychological well-being per se, such as dealing with patients with clinical depression, or they can be focused on well-being as a determinant of adherence to an exercise programme. If exercise produces feelings of well-being, adherence is likely to be enhanced. Mutrie (1999) provides a summary of issues associated with exercise adherence for various clinical groups such as COPD, cardiac rehabilitation, diabetes, cancers, HIV/AIDS, arthritis, osteoporosis, and low back pain. Physical activity can have an important role to play for all of these conditions yet adopting and maintaining involvement is critical. If programmes are devised with psychological as well as physical outcomes in mind, adherence should be enhanced. Programmes, therefore, will need an element of choice, a climate of self-improvement and personal mastery, enjoyment, and will normally be of moderate intensity.

Direct interventions could involve a number of psychological conditions, such as alcohol abuse and drug rehabilitation (Mutrie, 1999), schizophrenia (Faulkner & Biddle, 1999; Faulkner & Sparkes, 1999), as well as the areas addressed in this book. The most likely avenue for interventions will occur through the expanding number of GP referral schemes in the UK. GPs will be increasingly likely to refer patients to such programmes to alleviate more common conditions such as depression and anxiety. A recent development involves referrals from Community Mental Health Team (CMHT) members, particularly Community Psychiatric Nurses (CPNs), onto existing GP referral programmes or programmes and services established specifically for mental health service clients. Initiatives, similar to a brokerage service, are also developing that provide physical activity and leisure opportunities for mental health clients in the community. Finally, many in-patient and out-patient units provide exercise and sporting activities for patients and clients. For further information on such initiatives, readers are referred to the Physical Activity and Mental Health: National Consensus Statements and Guidelines for Practice document produced in parallel with this research review (Grant, in press).

However, as discussed, barriers to implementation are still significant and promoting physical activity to improve psychological well-being is far from a nationally applied standard, nor is physical activity commonly considered in developing care plans for mental health service clients. This book has provided a realistic overview of the state of evidence for the effect of physical activity on psychological well-being. Positive results have been reported and some advice regarding the difficulties that need to be addressed for physical activity promotion to be put into practice has been offered. Physical activity is a critical domain within public health and its role in the promotion of psychological well-being is important. It demands serious consideration in contemporary health promotion efforts.

References

Abele, A., & Brehm, W. (1993). Mood effects of exercise versus sports games: Findings and implications for well-being and health. *International Review of Health Psychology*, 2, 53–80.

Abourez, T., & Toole, T. (1995). Effect of task complexity on the relationship between physical fitness and reaction time in older women. *Journal of Aging and Physical Activity*, 3, 251–260.

Aldana, S.G., Sutton, L.D., Jacobson, B.H., Quirk, M.G. (1996). Relationships between leisure time, physical activity and perceived stress. *Perceptual and Motor Skills*, 82, 315–321.

Alfermann, D., & Stoll, O. (1995). Effects of physical exercise on self-concept and subjective well-being: Results of field experiments. In R. Vanfraechem-Raway & Y. Vanden Auweele (Eds), *Proceedings of the 9th European Congress on Sport Psychology*, Part 1 (pp. 238–246). Brussels: Belgian Society of Sport Psychology.

Altchiler, L., & Motta, R. (1994). Effects of aerobic and nonaerobic exercise on anxiety, absenteeism, and job satisfaction. *Journal of Clinical Psychology*, 50, 829–840.

American College of Sports Medicine (ACSM)(4th Edition)(1991). *Guidelines for exercise testing and prescription* (4th edn). Philadelphia: Lea & Febiger.

American Psychiatric Association. (1980). *Diagnostic and statistical manual* (3rd edn). Washington, DC: APA.

American Psychiatric Association (1994). *Diagnostic and statistical manual of mental disorders, IV*. Washington DC: APA.

Ames, C. (1992). Achievement goals, motivational climate, and motivational processes. In G.C. Roberts (Ed.), *Motivation in sport and exercise* (pp. 161–176). Champaign, IL: Human Kinetics.

Anshel, M.H. (1991). A psycho-behavioral analysis of addicted versus non-addicted male and female exercisers. *Journal of Sport Behavior*, 14, 145–154.

Anspaugh, D.J., Hunter, S., & Dignan, M. (1996). Risk factors for cardiovascular disease among exercising versus nonexercising women. *American Journal of Health Promotion*, 10, 171–174.

Arito, H., & Oguri, M. (1990). Contingent negative variation and reaction time of physically-trained subjects in simple and discriminative tasks. *Industrial Health*, 28, 97–106.

Balogun, J.A. (1987). The interrelationships between measures of physical fitness and self-concept. *Journal of Human Movement Studies*, 13, 255–265.

Bane, S., & McAuley, E. (1998). Body image and exercise. In J.L. Duda (Ed.), *Advances in sport and exercise psychology measurement* (pp. 311–324). Morgantown, WV: Fitness Information Technology.

Barry, A.J., Steinmetz, J.R., Page, H.F., Birkhead, N.C., & Rodahl, K. (1966). The effects of physical conditioning on older individuals, II: Motor performance and cognitive function. *Journal of Gerontology,* 21, 192–199.

Bartholomew, J.B., & Linder, D.E. (1998). State anxiety following resistance exercise: The roles of gender and exercise intensity. *Journal of Behavioral Medicine,* 21, 205–219.

Bartlewski, P.P., Van Raalte, J.L., & Brewer, B.W. (1996). Effects of aerobic exercise on the social physique anxiety and body esteem of female college students. *Women in Sport and Physical Activity Journal,* 5, 49–62.

Baylor, A.M., & Spirduso, W.W. (1988). Systematic aerobic exercise and components of reaction time in older women. *Journal of Gerontology,* 43, 121–126.

Beck, A.T., Ward, C.H., Mendelsohn, M., Mock, J., & Erbaugh, H. (1961). An inventory for measuring depression. *Archives of General Psychiatry,* 4, 561–571.

Beesley, S., & Mutrie, N. (1997). Exercise is beneficial adjunctive treatment in depression. Letter to Editor, *British Medical Journal,* 315, 1542.

Bennett, P., & Murphy, S. (1997). *Psychology and health promotion.* Buckingham: Open University Press.

Ben-Shlomo, L.S., & Short, M.A. (1986). The effects of physical conditioning on selected dimensions of self-concept in sedentary females. *Occupational Therapy in Mental Health,* 5, 27–46.

Ben-Yishai, Y., & Diller, L. (1973). Changing of atmospheric environment to improve mental and behavioural function. *New York State Journal of Medicine,* 12, 2877–2880.

Berger, B. (1996). Psychological benefits of an active lifestyle: what we know and what we need to know. *Quest,* 48, 330–353.

Berger, B.G., & McInman, A. (1993). Exercise and the quality of life. In R.N. Singer, M. Murphey, & L.K. Tennant (Eds). *Handbook of research on sport psychology* (pp. 729–760). New York: Macmillan.

Berger, B.G., & Owen, D.R. (1992). Preliminary analysis of a causal relationship between swimming and stress reduction: Intense exercise may negate the effects. *International Journal of Sport Psychology,* 23, 70–85.

Berlin J.A., & Colditz, G.A. (1990). A meta-analysis of physical activity in the prevention of coronary heart disease. *American Journal of Epidemiology,* 132, 612–628.

Biddle, S. (1995). Exercise and psychosocial health. *Research Quarterly for Exercise and Sport,* 66, 292–297.

Biddle, S.J.H., & Mutrie, N. (1991). *Psychology of physical activity and exercise: A health-related perspective.* London: Springer-Verlag.

Biddle, S., Sallis, J., & Cavill, N, (1998). Young and active? Young people and health-enhancing physical activity: Evidence and implications. London: HEA.

Bills, R.E., Vance E.L., & McLean, O.S. (1951). An index of adjustment and values. *Journal of Consulting Psychology,* 15, 257–261.

Birren, J.E., Woods, A.M., & Williams, M.V. (1980). Behavioural slowing with age: Causes, organisation, and consequences. In L.W. Poona (Ed.), *Aging in the 1980s: Psychological issues* (pp. 293–308). Washington, DC: American Psychological Association.

Blair, S.N., & Hardman, A. (1995). Introduction: Physical activity, health and well-being – an international consensus conference. *Research Quarterly for Exercise and Sport*, 66, ii.

Blair, S.N., Kohl, H.W., Paffenberger, R.S., Clark, D.G., Cooper, K.H., & Gibbons, L.W. (1989). Physical fitness and all-cause mortality: A prospective study of healthy men and women. *Journal of the American Medical Association*, 262, 2395–2401.

Blaney, J., Sothmann, M., Raff, H., Hart, B., & Horn, T. (1990). Impact of exercise training on plasma adrenocorticotropin response to a well-learned vigilance task. *Psychoneuroendocrinology*, 15, 453–62.

Blumenthal, J.A., Emery, C.F. Madden, D.J., George, L.K., Coleman, E., Riddle, M.W., McKee, D.C., Reasoner, J., & Williams, R.S. (1989). Cardiovascular and behavioral effects of aerobic exercise training in healthy older men and women. *Journal of Gerontology: Medical Sciences*, 44, M147-M157.

Blumenthal, J.A., Emery, C.F., Madden, D.J., Schneibolk, S.S., Walsh-Riddle, M.W., George, L.K., McKee, D.C., Higgenbotham, M., Cobb, F.R., & Colman, R.E. (1991). Long term effects of exercise on psychological functioning in older men and women. *Journal of Gerontology*, 46, 352–361.

Blumenthal, J.A., Fredrikson, M., Kuhn, C., Ulmer, R.L., Walsh-Riddle, M., & Applebaum, M. (1990). Aerobic exercise reduces levels of cardiovascular and perceived stress in subjects without prior evidence of myocardial ischemia. *American Journal of Cardiology*, 65, 93–98.

Blumenthal, J.A., O'Toole, L.C., & Chang, J.L. (1984). Is running an analogue of anorexia nervosa? *Journal of the American Medical Association* (JAMA), 252, 520–523.

Blumenthal, J.A., & Madden, D.J. (1988). Effects of aerobic exercise training, age, and physical fitness on memory-search performance. *Psychology and Aging*, 3, 280–285.

Blumenthal, J.A., Rose, S., & Chang, J.L. (1985). Anorexia nervosa and exercise: Implications from recent findings. *Sports Medicine*, 2, 237–247.

Boone, J.B, Jr., Probst, M.M., Rogers, M.W., & Berger, R. (1993). Post-exercise hypotension reduces cardiovascular responses to stress. *Journal of Hypertension*, 11, 449–453.

Borg, G.A.V. (1973) Perceived exertion: A note on history and methods. *Medicine & Science in Sport*, 5, 190–193.

Bosscher, R.J. (1993). Running and mixed physical exercises with depressed psychiatric patients. *International Journal of Sport Psychology*, 24, 170–184.

Botwinick, J. (1973). *Aging and Behaviour*. New York: Springer.

Bouchard, C., Shephard, R.J., & Stephens, T. (Eds) (1994). *Physical activity, fitness, and health*. Champaign, IL: Human Kinetics.

Boutcher, S.H. (1990). Aerobic fitness: Measurement and issues. *Journal of Sport and Exercise Psychology*, 12, 235–247.

Boutcher, S. (1993). Emotion and aerobic exercise. In R.N. Singer, M. Murphey, & L.K. Tennant (Eds), *Handbook of research on sport psychology* (pp. 799–814). New York: Macmillan.

Boutcher, S.H., Nugent, F.W. & Weltman, A.L. (1995). Heart rate response to psychological stressors of individuals possessing resting bradycardia. *Behavioural Medicine*, 21, 40–46.

Bowling, A. (1995). *Measuring health: A review of quality of life measurement scales*. Buckingham: Open University Press.

Bozoian, S., & McAuley, E. (1994). Strength training effects on subjective well-being and physical function in the elderly (Abs.). *Medicine and Science in Sports and Exercise*, 26, S156.

Brandon, J.E., & Loftin, J.M. (1991). Relationship of fitness to depression, state and trait anxiety, internal health locus of control, and self-control. *Perceptual and Motor Skills*, 73, 563–568.

Brewer, B.W. (1993). The dark side of exercise and mental health. In S. Serpa (Ed.), *Proceedings: VIII World Congress of Sport Psychology* (pp. 531–534). Lisbon: International Society of Sport Psychology.

Brewerton, T.D., Stellefson, E.J., Hibbs, N., Hodges, E.L., & Cochrane, C.E. (1995). Comparison of eating disorder patients with and without compulsive exercising. *International Journal of Eating Disorders*, 17, 413–416.

Brown, D.R. (1992). Physical activity, ageing, and psychological well-being: An overview of the research. *Canadian Journal of Sports Science*, 17, 185–193.

Brown, D.R., & Harrison, J.M. (1986). The effects of a strength training program on the strength and self-concept of two female age groups. *Research Quarterly for Exercise and Sport*, 57, 315–320.

Brown, D.R., Morgan, W.P., & Raglin, J.S. (1993). Effects of exercise and rest on the state anxiety and blood pressure of physically challenged college students. *Journal of Sports Medicine and Physical Fitness*, 33, 300–305.

Brown, D.R., Wang, Y., Ward, A., Ebbeling, C.B., Fortlage, L., Puleo, E., Benson, H., & Rippe, J.M. (1995). Chronic psychological effects of exercise and exercise plus cognitive strategies. *Medicine and Science in Sports and Exercise*, 27, 765–775.

Brown, R.I.F. (1993). Some contributions of the study of gambling to the study of other addictions. In W.R. Eadington & J.A. Cornelius (Eds), *Gambling behavior and problem gambling* (pp. 241–272). Reno: University of Nevada Press.

Brown, S.W., Welsh, M.C., Labbe, E.E., Vitulli, W.F., & Kulkarni, P. (1992). Aerobic exercise in the psychological treatment of adolescents. *Perceptual and Motor Skills*, 74, 555–560.

Buckworth, J., Dishman, R.K., & Cureton, K.J. (1994). Autonomic responses of women with parental hypertension: Effects of physical activity and fitness. *Hypertension*, 24, 576–584.

Busse, E.W. (1969). Theories of aging. In E.W. Busse and E. Pfeiffer (Eds), *Behaviour and adaptation in later life* (pp. 11–32). Boston: Little Brown.

Buxton, M.J., O'Hanlon, M., & Rushby, J. (1990). A new facility for the measurement of health-related quality of life. *Health Policy*, 16, 199–208.

Buxton, M.J., O'Hanlon, M., & Rushby, J. (1992). EuroQol: A reply and reminder. *Health Policy*, 20, 329–332.

Byrne, A., & Byrne, D.G. (1993). The effect of exercise on depression, anxiety and other mood states. *Journal of Psychosomatic Research*, 37, 565–574.

Byrne, B.M. (1996). *Measuring self-concept across the lifespan*. Washington DC: American Psychological Association.

Calfas, K., & Cooper, D. (1996). Effect of a 5 week exercise training program on self-worth among adolescent girls: A randomised controlled study. *Medicine and Science in Sports and Exercise*, 28, S135.

Calfas, K. J., & Taylor, C. (1994). Effects of physical activity on psychological variables in adolescents. *Pediatric Exercise Science*, 6, 406–423.

Calvo, M.G., Alamo, L., & Ramos, P. (1990). Test anxiety, motor performance and learning: Attentional and somatic interference. *Personality and Individual Differences*, 11, 29–38.

Calvo, M.G., Szabo, A., & Capafons, J. (1996). Anxiety and heart rate under psychological stress: The effects of exercise training. *Anxiety, Stress and Coping*, 9, 321–337.

Camacho, T.C., Roberts, R.E., Lazarus, N.B., Kaplan, G.A., & Cohen, R.D. (1991). Physical activity and depression: Evidence from the Alameda county study. *American Journal of Epidemiology*, 134, 220–231.

Cameron, O.G., & Hudson, C.J. (1986). Influence of exercise on anxiety level in patients with anxiety disorders. *Psychosomatics*, 27, 720–723.

Campbell, D.T., & Stanley, J.C. (1963). *Experimental and quasi-experimental designs for research*. Chicago: Rand McNally.

Campbell, R.N. (1984). *The new science: Self-esteem psychology*. Lanham, MD: University Press of America.

Carmack, M.A., & Martens, R. (1979). Measuring commitment to running: A survey of runners' attitudes and mental states. *Journal of Sport Psychology*, 1, 2542.

Carrieri-Kohlman, V., Gormley, J.M., Douglas, M.K., Paul, S.M., & Stulbarg, M.S. (1996). Exercise training decreases dyspnea and the distress and anxiety associated with it. Monitoring alone may be as effective as coaching. *Chest*, 110, 1526–1535.

Carroll, D., Smith, G.D., Sheffield, D., Shipley, M.J., & Marmot, M.G. (1995). Pressor reactions to psychological stress and prediction of future blood pressure: Data from the Whitehall II study. *British Medical Journal*, 310, 771–776.

Chaouloff, F. (1997). The serotonin hypothesis. In W.P. Morgan (Ed.), *Physical activity and mental health* (pp. 179–198). Washington, DC: Taylor & Francis.

Chapman, C.L., & De Castro, J.M. (1990). Running addiction: Measurement and associated psychological characteristics. *Journal of Sports Medicine and Physical Fitness*, 30, 283–290.

Chodzko-Zajko. W.J., & Moore, K.A. (1994). Physical fitness and cognitive functioning in aging. *Exercise and Sport Sciences Reviews*, 22, 195–220.

Choi, P.Y.L., & Salmon, P. (1995). Stress responsivity in exercisers and non-exercisers during different phases of the menstrual cycle. *Social Science and Medicine*, 6, 769–777.

Clarkson-Smith, L., & Hartley, A.A. (1989). Relationships between physical exercise and cognitive abilities in older adults. *Psychology and Aging*, 4, 183–189.

Claytor, R.P. (1991). Stress reactivity: Hemodynamic adjustments in trained and untrained humans. *Medicine and Science in Sports and Exercise*, 23, 873–881.

Clore, G.L., Ortony, A., & Foss, M.A. (1987). The psychological foundations of the affective lexicon. *Journal of Personality and Social Psychology*, 53, 751–766.

Cockerill, I.M., & Riddington, M.E. (1996). Exercise dependence and associated disorders: A review. *Counselling Psychology Quarterly*, 9, 119–129.

Cocklin, J.C. (1989). The effects of physical fitness and body cathexis on self-concept change in women after aerobic conditioning. Doctoral dissertation, Oklahoma State University, *Dissertation Abstracts International*, 49 (10), 4594–B.

Collingwood, T.R. (1972). The effects of physical training upon behaviour and self-attitudes. *Journal of Clinical Psychology*, 28, 583–585.

Conboy, J.K. (1994). The effects of exercise withdrawal on mood states of runners. *Journal of Sport Behavior*, 17, 188–203.

Cooper, C. & Cartwright, S. (1996). *Mental health and stress in the workplace.* London: HMSO.

Coopersmith, S. (1967). *The antecedents of self-esteem.* San Francisco, CA: Freeman.

Cottman, C.W., & Holets, V.R. (1985). Structural changes at synapses with age: Plasticity regeneration. In C.E. Finch & E.L. Schneider (Eds), *Handbook of the biology of aging* (2nd edn) (pp. 617–644). New York: Nostrand & Rinehold.

Cox, R.H. (1985). *Sport psychology: Concepts and applications.* Dubuque, IA: W.C. Brown.

Craft, L.L., & Landers, D.M. (1998). The effect of exercise on clinical depression and depression resulting from mental illness: A meta-analysis. *Journal of Sport and Exercise Psychology,* 20, 339–357.

Cramer, S.R., Nieman, D.C., & Lee, J.W. (1991). The effects of moderate exercise training on psychological well-being and mood state in women. *Journal of Psychosomatic Research,* 35, 437–49.

Crews D.J. & Landers, D.M. (1987). A meta-analytic review of aerobic fitness and reactivity to psychosocial stressors. *Medicine and Science in Sports and Exercise,* 19 (Suppl.), S114–S120.

Crisp, A.H., Hsu, L.K.G., Harding, B., & Hartshorn, J. (1980). Clinical features of anorexia nervosa: A study of a consecutive series of 102 female patients. *Journal of Psychosomatic Research,* 24, 179–191.

Crocker, P.R., & Grozelle, C. (1991). Reducing induced state anxiety: Effects of acute aerobic exercise and autogenic relaxation. *Journal of Sports Medicine and Physical Fitness,* 31, 277–282.

Crossman, J., Jamieson, J., & Henderson, L. (1987). Responses of competitive athletes to lay-offs in training: Exercise addiction or psychological relief? *Journal of Sport Behavior,* 10, 28–38.

Cusumano, J.A., & Robinson, S.E. (1992). The short term psychophysiological effects of hatha yoga and progressive relaxation on female Japanese students. *Applied Psychology: An International Review,* 42, 77–90.

Czajkowski, S.M., Hidelang, R.D., Dembroski, T.M., Mayerson, S.E., Parks, E.B., & Holland, J.C. (1990). Aerobic fitness, psychological characteristics, and cardiovascular reactivity to stress. *Health Psychology,* 9, 676–692.

Davis, C. (1990a). Body image and weight preoccupation: A comparison between exercising and non-exercising women. *Appetite,* 15, 13–21.

Davis, C. (1990b). Weight and diet preoccupation and addictiveness: The role of exercise. *Personality and Individual Differences,* 11, 823–827.

Davis, C. (1997). Body image, exercise, and eating behaviors. In K.R. Fox (Ed.), *The physical self: From motivation to well-being* (pp. 143–174). Champaign, IL: Human Kinetics.

Davis, C., Brewer, H., & Ratusny, D. (1993). Behavioral frequency and psychological commitment: Necessary concepts in the study of excessive exercising. *Journal of Behavioral Medicine,* 16, 611–628.

Davis, C., Kennedy, S.H., Ralevski, E., Dionne, M., Brewer, H., Neitzert, C., & Ratusny, D. (1995). Obsessive compulsiveness and physical activity in anorexia nervosa and high-level exercising. *Journal of Psychosomatic Research,* 39, 967–976.

Davis, W.M. (1971). The effects of a cardiovascular conditioning program on selected psychological responses of college males (Doctoral dissertation, University of Oklahoma, 1970). *Dissertation Abstracts International,* 32, 221A.

De Coverley Veale, D.M.W. (1987). Exercise dependence. *British Journal of Addiction*, 82, 735–740.

de Geus, E.C.J., Lorenz, J.P., Van Doornen, L.J.P., de Visser, D.C., & Orlebeke, J.F. (1990). Existing and training induced differences in aerobic fitness: Their relationship to physiological response patterns during different types of stress. *Psychophysiology*, 27, 457–478.

de Geus, E.J., Lorenz, J.P., Van Doornen, L.J., & Orlebeke, J.F. (1993). Regular exercise and aerobic fitness in relation to psychological make-up and physiological stress reactivity. *Psychosomatic Medicine*, 55, 347–363.

Del Rey, P. (1982). Effects of contextual interference on the memory of older females differing in levels of physical activity. *Perceptual and Motor Skills*, 55, 171–180.

Department of Health (1994a). *Health of the nation: Key area handbook mental illness*. London: HMSO.

Department of Health (1994b). *More people, more active, more often*. London: Department of Health.

Department of Health. NHS Executive. (1996). *Burdens of disease: a discussion document*. London: Department of Health.

Department of Health (1999). White Paper. *Saving lives: Our healthier nation*. London: HMSO.

Derogatis, L.R. (1980). *SCL-90: Administration, scoring and interpretation manual* (Rev. edn). Baltimore, MD: Clinical Psychometrics Research Unit, John Hopkins University School of Medicine.

Derogatis, L., Lipman, R., & Covi, L. (1973). The SCL-90: An outpatient psychiatric rating scale. *Psychopharmacology Bulletin*, 9, 13–28.

Desharnais, R., Jobin, J., Cote, C., Levesque, L., & Godin, G. (1993). Aerobic exercise and the placebo effect. *Psychosomatic Medicine*, 55, 149–154.

Diener, E. (1984). Subjective well-being. *Psychological Bulletin*, 95, 542–575.

Dishman, R.K. (Ed.) (1988). *Exercise adherence: Its impact on public health*. Champaign, IL: Human Kinetics.

Dishman, R.K. (1993). Exercise adherence. In R.N. Singer, M. Murphey, & L.K. Tennant (Eds), *Handbook of research on sport psychology* (pp. 779–798). New York: Macmillan.

Dishman, R.K. (1995). Physical activity and public health: Mental health. *Quest*, 47, 362–385.

Dishman, R.K. (1997). The norepinephrine hypothesis. In W.P. Morgan (Ed.), *Physical activity and mental health* (pp. 199–212). Washington, DC: Taylor & Francis.

Dishman, R.K., Farquhar, R.P., & Cureton, K.J. (1994). Responses to preferred intensities of exertion in men differing in activity levels. *Medicine and Science in Sports and Exercise*, 26, 783–790.

Dixhoorn, J., Duivenvoorden, H.J., Pool, J., & Verhage, F. (1990). Psychic effects of physical therapy after myocardial infarction. *Journal of Psychosomatic Research*, 34, 327–337.

Dixon, P., Heaton, J., Long, A., & Warburton, A. (1994). Reviewing and applying the SF-36. *Outcomes Briefing*, 4, 3–25.

Doan, B.T., Plante, T.G., DiGregorio, M., & Manuel, G. (1995). The influence of aerobic exercise and relaxation training on coping with test-taking anxiety. *Anxiety, Stress, and Coping*, 8, 101–111.

Doan, R.E., & Scherman, A. (1987). The therapeutic effect of physical fitness on measures of personality: A literature review. *Journal of Counseling and Development*, 66, 28–36.

Donaghy, M.E., & Mutrie, N. (1998). A randomised controlled study to investigate the effect of exercise on the physical self-perceptions of problem drinkers. *Physiotherapy*, 84, 169.

Doyne, E.J., Ossip-Klein, D.J., Bowman, E., Osborn, K.M., McDougall-Wilson, I.B., & Neimeyer, R.A. (1987). Running versus weight lifting in the treatment of depression. *Journal of Consulting and Clinical Psychology*, 55, 748–754.

Duda, J.L. (1993). Goals: A social-cognitive approach to the study of achievement motivation in sport. In R.N. Singer, M. Murphey, & L.K. Tennant (Eds). *Handbook of research on sport psychology* (pp. 421–436). New York: Macmillan.

Dunn, A.L. & Dishman, R.K. (1991). Exercise and the neurobiology of depression. *Exercise and Sport Sciences Reviews*, 19, 41–98.

Dustman, R.E., Emmerson, R.Y., Ruhling, R.O., Shearer, D.E., Steinhaus, L.A., Johnson, S.C., Bonekat, H.W., & Shigeoka, J.W. (1990). Age and fitness effects on EEG, ERPs, visual sensitivity, and cognition. *Neurobiology of Aging*, 11, 193–200.

Dustman, R.E., Emmerson, R.Y., & Shearer, D.E. (1990). Electrophysiology and aging: slowing, inhibition, and aerobic fitness. In M.L Howe, M.J. Stones, & C.J. Brainerd (Eds), *Cognitive and behavioural performance factors in atypical aging* (pp. 103–149). New York: Springer-Verlag.

Dustman, R.E., Ruhling, R.O., Russell, E.M., Shearer, D.E., Bonekat, H.W., Shigeoka, J.W., Wood, J.S., & Bradford, D.C. (1984). Aerobic exercise training and improved neuropsychological function of older individuals. *Neurobiology of Aging*, 5, 35–42.

Elsayed, M., Ismail, A.H., & Young, R.J. (1980). Intellectual differences of adult men related to age and physical fitness before and after an exercise program. *Journal of Gerontology*, 35, 383–387.

Emery, C.F., & Gatz, M. (1990). Psychological and cognitive effects of an exercise program for community-residing older adults. *The Gerontologist*, 30, 184–188.

Enns, M.P., Drewnowski, A., & Grinker, J.A. (1987). Body composition, body-size estimation and attitudes toward eating in male college athletes. *Psychosomatic Medicine,* 49, 56–64.

Era, P. (1988). Sensory, psychomotor, and motor functions in men of different ages. *Scandinavian Journal of Social Medicine*, 39 (Suppl.), 9–77.

Estok, P.J., & Rudy, E.B. (1986). Physical, psychosocial, menstrual changes/risks and addiction in female marathon and nonmarathon runners. *Health Care for Women International*, 7, 187–202.

Etnier, J.L., Salazar, W., Landers, D.M., Petruzzello, S.J., Han, M., & Nowell, P. (1997). The influence of physical fitness and exercise upon cognitive functioning: A meta-analysis. *Journal of Sport and Exercise Psychology*, 19, 249–274.

Farmer, M., Locke, B., Moscicki, E., Dannenberg, A., Larson, D., & Radloff, L. (1988). Physical activity and depressive symptoms: The NHANES I epidemiologic follow-up study. *American Journal of Epidemiology*, 128, 1340–1351.

Faulkner, G., & Biddle, S.J.H. (1999). Exercise as therapy for schizophrenia: A review. *Journal of Mental Health*, 8, 441–457.

Faulkner, G., & Sparkes, A.C. (1999). Exercise as therapy for schizophrenia: An ethnographic study. *Journal of Sport and Exercise Psychology*, 21, 52–69.

Fillingim, R.B., & Blumenthal, J.A. (1993). Psychological effects of exercise among the elderly. In P. Seraganian (Ed.), *Exercise psychology* (pp. 237–253). New York: John Wiley.

Fisher, E., & Thompson, J.K. (1994). A comparative evaluation of cognitive-behavioral therapy (CBT) versus exercise therapy (ET) for the treatment of body image disturbance. Preliminary findings. *Behavior Modification*, 18, 171–85.

Fitts, W.H. (1965). *Tennessee Self-Concept Scale: Manual*. Los Angeles: Western Psychological Services.

Floeter, M.K., & Greenough, W.T. (1979). Cerebrellar plasticity: Modification of Purkinge cell structure by differential rearing in monkeys. *Science*, 206, 227–229.

Flory, J.D., & Holmes, D.S. (1991). Effects of an acute bout of aerobic exercise on cardiovascular and subjective cognitive work. *Journal of Psychosomatic Research*, 35, 225–230.

Folkins, C.H., & Sime, W.E. (1981). Physical fitness training and mental health. *American Psychologist*, 36, 373–389.

Fox, K.R. (1990). *The Physical Self-Perception Profile Manual*. DeKalb, IL: Office for Health Promotion, Northern Illinois University.

Fox. K.R. (1997). The physical self and processes in self-esteem development. In K.R. Fox (Ed.), *The physical self: From motivation to well-being* (pp. 111–140). Champaign, IL: Human Kinetics.

Fox, K.R. (1998). Advances in the measurement of the physical self. In J.L. Duda (Ed.), *Advances in sport and exercise psychology measurement* (pp. 295–310). Morgantown, WV: Fitness Information Technology.

Fox, K., Biddle, S.J.H., Edmunds, L., Bowler, I., & Killoran, A. (1997). Physical activity promotion through primary health care in England. *British Journal of General Practice*, 47, 367–369.

Fox, K.R., & Corbin, C.B. (1989). The Physical Self-Perception Profile: Development and preliminary validation. *Journal of Sport and Exercise Psychology*, 11, 408–430.

Fox, K.R., Page, A., Armstrong, N., & Kirby, B. (1994). Dietary restraint and self-perceptions in early adolescence. *Personality and Individual Differences*, 17, 87–96.

Frederick, C.M., & Morrison, C.S. (1996). Social physique anxiety: personality constructs, motivations, exercise attitudes, and behaviors. *Perceptual and Motor Skills*, 82, 963–72.

Freemantle, N., Long, A., Mason, J., Sheldon, T., Song, F., Watson, P., & Wilson, C. (1993). The treatment of depression in primary care. *Effective Health Care*, Issue 5.

Fremont, J., & Craighead, L. W. (1987). Aerobic exercise and cognitive therapy in the treatment of dysphoric moods. *Cognitive Therapy and Research*, 11, 241–251.

French, S.A., Perry, C.L., Leon, G.R., & Fulkerson, J.A. (1994). Food preferences, eating patterns, and physical activity among adolescents: Correlates of eating disorders symptoms. *Journal of Adolescent Health*, 15, 286–294.

French, S.A., Perry, C.L., Leon, G.R., & Fulkerson, J.A. (1995). Changes in psychological variables and health behaviors by dieting status over a three-year period in a cohort of adolescent females. *Journal of Adolescent Health,* 16, 438–447.

French, S.A., Story, M., & Perry, C.L. (1995). Self-esteem and obesity in children and adolescents: A literature review. *Obesity Research*, 3, 479–490.

Furst, D.M., & Germone, K. (1993). Negative addiction in male and female runners and exercisers. *Perceptual and Motor Skills*, 77, 192–194.

Gabler-Halle, D., Halle, J.W., & Chung, Y.B. (1993). The effects of aerobic exercise on psychological and behavioral variables of individuals with developmental disabilities: A critical review. *Research in Development Disabilities*, 14, 359–386.

Gauvin, L. (1990). An experiential perspective on the motivational features of exercise and lifestyle. *Canadian Journal of Sport Sciences*, 15, 51–58.

Gauvin, L., & Rejeski, W.J. (1993). The Exercise-Induced Feeling Inventory: Development and initial validation. *Journal of Sport and Exercise Psychology*, 15, 403–423.

Gauvin, L., & Spence, J.C. (1996). Physical activity and psychological well-being: Knowledge base, current issues, and caveats. *Nutrition Reviews*, 54, S53–65.

Gauvin, L., & Spence, J.C. (1998). Measurement of exercise-induced changes in feeling states, affect, mood, and emotions. In J.L. Duda (Ed.), *Advances in sport and exercise psychology measurement* (pp. 325–336). Morgantown, WV: Fitness Information Technology.

Glasser, W. (1976). *Positive Addiction*. New York, NY: Harper & Row.

Gleser, J., & Mendelberg, H. (1990). Exercise and sport in mental health: A review of the literature. *Israel Journal of Psychiatry and Related Sciences*, 27, 99–112.

Goldberg, D.P., Cooper, B., Eastwood, M.R., Kedward, H.B., & Shepherd, M. (1970). A standardised psychiatric interview for use in community surveys. *British Journal of Preventative and Social Medicine*, 24, 18–23.

Graham, R.E., Zelchner, A., Peacock, L.J., & Dishman, R.K. (1996). Bradycardia during baroreflex stimulation and active or passive stressor tasks. *Cardio-respiratory Fitness and Psychophysiology*, 33, 566–575.

Grant, T. (Ed.)(in press). *Physical activity and mental health: National consensus statements and guidelines for practice*. London: Health Education Authority.

Greist, J.H., Klein, M.H., Eischens, R.R., Faris, J.W., Gurman, A.S., & Morgan, W.P. (1979). Running as a treatment for depression. *Comprehensive Psychiatry*, 20, 41–54.

Griffiths, M. (1997). Exercise addiction: A case study. *Addiction Research*, 5, 161–168.

Gruber, J.J. (1986). Physical activity and self-esteem development in children: A meta-analysis. *American Academy of Physical Education Papers*, 19, 330–48.

Hailey, B.J., & Bailey, L.A. (1982). Negative addiction in runners: A quantitative approach. *Journal of Sport Behavior*, 5, 150–153.

Hale, A.S. (1997). ABC of mental health: Depression. *British Medical Journal*, 315, 43–46.

Hamilton, M. (1960). A rating scale for depression. *Journal of Neurosurgical Psychiatry*, 23, 56–61.

Hannaford, C. (1984). The psychophysiological effects of a running program on depression, self-esteem and anxiety. *Dissertation Abstracts International*, 44, 3527B.

Hardy, C.J., & Rejeski, W.J. (1989). Not what, but how one feels: The measurement of affect during exercise. *Journal of Sport and Exercise Psychology*, 11, 304–317.

Hart, B. (1981). The effect of age and habitual activity on the fractionated components of resisted and unresisted response time. *Medicine and Science in Sports and Exercise*, 13, 78.

Hart, E.A., Leary, M.R., & Rejeski, W.J. (1989). The measurement of social physique anxiety. *Journal of Sport and Exercise Psychology*, 11, 94–104.

Hart, M.E., & Shay, C.T. (1964). Relationship between physical fitness and academic success. *Research Quarterly*, 35, 443–445.

Harter, S. (1988). *Manual for the Self-Perception Profile for Adolescents*. Denver, CO: University of Denver.

Hasher, L., & Zacks, R.T. (1988). Automatic and effortful processes in memory. *Journal of Experimental Psychology*, 108, 356–388.

Hawkins, H.L., Kramer, A.F., & Capaldi, D. (1992). Aging, exercise, and attention. *Psychology and Aging*, 7, 643–653.

Head, A., Kendall, M.J., Ferner, R., & Eagles, C. (1996). Acute effects of beta blockade and exercise on mood and anxiety. *British Journal of Sports Medicine*, 30, 238–242.

Health Education Authority (1995). *Health update 5: Physical activity*. London: Health Education Authority.

Hertzog, C.K. (1989). Influences of cognitive slowing on age differences in intelligence. *Developmental Psychology*, 25, 636–651.

Hertzog, C., Schaie, K.W., & Gribbin, K. (1978). Cardiovascular disease and changes in intellectual functioning from middle to old age. *Journal of Gerontology*, 33, 872–883.

Hill, A.B. (1965). The environment and disease: Association or causation? *Proceedings of the Royal Society of Medicine*, 58, 295–300.

Hill, R.D., Storandt, M., & Malley, M. (1993). The impact of long-term exercise training on psychological function in older adults. *Journal of Gerontology: Psychological Sciences*, 48, 12–17.

Hill, S., Harries, U., & Popay, J. (1996). Is the short form 36 (SF-36) suitable for routine health outcomes assessment in health care for older people? Evidence from preliminary work in community based health services in England. *Journal of Epidemiology and Community Health*, 50, 94–98.

Hilyer, J.C., & Mitchell, W. (1979). Effect of systematic physical fitness training combined with counseling on the self-concept of college students. *Journal of Counseling Psychology*, 26, 427–436.

Hilyer, J.C., Wilson, D.G., Dillon, C., Caro, L., Jenkins, C., Spencer, W.A., & Booker, A. (1982). Physical fitness training and counseling treatment for youth offenders. *Journal of Counseling Psychology*, 29, 292–303.

Hobson, M.L., & Rejeski, W.J. (1993). Does the dose of acute exercise mediate psychophysiological responses to mental stress? *Journal of Sport and Exercise Psychology*, 15, 77–87.

Hoffmann, P. (1997). The endorphin hypothesis. In W.P. Morgan (Ed.), *Physical activity and mental health* (pp. 163–177). Washington, DC: Taylor & Francis.

Houtmann, I.L.D., & Bakker, F.C. (1991). Individual differences in reactivity to and coping with the stress of lecturing. *Journal of Psychosomatic Research*, 35, 11–24.

Hoyer, W.J., Labouvie, G.V., & Baltes, P.B. (1973). Modification of response speed deficits and intellectual performance in the elderly. *Human Development*, 16, 233–242.

Hull, E., Young, S., & Ziegler, M. (1984). Aerobic fitness affects cardiovascular responses to stressors. *Psychophysiology*, 21, 353–360.

Hunt, S.M., McEwan, J., & McKenna, S.P. (1986). *Measuring health status*. London: Croom Helm.

Hurst, D.F., Boswell, D.L., Boogard, S.E., & Watson, M.W. (1997). The relationship of self-esteem to the health-related behaviors of the patients of a primary care clinic. *Archives of Family Medicine*, 6, 67–70.

Hutzler, Y., & Bar-Eli, M. (1993). Psychological benefits for sports for disabled people: A review. *Scandinavian Journal of Medicine and Science in Sports*, 3, 217–228.

Ismail, A.H., & El-Naggar, A.M. (1981). Effect of exercise on cognitive processing in adult men. *Journal of Human Ergology*, 10, 83–91.

Jambor, E.A., Rudisill, M.E., Weekes, E.M., & Michaud, T.J. (1994). Association among fitness components, anxiety, and confidence following aerobic training in aquarunning. *Perceptual and Motor Skills*, 78, 595–602.

Jenkinson, C., Layte, R., Coulter, A., & Wright, L. (1996). Evidence for the sensitivity of the SF-36 health status measure to inequalities in health: Results from the Oxford Healthy Lifestyles Survey. *Journal of Epidemiology and Community Health*, 50, 377–380.

Jex, S.M. (1991). The psychological benefits of exercise in work settings: A review, critique, and dispositional model. *Work and Stress*, 5, 133–147.

Jin, P. (1992). Efficacy of Tai Chi, brisk walking, meditation, and reading in reducing mental and emotional stress. *Journal of Psychosomatic Research*, 36, 361–370.

Johnson, R. (1995). Exercise dependence: When runners don't know when to quit. *Sports Medicine and Arthroscopy Review*, 3, 267–273.

Johnston, B. (1970). A study of the relationships among self-concept, movement concept and physical fitness and the effects of a physical conditioning program upon self-concept and movement concept (Doctoral dissertation, Florida State University, 1969). *Dissertation Abstracts International,* 30, 5270A–5271A.

Kaplan, G.A., Roberts, R.E., Camacho, T.C., & Coyne, J.C. (1987). Psychosocial predictors of depression. *American Journal of Epidemiology*, 125, 206–220.

Kennedy, R.S., Dunlap, W.P., Bandert, L.E., Smith, M.G., & Houston, C.S. (1989). Cognitive performance in a simulated climb of Mount Everest: Operation Everest II. *Aviation and Space Environmental Medicine*, 60, 99–104.

Killoran, A., Fentem, P., & Caspersen, C. (Eds) (1994*). Moving on: International perspectives on promoting physical activity*. London: Health Education Authority.

King, B., & Cotes, J.E. (1989). Relation of lung function and exercise capacity to mood and attitudes to health. *Thorax*, 44, 402–409.

King, A.C., Taylor, C. & Haskell, W.L. (1993). Effects of differing intensities and formats of 12 months of exercise training on psychological outcomes in older adults. *Health Psychology*, 12, 292–300.

King, A.C., Taylor, C.B., Haskell, W.L., & DeBusk, R.F. (1989). Influence of regular aerobic exercise on psychological health: A randomized, controlled trial of healthy middle-aged adults. *Health Psychology*, 8, 305–324.

Klein, M.J., Griest, J.H., Gurman, A.S., Neimeyer, R.A., Lesser, D.P., Bushnell, N.J., & Smith, R.E. (1985). A comparative outcome study of group psychotherapy vs. exercise treatments for depression. *International Journal of Mental Health*, 13, 148–177.

Knight, P.O., Schocken, D.D., Powers, P.S., Feld, J., & Smith, J.T. (1987). Gender comparison in anorexia nervosa and obligate running (abstract). *Medicine and Science in Sports and Exercise*, 19(2: Suppl.), S66.

Kobasa, S.C., Maddi, J.R., & Puccetti, M.C. (1982). Personality and exercise as buffers in the stress-illness relationship.*Journal of Behavioral Medicine*,5,391–404.

Koltyn, K.F. (1997). The thermogenic hypothesis. In W.P. Morgan (Ed.), *Physical activity and mental health* (pp. 213–226). Washington, DC: Taylor & Francis.

Kubitz, K.A., & Landers, D.M. (1993). The effects of aerobic training on cardio-vascular responses to mental stress: An examination of underlying mechanisms. *Journal of Sport and Exercise Psychology*, 15, 326–337.

Kubitz, K.A., & Pothakos, K. (1997). Does aerobic exercise decrease brain activation? *Journal of Sport and Exercise Psychology*, 19, 291–301.

Kugler, J., Dimsdale, J.E., Hartley, L.H., & Sherwood, J. (1990). Hospital supervised vs. home exercise in cardiac rehabilitation: Effects on aerobic fitness, anxiety, and depression. *Archives of Physical Medicine and Rehabilitation*, 71, 322–325.

Kugler, J., Seelbach, H., & Kruskemper, G.M. (1994). Effects of rehabilitation exercise programmes on anxiety and depression in coronary patients: A meta-analysis. *British Journal of Clinical Psychology*, 33, 401–410.

Kurtz, Z. (Ed.) (1992). *With health in mind*. London: Action for Sick Children.

La Forge, R. (1995). Exercise-associated mood alterations: A review of interactive neurobiological mechanisms. *Medicine, Exercise, Nutrition and Health*, 4, 17–32.

Landers, D.M., & Petruzzello, S.J. (1994). Physical activity, fitness and anxiety. In C. Bouchard, R.J. Shephard, & T. Stephens (Eds), *Physical activity, fitness and health: International proceeedings and consensus statement*. Champaign, IL: Human Kinetics.

LaPerriere, A.R., Antoni, M.H., Schneiderman, N., Ironson, G., Klimas, N., Caralis, P., & Fletcher, M.A. (1990). Exercise intervention attenuates emotional distress and natural killer cell decrements following notification of positive serologic status for HIV-1. *Biofeedback and Self Regulation*, 15, 229–242.

Lazarus, R.S. (1991). *Emotion and adaptation*. New York: Oxford University Press.

Leary, M.R. (1992). Self-presentational processes in exercise and sport. *Journal of Sport and Exercise Psychology*, 14, 339–351.

Lefebvre, R., & Sanford, S. (1984). A multi-modal questionnaire for stress. *Journal of Human Stress*, 11, 69–75.

Leith, L.M. (1994). *Foundations of exercise and mental health*. Morgantown, WV: Fitness Information Technology.

Leith, L.M., & Taylor, A.H. (1990). Psychological aspects of exercise: A decade literature review. *Journal of Sport Behavior*, 13, 219–239.

Levine, M.D., Marcus, M.D., & Moulton, P. (1996). Exercise in the treatment of binge eating disorder. *International Journal of Eating Disorders*, 19, 171–177.

Lirgg, C. (1991). Gender differences in self-confidence in physical activity: A meta-analysis of recent studies. *Journal of Sport and Exercise Psychology*, 13, 294–310.

Lobstein, D.D., Ismail, A.H., & Rasmussen, C.L. (1989). Beta-endorphin and components of emotionality discriminate between physically active and sedentary men. *Biological Psychiatry*, 26, 3–14.

Long, B.C. (1991). Physiological and psychological stress recovery of physically fit and unfit women. *Canadian Journal of Behavioural Science*, 23, 53–65.

Long, B.C., & Van Stavel, R. (1995). Effects of exercise training on anxiety: A meta-analysis. *Journal of Applied Sport Psychology*, 7, 167–189.

Lubin, A. (1965). Adjective checklists for measurement of depression. *Archives of General Psychiatry*, 12, 57–62.

MacMahon, J.R., & Gross, R.T. (1988). Physical fitness and psychosocial effects of aerobic exercise in delinquent adolescent males. *Sports Medicine*, 142, 1361–1366.

Mactavish, J.B., & Searle, M.S. (1992). Older individuals with mental retardation and the effect of a physical activity intervention on selected social psychological variables. *Therapeutic Recreation Journal*, 26, 38–47.

Madden, D.J., Blumenthal, J.A., Allen, P.A., & Emery, C.F. (1989). Improving aerobic capacity in healthy older adults does not necessarily lead to improved cognitive performance. *Psychology and Aging*, 4, 307–320.

Markland, D., Emberton, M., & Tallon, R. (1997). Confirmatory factor analysis of the Subjective Exercise Experiences Scale among children. *Journal of Sport and Exercise Psychology*, 19, 418–433.

Marsh, H.W. (1992a). *Self-Description Questionnaire II: Manual*. Publication Unit, Faculty of Education, University of Western Sydney.

Marsh, H.W. (1992b). *Self-Description Questionnaire (SDQ) III: A theoretical and empirical basis for the measurement of multiple dimensions of late adolescent self-concept. An interim test manual and research monograph*. Macarthur, New South Wales, Australia: University of Western Sydney, Faculty of Education.

Marsh, H.W. (1997). The measurement of physical self-concept: A construct validation approach. In K.R.Fox (Ed.), *The physical self: From motivation to well-being* (pp. 27–58). Champaign, IL: Human Kinetics.

Marsh, H.W., & Peart, N.D. (1988). Competitive and co-operative physical fitness training programs for girls: Effects on physical fitness and multidimensional self-concepts. *Journal of Sport and Exercise Psychology*, 10, 390–407.

Marsh, H.W., & Richards, G.E. (1988). The Tennesse Self-Concept Scales: Reliability, internal structure, and construct validity. *Journal of Personality and Social Psychology*, 55, 612–624.

Marsh, H.W., Richards, G.E., Johnson, S., Roche, L., & Tremayne, P. (1994). Physical Self-Description Questionnaire: Psychometric properties and multitrait-multimethod analysis of relations to existing instruments. *Journal of Sport and Exercise Psychology*, 16, 270–305.

Martens, R., Vealey, R.S., & Burton, D. (1990). *Competitive Anxiety in Sport*. Champaign, IL: Human Kinetics.

Martinek, T.J., Cheffers, J.T., & Zaichkowsky, L.D. (1978). Physical activity, motor development, self-concept: Race and age differences. *Perceptual and Motor Skills,* 26, 147–154.

Martinek, T.J., & Zaichkowsky, L.D. (1977). *Manual and scale for the Martinek-Zaichkowsky self-concept scale for children*. Jacksonville, IL: Psychologists and Educators.

Martinsen, E.W. (1989). The role of aerobic exercise in the treatment of depression. *Stress Medicine*, 3, 93–100.

Martinsen, E.W. (1993). Therapeutic implications of exercise for clinically anxious and depressed patients. *International Journal of Sport Psychology*, 24, 185–199.

Martinsen, E.W. (1994). Physical activity and depression: Clinical experience. *Acta Psychiatrica Scandinavica*, 377, 23–27.

Martinsen, E.W., Hoffart, A., & Solberg, O. (1989). Comparing aerobic and non-aerobic forms of exercise in the treatment of clinical depression: A randomized trial. *Comprehensive Psychiatry*, 30, 324–331.

Martinsen, E.W., Medhus, A., & Sandvik, L. (1985). Effects of aerobic exercise on depression: A controlled trial. *British Medical Journal*, 291, 100.

Martinsen, E.W., Sandvik, L., & Kolbjornsrud, O.B. (1989). Aerobic exercise in the treatment of non-psychotic mental disorders: An exploratory study. *Nord. Psykiatr. Tidsskr.*, 44, 35–43.

Martinsen, E.W. & Stephens, T. (1994). Exercise and mental health in clinical and free-living populations. In R.K. Dishman (Ed.), *Advances in exercise adherence* (pp. 55–72). Champaign, IL: Human Kinetics.

Martinsen, E.W., Strand, J., Paulson, G., & Kaggestad, J. (1989). Physical fitness level in patients with anxiety and depressive disorders. *International Journal of Sports Medicine*, 10, 58–61.

McAuley, E. (1994). Physical activity and psychosocial outcomes. In C. Bouchard, R.J. Shephard, & T. Stephens (Eds), *Physical activity, fitness and health* (pp. 551–568). Champaign, IL: Human Kinetics.

McAuley, E., Bane, S.M., Rudolph, D.L., & Lox, C.L. (1995). Physique anxiety and exercise in middle-aged adults. *Journal of Gerontology*, 50B, 229–235.

McAuley, E., & Courneya, K. (1994). The Subjective Exercise Experiences Scale (SEES): Development and preliminary validation. *Journal of Sport and Exercise Psychology*, 16, 163–177.

McAuley, E., Courneya, K.S. & Lettunich, J. (1991). Effects of acute and long-term exercise on self-efficacy responses in sedentary, middle-aged males and females. *The Gerontologist*, 31: 4, 534–542.

McAuley, E., & Mihalko, S.L. (1998). Measuring exercise-related self-efficacy. In J.L. Duda (Ed.), *Advances in sport and exercise psychology measurement* (pp. 371–392). Morgantown, WV: Fitness Information Technology.

McAuley, E., Mihalko, S.L., & Bane, S.M. (1995). Exercise and self-esteem in middle-aged adults: Multidimensional relationships and physical fitness and self-efficacy influences. *Journal of Behavioral Medicine*, 20, 67–83.

McAuley, E., Mihalko, S.L., & Bane, S.M. (1996). Acute exercise and anxiety reduction: Does the environment matter? *Journal of Sport and Exercise Psychology*, 18, 408–419.

McAuley, E., & Rudolph, D. (1995). Physical activity, aging, and psychological well-being. *Journal of Aging and Physical Activity*, 3, 67–96.

McCann, I.L., & Holmes, D. S. (1984). Influence of aerobic exercise on depression. *Journal of Personality and Social Psychology*, 46, 1142–1147.

McCarrick, A.K., Manderscheid, R.W., Bertolucci, D.E., Goldman, H., & Tessler, R.C. (1986). Chronic medical problems in the chronic mentally ill. *Hospital and Community Psychiatry*, 37, 289–291.

McCubbin, J.A., Cheung, R., Montgomery, T.B., Bulbulian, R., & Wilson, J.F. (1992). Aerobic fitness and opioidergic inhibition of cardiovascular stress reactivity. *Psychophysiology*, 29, 687–697.

McDonald, D.G., & Hodgdon, J.A. (1991). *Psychological effects of aerobic fitness training: Research and theory*. New York: Springer-Verlag.

McEntee, D.J., & Halgin, R.P. (1996). Therapists' attitudes about addressing the role of exercise in psychotherapy. *Journal of Clinical Psychology*, 52, 48–60.

McFarland, R.A. (1963). Experimental evidence of the relationship between aging and oxygen want: In search of a theory of aging. *Ergonomics*, 6, 339–366.

McGowan, R.W., Jarman, B,O. & Pedersen, D.M. (1974). Effects of a competitive endurance training program on self-concept and peer approval. *Journal of Psychology*, 86, 57–60.

McKenna, J., Naylor, P-J., & McDowell, N. (1998). Barriers to physical activity promotion by GPs and practice nurses. *British Journal of Sports Medicine*, 32, 242–247.

McNair, D.M., Lorr, M., & Droppleman, L.F. (1971). *Manual for the Profile of Mood States.* San Diego, CA: Educational and Industrial Testing Service.

McNeil, J.K., LeBlanc, E.M., & Joyner, M. (1991). The effects of exercise on depressive symptoms in the moderately depressed elderly. *Psychology and Aging,* 6, 487–488.

Milligan, W.L., Powell, D.A., Harley, C., & Furchtgott, E. (1984). A comparison of physical health and psychosocial variables as predictors of reaction time and serial learning performance in elderly men. *Journal of Gerontology,* 39, 704–710.

Mock, V., Dow, K.H., Meares, C.J., Grimm, P.M., Dienemann, J.A., Haisfield-Wolfe, M.E., Quitasol, W., Mitchell, S., Chakravarthy, A., & Gage, I. (1997). Effects of exercise on fatigue, physical functioning, and emotional distress during radiation therapy for breast cancer. *Oncology Nursing Forum,* 24, 991–1000.

Molloy, D.W., Beerschoten, D.A., Borrie, M.J., Crilly, R.G., & Cape, R.D.T. (1988). Acute effects of exercise on neuropsychological function in elderly subjects. *Journal of the American Geriatrics Society,* 36, 29–33.

Morgan, W.P. (1968). Selected physiological and psychomotor correlates of depression in psychiatric patients. *Research Quarterly,* 39, 1037–1043.

Morgan, W.P. (1969). A pilot investigation of physical working capacity in depressed and non-depressed psychiatric males. *Research Quarterly,* 40, 859–861.

Morgan, W.P. (1970a). Physical fitness correlates of psychiatric hospitalization. In G.S. Kenyon (Ed.), *Contemporary psychology of sport* (pp. 297–300). Chicago: Athletic Institute.

Morgan, W.P. (1970b). Physical working capacity in depressed and non-depressed psychiatric females: A preliminary study. *American Corrective Therapy Journal,* 24, 14–16.

Morgan, W.P. (1979). Negative addiction in runners. *The Physician and Sportmedicine,* 7, 57–63; 67–70.

Morgan, W.P. (1994). Physical activity, fitness and depression. In C. Bouchard, R. J. Shephard, & T. Stephens (Eds), *Physical activity, fitness, and health* (pp. 851–867). Champaign, IL: Human Kinetics.

Morgan, W.P. (Ed.) (1997). *Physical activity and mental health.* Washington, DC: Taylor & Francis.

Morgan, W.P., & Goldston, S.E. (Eds) (1987). *Exercise and mental health.* Washington: Hemisphere.

Morgan, W.P., & Sonstroem, R.J. (1989). Exercise and self-esteem: Rationale and model. *Medicine and Science in Sports and Exercise,* 21, 329–337.

Morris, M. (1989). Running round the clock. *Running,* 104, 44–45.

Morris, J. (1994). Exercise in the prevention of coronary heart disease: Today's best buy in public health. *Medicine and Science in Sports and Exercise,* 26, 807–814.

Moses, J., Steptoe, A., Mathews, A., & Edwards, S. (1989). The effects of exercise training on mental well-being in the normal population: A controlled trial. *Journal of Psychosomatic Research,* 33, 47–61.

Moul, J.L., Goldman, B., & Warren, B. (1995). Physical activity and cognitive performance in the older population. *Journal of Aging and Physical Activity,* 3, 135–145.

Muraki, S., Maehara, T., Ishii, K., Ajimoto, M., & Kikuchi, K. (1993). Gender difference in the relationship between physical fitness and mental health. *Annals of Physiological Anthropology,* 12, 379–384.

Murphy, G. (1947). *Personality: A biosocial approach to origins and structure.* New York: Harper & Row.

Murphy, M.H., & Hardman, A.E. (1998). Training effects of short and long bouts of brisk walking in sedentary women. *Medicine and Science in Sports and Exercise,* 30, 152–157.

Mutrie, N. (1988). Exercise as a treatment for moderate depression in the UK National Health Service. In *Sport, Health, Psychology and Exercise Symposium Proceedings* (pp. 96–105). London: The Sports Council and Health Education Authority.

Mutrie, N. (1997). The therapeutic effects of exercise on the self. In K.R. Fox (Ed.), *The physical self: From motivation to well-being* (pp. 287–314). Champaign, IL: Human Kinetics.

Mutrie, N. (1999). Exercise adherence and clinical populations. In S.J. Bull (Ed.), *Adherence issues in sport and exercise* (pp. 75–109). Chichester: John Wiley.

Mutrie, N., & Biddle, S.J.H. (1995). The effects of exercise on mental health in non-clinical populations. In S.J.H. Biddle (Ed.), *European perspectives on exercise and sport psychology* (pp. 50–70). Champaign, IL: Human Kinetics.

Mutrie, N., & Davison, R. (1994). Physical self-perceptions in exercising older adults. *Journal of Sports Sciences,* 12, 203.

National Forum for Coronary Heart Disease Prevention (1995). *Physical activity: An agenda for action.* London: Health Education Authority.

Neal, R. (1977). Effect of group counseling and physical fitness programs on self-esteem and cardiovascular fitness (Doctoral dissertation, Boston University, 1977). *Dissertation Abstracts International,* 38, 1911A–1912A.

NHS Health and Advisory Service (1995). *Child and adolescent mental health services.* London: HMSO.

Norris, R., Carroll, D., & Cochrane, R. (1990). The effects of aerobic and anaerobic training on fitness, blood pressure and psychological stress and well-being. *Journal of Psychosomatic Research,* 34, 367–375.

Norris, R., Carroll, D., & Cochrane, R. (1992). The effects of physical activity and exercise training on psychological stress and well-being in an adolescent population. *Journal of Psychosomatic Research,* 36, 55–65.

North, T.C., McCullagh, P., & Tran, Z.V. (1990). The effect of exercise on depression. *Exercise and Sport Sciences Reviews,* 18, 379–415.

Norvell, N., & Belles, D. (1993). Psychological and physical benefits of circuit weight training in law enforcement personnel. *Journal of Consulting and Clinical Psychology,* 61, 520–527.

Norvell, N., Martin, D., & Salamon, A. (1991). An examination of the psychological and physiological benefits of passive and aerobic exercise in sedentary middle-aged women. *Journal of Nervous and Mental disease,* 147, 95–96.

Nouri, S., & Beer, J. (1989). Relations of moderate physical exercise to scores on hostility, aggression, and trait-anxiety. *Perceptual and Motor Skills,* 68, 1191–1194.

Ntoumanis, N., & Biddle, S.J.H. (1999a). Affect and achievement goals in physical activity: A meta-analysis. *Scandinavian Journal of Medicine and Science in Sports,* 9, 315–332.

Ntoumanis, N., & Biddle, S.J.H. (1999b). A review of motivational climate in physical activity. *Journal of Sports Sciences,* 17, 643–665.

O'Connor, P.J., Bryant, C.X., Veltri, J.P., & Gebhardt, S.M. (1993). State anxiety and ambulatory blood pressure following resistance exercise in females. *Medicine and Science in Sports and Exercise*, 25, 516–521.

O'Connor, P.J., & Davis, J.C. (1992). Psychobiologic responses to exercise at different times of day. *Medicine and Science in Sports and Exercise*, 24, 714–719.

O'Connor, P.J., Petruzzello, S.J., Kubitz, K.A., & Robinson, T.L. (1995). Anxiety responses to maximal exercise testing. *British Journal of Sports Medicine*, 29, 97–102.

Offenbach, S.I., Chodko-Zajko, W.J., & Ringel, R.L. (1990). Relationship between physiological status, cognition, and age in adult men. *Bulletin of the Psychonomic Society*, 28, 112–114.

Ojanen, M. (1994). Can the true effects of exercise on psychological variables be separated from placebo effects? *International Journal of Sport Psychology*, 25, 63–80.

Olfman, S. (1987). Relationships among physical fitness, cognitive performance and self-concept in older adults. (Doctoral dissertation, Concordia University, 1986). *Dissertation Abstracts International*, 48, B271.

O'Neill, M.P. (1989). Physical self-concept and psychological mood states: Their relationship to aerobic exercise. (Doctoral dissertation, Washington State University). *Dissertation Abstracts International*, 50, B4780.

Ossip-Klein, D.J., Doyne, E.J., Bowman, E.D., Osborn, K.M., McDougall-Wilson, J.B., & Neimeyer, R.A. (1989). Effects of running or weight lifting on self-concept in clinically depressed women. *Journal of Consulting and Clinical Psychology*, 57, 158–161.

Paas, F.G., Adams, J.J., Janssen, G.M.E., Vrencken, J.G.P., & Bovens, A.M.P.M. (1994). Effects of a 10-month endurance training program on performance of a speeded perceptual-motor task. *Perceptual and Motor Skills*, 78, 1267–1273.

Paffenbarger, R.S., Lee, I.-M., & Leung, R. (1994). Physical activity and personal characteristics associated with depression and suicide in American college men. *Acta Psychiatrica Scandinavia*, 89, 16–22.

Palmer, L.K. (1995). Effects of a walking program on attributional style, depression and self-esteem in women. *Perceptual and Motor Skills*, 81, 891–898.

Panton, L.B., Graves. J.E., Pollock, M.L., Hayhery, J.M., & Chen, W. (1990). Effect of aerobic and resistance training on fractionated reaction time and speed of movement. *Journals of Gerontology*, 45, M26–M31.

Parfitt, G., Eston, R., & Connolly, D. (1996). Psychological affect at different ratings of perceived exertion in high- and low-active women: A study using a production protocol. *Perceptual and Motor Skills*, 82, 1035–1042.

Parfitt, G., Markland, D., & Holmes, C. (1994). Responses to physical exertion in active and inactive males and females. *Journal of Sport and Exercise Psychology*, 16, 178–186.

Pasman, L., & Thompson, J.K. (1988). Body image and eating disturbance in obligatory runners, obligatory weight lifters, and sedentary individuals. *International Journal of Eating Disorders*, 7, 759–777.

Pate, R.R., Pratt, M., Blair, S.N., Haskell, W.L., Macera, C.A., Bouchard, C., Buchner, D., Ettinger, W., Heath, G.W., King, A.C., Kriska, A., Leon, A.S., Marcus, B.H., Morris, J., Paffenbarger, R.S., Patrick, K., Pollock, M.L., Rippe, J.M., Sallis, J., & Wilmore, J.H. (1995). Physical activity and public health. *Journal of the American Medical Association*, 273, 402–407.

Paykel, E.S., & Priest, R.G. (1992). Recognition and management of depression in general practice: A consensus statement. *British Medical Journal*, 305, 1198–1202.

Percy, L.E., Dzuiban, C.D., & Martin, J.B. (1981). Analysis of the effects of distance running on self-concepts of elementary students. *Perceptual and Motor Skills*, 52, 42.

Perlmutter, M., & Nyquist, L. (1990). Relationships between self-reported physical and mental health and intelligence performance across adulthood. *Journal of Gerontology: Sciences*, 45, 145–155.

Perronet, F., Massicotte, D., Paquet, J.E., Brisson, G., & de Champlain, J. (1989). Blood pressure and plasma catecholamine responses to various challenges during exercise recovery in man. *European Journal of Applied Physiology*, 58, 551–555.

Petruzzello, S.J., Jones, A.C., & Tate, A.K. (1997). Affective responses to acute exercise: A test of opponent process theory. *Journal of Sports Medicine and Physical Fitness*, 37, 205–212.

Petruzzello, S.J., & Landers, D.M. (1994a). State anxiety reduction and exercise: Does hemispheric activation reflect such changes? *Medicine and Science in Sports and Exercise*, 26, 1028–1035.

Petruzzello, S.J., & Landers, D.M. (1994b). Varying the duration of acute exercise: Implications for changes in affect. *Anxiety, Stress and Coping*, 6, 301–310.

Petruzzello, S.J., Landers, D.M., Hatfield, B.D., Kubitz, K.A., & Salazar, W. (1991). A meta-analysis on the anxiety-reducing effects of acute and chronic exercise: Outcomes and mechanisms. *Sports Medicine*, 11, 143–182.

Petruzzello, S.J., Landers, D.M., & Salazar, W. (1993). Exercise and anxiety reduction: Examination of temperature as an explanation for affective change. *Journal of Sport and Exercise Psychology*, 15, 63–70.

Petruzzello, S.J., & Tate, A.K. (1997). Brain activation, affect and aerobic exercise: An examination of both state-independent and state-dependent relationships. *Psychophysiology*, 34, 527–533.

Pierce, E.F. (1994). Exercise dependence syndrome in runners. *Sports Medicine*, 18, 149–155.

Pierce, E.F., Daleng, M.L., & McGowan, R.W. (1993). Scores of exercise dependence among dancers. *Perceptual and Motor Skills*, 76, 531–535.

Pierce, T.W., Madden, D.J., Siegel, W.C., & Blumenthal, J.A. (1993). Effects of aerobic exercise on cognitive and psychosocial functions in patients with hypertension. *Health Psychology*, 12, 286–291.

Piers, E.V. (1984). *Piers-Harris Children's Self-Concept Scale: Revised manual*. Los Angeles: Western Psychological Services.

Pistacchio, T., Weinberg, R., & Jackson, A. (1989). The development of a psychobiologic profile of individuals who experience and those who do not experience exercise related mood enhancement. *Journal of Sport Behavior*, 12, 151–166.

Plante, T.G. (1993). Aerobic exercise in prevention and treatment of psychopathology. In P. Seraganian (Ed.), *Exercise psychology: The influence of physical exercise on psychological processes* (pp. 358–379). New York: Wiley.

Powell K.E., & Blair S. (1994). The public health burdens of sedentary living habits: Theoretical but realistic estimates. *Medicine and Science in Sports and Exercise*, 26, 851–856.

188   *References*

Powell K.E., Thompson, P.D., Casperson, C.J., & Kendrick, J.S. (1987). Physical activity and the incidence of coronary heart disease. *Annual Review of Public Health*, 8, 253–287.

Pysh, J.J., & Weiss, G.M. (1979). Exercise during development induces an increase in Purkinge cell dendritic tree size. *Science*, 206, 230–231.

Radloff, L.S. (1977). The CES-D scale: A self-report depression scale for research in the general population. *Applied Psychological Measurement*, 1, 385–401.

Raglin, J.S. (1993). Overtraining and staleness: Psychometric monitoring of endurance athletes. In R.N. Singer, M. Murphey, & L.K. Tennant (Eds), *Handbook of research on sport psychology* (pp. 840–850). New York: Macmillan.

Raglin, J.S. (1997). Anxiolytic effects of physical activity. In W.P. Morgan (Ed.), *Physical activity and mental health* (pp. 107–126). Washington, DC: Taylor & Francis.

Raglin, J.S., Eksten, F., & Garl, T. (1995). Mood state responses to a pre-season conditioning program in male collegiate basketball players. *International Journal of Sport Psychology*, 26, 214–225.

Raglin, J.S., Koceja, D.M., Stager, J.M., & Harms, C.A. (1996). Mood, neuromuscular function, and performance during training in female swimmers. *Medicine and Science in Sports and Exercise*, 28, 372–375.

Raglin, J.S., & Morgan, W.P. (1987). Influence of exercise and quiet rest on state anxiety and blood pressure. *Medicine and Science in Sports and Exercise*, 19, 456–463.

Raglin, J.S., Turner, P.E., & Eksten, F. (1993). State anxiety and blood pressure following 30 minutes of leg ergometry or weight training. *Medicine and Science in Sports and Exercise*, 25, 1044–1048.

Raglin, J.S., & Wilson, M. (1996). State anxiety following 20 minutes of bicycle ergometer exercise at selected intensities. *International Journal of Sports Medicine*, 17, 467–471.

Reed, D.L., Thompson, J.K., & Coovert, D.L. (1991) Development and validation of the Physical Appearance State and Trait Anxiety Scale (PASTAS). *Journal of Anxiety Disorders*, 5, 323–332.

Rejeski, W.J., Brawley, L.R., & Schumaker, S.A. (1996). Physical activity and health-related quality of life. *Exercise and Sport Sciences Reviews*, 24, 71–108.

Rejeski W.J., Gregg, E., Thompson, A., & Berry, M. (1991). The effects of varying doses of acute aerobic exercise on psychophysiological stress responses in highly trained cyclists. *Journal of Sport and Exercise Psychology*, 13, 188–199.

Rejeski, W.J., Hardy, C.J., & Shaw, J. (1991). Psychometric confounds of assessing state anxiety in conjunction with acute bouts of vigorous exercise. *Journal of Sport and Exercise Psychology*, 13, 65–74.

Rejeski, W.J., Thompson, A., Brubaker, P.H., & Miller, H.S. (1992). Acute exercise: Buffering psychosocial stress responses in women. *Health Psychology*, 11, 355–362.

Richards, S., Musser, W.S., & Gershon, S. (1999). *Maintenance pharmacotherapies for neuropsychiatric disorders*. Philadelphia, PA: Brunner/Mazel.

Richert, A.J., & Hummers, J.A. (1986). Patterns of physical activity in college students at possible risk for eating disorder. *International Journal of Eating Disorders*, 5, 775–763.

Riddoch, C., Puig-Ribera, A., & Cooper, A. (1998). *Effectiveness of physical activity promotion schemes in primary care: A review*. London: Health Education Authority.

Rikli, R.E., & Busch, S. (1986). Motor performance of women as a function of age and physical activity level. *Journal of Gerontology*, 41, 645–649.

Rikli, R.E., & Edwards, D.J. (1991). Effects of a three year exercise program on motor function and cognitive processing speed in older women. *Research Quarterly of Exercise and Sport*, 62, 61–67.

Roberts, B.L. (1990). Effects of walking on reaction and movement times among elders. *Perceptual and Motor Skills*, 71, 131–140.

Rosenberg, M. (1965). *Society and the adolescent self-image*. Princeton, NJ: Princeton University.

Roth, D.L. (1989). Acute emotional and psychophysiological effects of aerobic exercise. *Psychophysiology*, 26, 593–602.

Roy, M., & Steptoe, A. (1991). The inhibition of cardiovascular responses to mental stress following aerobic exercise. *Psychophysiology*, 28, 680–699.

Rozin, P., & Stoess, C. (1993). Is there a general tendency to become addicted? *Addictive Behaviors*, 18, 81–87.

Ruck, J., & Taylor, A.H. (1991). The effects of aerobic exercise and quiet rest on state anxiety and blood pressure following a psychological stressor (abstract). *Journal of Sports Sciences*, 9, 447–448.

Rudy, E.B., & Estok, P.J. (1989). Measurement and significance of negative addiction in runners. *Western Journal of Nursing Research*, 11, 548–558.

Rudy, E.B., & Estok, P.J. (1990). Running addiction and dyadic adjustment. *Research in Nursing and Health*, 13, 219–225.

Russell, J.A. (1980). A circumplex model of affect. *Journal of Personality and Social Psychology*, 39, 1161–1178.

Rutter, M., & Smith D.J. (Eds). (1995*). Psychosocial disorders in young people: Time trends and their causes*. New York: John Wiley.

Ryckman, R.M., Robbins, M.A., Thornton, B. & Cantrell, P. (1982). Development and validation of a physical self-efficacy scale. *Journal of Personality and Social Psychology*, 42, 891–900.

Sachs, M.L. (1981). Running addiction. In M. Sacks & M. Sachs (Eds), *Psychology of Running* (pp. 116–126). Champaign, IL: Human Kinetics.

Sachs, M.L., & Pargman, D. (1979). Running addiction: A depth interview examination. *Journal of Sport Behavior*, 2, 143–155.

Sachs, M.L., & Pargman, D. (1984). Running addiction. In M.L. Sachs & G.W. Buffone (Eds), *Running as therapy: An integrated approach* (pp. 231–252). Lincoln, NE: University of Nebraska Press.

Sallis, J.F., & Patrick, K. (1994). Physical activity guidelines for adolescents: Consensus statements. *Pediatric Exercise Science*, 6, 302–314.

Salthouse, T.T. (1985). *A theory of aging*. Amsterdam: North-Holland.

Sarason, I.G. (1975). Test anxiety, attention and general problems of anxiety. In C.D. Spielberger & I.G. Sarason (Eds), *Stress and anxiety: Volume 1* (pp. 381–403). Washington DC: Hemisphere/Wiley.

Schempp, P.G., Cheffers, J.T.F., & Zaichowsky, L.D. (1983). Influence of decision-making on attitudes, creativity, motor skill and self-concept in elementary children. *Research Quarterly for Exercise and Sport,* 54, 183–189.

Schlicht, W. (1994). Sport und seelische gesundheit: Eine meta-analyse. In J. Nitsch & R. Seiler (Eds), *Health sport – movement therapy: Proceedings of the 8th European Congress of Sport Psychology 1991: Volume 4* (pp. 57–63). Sankt Augustin, Germany: Academia Verlag.

Scott, J. (1996). Cognitive therapy of affective disorders: A review. *Journal of Affective Disorders*, 37, 1–11.

Seamonds, B.C. (1982). Stress factors and their effects on absenteeism in a corporate employee group. *Journal of Occupational Medicine*, 24, 393–397.

Secord, P.F., & Jourard, S.M. (1953). The appraisal of body cathexis: Body cathexis and the self. *Journal of Consulting Psychology,* 17, 343–347.

Sedlock, D.A., & Duda, J.L. (1994). The effect of trait anxiety and fitness level on heart rate and state anxiety responses to a mental arithmetic stressor among college-age women. *International Journal of Sport Psychology*, 25, 218–229.

Selye, H. (1956). *The stress of life*. New York: McGraw-Hill.

Sexton, H., Maere, A., & Dahl, N.H. (1989). Exercise intensity and reduction in neurotic symptoms: A controlled follow-up study. *Acta Psychiatrica Scandinavica*, 80, 231–235.

Shavelson, R.J., Hubner, J.J., & Stanton, G.C. (1976). Self-concept: Validation of construct interpretations. *Review of Educational Research*, 46, 407–41.

Sherrill, C. (1997). Disability, identity, and involvement in sport and exercise. In K.R. Fox (Ed.), *The physical self: From motivation to well-being* (pp. 257–286). Champaign, IL: Human Kinetics.

Sherwood, A., Light, K.C., & Blumenthal, J.A. (1989). Effects of aerobic exercise training on hemodynamic responses during psychosocial stress in normotensive and borderline hypertensive type A men: A preliminary report. *Psychosomatic Medicine*, 51, 123–136.

Sherwood, D.E., & Selder, D.J. (1979). Cardiorespiratory health, reaction time, and aging. *Medicine and Science in Sports*, 11, 186–189.

Short, M.A., DiCarlo, S., Steffee, W.P., & Pavlou, K. (1984). Effects of physical conditioning on self-concept of adult obese males. *Physical Therapy,* 64, 194–198.

Smith, T.P. (1984). An evaluation of the psychological effects of physical education on children (Doctoral dissertation, De Paul University, 1983). *Dissertation Abstracts International*, 44, 3260B.

Sonstroem, R.J. (1978). Physical estimation and attraction scales: Rationale and research. *Medicine and Science in Sports*, 10, 97–102.

Sonstroem, R.J. (1984). Exercise and self-esteem. *Exercise and Sport Sciences Reviews*, 12, 123–155.

Sonstroem, R.J. (1997a). Physical activity and self-esteem. In W.P. Morgan (Ed.), *Physical activity and mental health* (pp. 128–143). Washington DC: Taylor & Francis.

Sonstroem, R.J. (1997b). The physical self-system: A mediator of exercise and self-esteem. In K.R. Fox (Ed.), *The physical self: From motivation to well-being* (pp. 3–26). Champaign, IL: Human Kinetics.

Sonstroem, R.J., Harlow, L.L., & Josephs, L. (1994). Exercise and self-esteem: Validity of model expansion and exercise associations. *Journal of Sport and Exercise Psychology*, 16, 29–42.

Sonstroem, R.J., & Morgan, W.P. (1989). Exercise and self-esteem: Rationale and model. *Medicine and Science in Sports and Exercise*, 21, 329–337.

Sonstroem, R.J., & Potts, S.A. (1996). Life adjustment correlates of physical self-concepts. *Medicine and Science in Sports and Exercise*, 28, 619–625.

Sonstroem, R.J., Speliotis, E.D., & Fava, J.L. (1992). Perceived physical competence in adults: An examination of the Physical Self-Perception Profile. *Journal of Sport and Exercise Psychology*, 14, 207–221.

Sothmann, M.S., Buckworth, J., Claytor, R.P., Cox, R.H., White-Welkley, J.E., & Dishman, R.K. (1996). Exercise training and the cross-stressor adaptation hypothesis. *Exercise and Sport Sciences Reviews*, 24, 267–287.

Sothmann, M.S., Hart, B.A., & Horn, T.S. (1991). Plasma catecholamine response to acute psychological stress in humans: Relation to aerobic fitness and exercise training. *Medicine and Science in Sports and Exercise*, 23, 7.

Speith, W. (1965). Slowness of task performance and cardiovascular diseases. In A.T. Welford & J.E. Birren (Eds), *Behavior, aging, and the nervous system* (pp. 366–400). Springfield, IL: Thomas.

Spence, J.C. (unpublished). The effects of exercise on self-esteem. Edmonton: University of Alberta.

Spence, J.C., & Poon, P. (1997). The effect of physical activity on self-concept: A meta-analysis. *Alberta Centre for Well-Being: Research Update*, 4, 4.

Spielberger, C.D., Gorsuch, R.L., Lushene, R., Vagg, P.R., & Jacobs, G.A. (1983). *Manual for the State-trait Anxiety Inventory (Form YI)*. Palo Alto, CA: Consulting Psychologists Press.

Spirduso, W.W. (1975). Reaction and movement time as a function of age and physical activity level. *Journal of Gerontology*, 30, 435–440.

Spirduso, W.W. (1980). Physical fitness, aging, and psychomotor speed: A review. *Journal of Gerontology*, 35, 850–865.

Spirduso, W.W. (1994). *Physical dimensions of aging*. Champaign, IL: Human Kinetics.

Spirduso, W.W., & Clifford, P. (1978). Replication of age and physical activity effects on reaction and movement time. *Journal of Gerontology*, 33, 26–30.

Spitzer, R.L., Endicott, J., & Robins, E. (1978). Research diagnostic criteria. *Archives of General Psychiatry*, 35, 773–782.

Sports Council & Health Education Authority (1992). *Allied Dunbar National Fitness Survey: Main findings*. London: Author.

Stacey, C., Kozma, A., & Stones, M.J. (1985). Simple cognitive and behavioral changes resulting from improved physical fitness in persons over 50 years of age. *Canadian Journal on Aging*, 4, 67–73.

Stein, P.K., & Boutcher, S.H. (1992). The effect of participation in an exercise training program on cardiovascular reactivity in sedentary middle-aged males. *International Journal of Psychophysiology*, 13, 215–223.

Stelmach, G. (1994). Physical activity and aging: Sensory and perceptual processing. In C. Bouchard (Ed.), *Physical activity, fitness, and health: International proceedings and consensus statement* (pp.521–529). Champaign, IL: Human Kinetics.

Stephens, T. (1988). Physical activity and mental health in the United States and Canada: Evidence from four population surveys. *Preventive Medicine*, 17, 35–47.

Steptoe, A. (1992). Physical activity and psychological well-being. In N. Norgan (Ed.), *Physical activity and health* (pp. 207–229). Cambridge: Cambridge University Press.

Steptoe, A., & Bolton, J. (1988). The short-term influence of high and low intensity physical exercise on mood. *Psychology and Health*, 2, 91–106.

Steptoe, A., & Butler, N. (1996). Sports participation and emotional well-being in adolescents. *The Lancet*, 347, 1789–1792.

Steptoe, A., & Cox, S. (1988). Acute effects of aerobic exercise on mood. *Health Psychology*, 7, 329–340.

Steptoe, A., Edwards, S., Moses, J., & Mathews, A. (1989). The effects of exercise training on mood and perceived coping ability in anxious adults from the general population. *Journal of Psychosomatic Research*, 33, 537–547.

Steptoe, A., Kearsley, N., & Walters, N. (1993). Cardiovascular activity during mental stress following vigorous exercise in sportsmen and inactive men. *Psychophysiology*, 30, 245–252.

Steptoe, A., Moses, J., Edwards, S., & Mathews, A. (1993). Exercise and responsivity to mental stress: Discrepancies between the subjective and physiological effects of aerobic training. *International Journal of Sport Psychology*, 24, 110–129.

Steptoe, A.M., Moses, J., Mathews, A., & Edwards, S. (1990). Aerobic fitness, physical activity, and psychophysiological reactions to mental tasks. *Psychophysiology*, 27, 264–274.

Stewart, A.L., Hays, R.D., Wells, K.B., Rogers, W.H., Spritzer, K.L., & Greenfield, S. (1994). Long-term functioning and well-being outcomes associated with physical activity and exercise in patients with chronic conditions in the Medical Outcomes Study. *Journal of Clinical Epidemiology*, 47, 719–730.

Stones, M.J., & Kozma, A. (1989). Age, exercise, and coding performance. *Psychology and Aging*, 4, 190–194.

Summers, J.J., & Hinton, E.R. (1986). Development of scales to measure participation in running. In L.E. Unestahl (Ed.), *Contemporary Sport Psychology* (pp. 73–84). Orebro, Sweden: Veje.

Suominen, H., Heikkinen, E., Parkatti, T., Forsberg, S., & Kiiskinen, A. (1980). Effects of 'lifelong' physical training on functional aging in men. *Scandinavian Journal of Social Medicine*, 55, 225–240.

Szabo, A. (1995). The impact of exercise deprivation on well-being of habitual exercisers. *The Australian Journal of Science and Medicine in Sport*, 27, 68–75.

Szabo, A. (1997). Cross sectional research on the Internet. *Journal of Physical Education and Sport Sciences*, 10, 14–22.

Szabo, A., Brown, T.G., Gauvin, L., & Seraganian, P. (1993). Aerobic fitness does not influence *directly* heart rate *reactivity* to mental stress. *Acta Psychologica Hungarica*, 81, 229–237.

Szabo, A., Frenkl, R., & Caputo, A. (1996). Deprivation feelings, anxiety, and commitment to various forms of physical activity: A cross-sectional study on the Internet. *Psychologia*, 39, 223–230.

Szabo, A., Frenkl, R., & Caputo, A. (1997). Relationships between addiction to running, commitment to running, and deprivation from running. *European Yearbook of Sport Psychology*, 1, 130–147.

Szabo, A., Frenkl, R., Janek, G., Kalman, L., & Laszay, D. (1998). Runners' anxiety and mood on running and non-running days: An in situ daily monitoring study. *Psychology, Health and Medicine*, 3, 193–199.

Szabo, A., & Gauvin, L. (1992). Reactivity to written mental arithmetic: Effects of exercise lay-off and habituation. *Physiology and Behavior*, 51, 501–506.

Szabo, A., Peronnet, F., Boudreau, G., Cote, L., Gauvin, L., & Seraganian, P. (1993). Psychophysiological profiles in response to various challenges during recovery from acute aerobic exercise. *International Journal of Psychophysiology*, 14, 285–292.

Szafran, J. (1966). Age, cardiac output, and choice reaction time. *Nature*, 209, 836–837.

Szymanski, L.A., & Chrisler, J.C. (1990). Eating disorders, gender role, and athletic activity. *Psychology: A Journal of Human Behavior*, 27, 20–29.

Talbot, H.M., & Taylor, A.H. (1998). Changes in physical self-perceptions: Findings from a randomised controlled study of a GP exercise referral scheme. *Journal of Sports Sciences*, 16, 105–106.

Tate, A.K., & Petruzzello, S.J. (1995). Varying the intensity of acute exercise: Implications for changes in affect. *Journal of Sports Medicine and Physical Fitness*, 35, 295–302.

Taylor, J.A. (1953). A personality scale of manifest anxiety. *Journal of Abnormal Social Psychology*, 48, 285–290.

Thaxton, L. (1982). Physiological and psychological effects of shortterm exercise addiction on habitual runners. *Journal of Sport Psychology*, 4, 7380.

Thayer, R.E. (1967). The measurement of activation through self-report. *Psychological Reports*, 20, 663–678.

Thiel, A., Gottfried, H., & Hesse, F.W. (1993). Subclinical eating disorders in male athletes. *Acta Psychiatrica Scandinavica*, 88, 259–265.

Thirlaway, K., & Benton, D. (1996). Exercise and mental health: The role of activity and fitness. In J. Kerr, A. Griffiths, & T. Cox (Eds), *Workplace health, employee fitness and exercise* (pp. 69–82). London: Taylor & Francis.

Thomas, J.R., Landers, D.M., Salazar, W., & Etnier, J. (1994). Exercise and cognitive function. In C. Bouchard, R.J. Shepherd, & T. Stephens (Eds), *Physical activity, fitness, and health* (pp. 521–529). Champaign, IL: Human Kinetics.

Thomas, J.R., & Nelson, J.K. (1996). *Research Methods in Physical Activity* (3rd edn). Champaign, IL: Human Kinetics.

Thompson, J.K., & Blanton, P. (1987). Energy conservation and exercise dependence: A sympathetic arousal hypothesis. *Medicine and Science in Sports and Exercise*, 19, 91–97.

Thornton, E.W., & Scott, S.E. (1995). Motivation in the committed runner: Correlations between self-report scales and behaviour. *Health Promotion International*, 10, 177–184.

Tilford, S., Delaney, F., & Vegells, M. (1997). *Effectiveness of mental health promotion interventions: A review*. London: Health Education Authority.

Tkachuk, G.A., & Martin, G.L. (1999). Exercise therapy for patients with psychiatric disorders: Research and clinical implications. *Professional Psychology: Research and Practice*, 30, 275–282.

Topp, R. (1989). Effect of relaxation or exercise on undergraduates' test anxiety. *Perceptual and Motor Skills*, 69, 35–41.

Torres, R., & Fernandez, F. (1995). Self-esteem and the value of health as determinants of adolescent health behavior. *Journal of Adolescent Health Care*, 16, 60–63.

Trine, MR., & Morgan, WP. (1997). Influence of time of day on the anxiolytic effects of exercise. *International Journal of Sports Medicine*, 18, 161–168.

Trujillo, C.M. (1983). The effect of weight training and running exercise intervention programs on the self-esteem of college women. *International Journal of Sport Psychology*, 14, 162–173.

Tucker, L.A. (1987). Effect of weight training on body attitudes: Who benefits most? *Journal of Sports Medicine*, 27, 70–78.

Tucker, L.A., & Mortell, R. (1993). Comparison of the effects of walking and weight training programs on body image in middle-aged women: An experimental study. *American Journal of Health Promotion*, 8, 34–42.

Tuson, K.M., & Sinyor, D. (1993). On the affective benefits of acute aerobic exercise: Taking stock after twenty years of research. In P. Seraganian (Ed.), *Exercise psychology* (pp. 80–121). New York: John Wiley.

US Department of Health and Human Services (PHS). (1996). *Physical activity and health: A report of the Surgeon General (executive summary)*. Pittsburgh, PA: Superintendent of Documents.

Ussher, M., Taylor, A.H., West, R., & McEwen A. (in press). Does exercise aid smoking cessation? A sytematic review. *Journal of Addiction*.

Van Doornen, L.J., & de Geus, E.J. (1989). Aerobic fitness and the cardiovascular response to stress. *Psychophysiology*, 26, 17–28.

Veale, D., Le Fevre, K., Pantelis, C., de Souza, V., Mann, A., & Sargeant, A. (1992). Aerobic exercise in the adjunctive treatment of depression: A randomised controlled trial. *Journal of the Royal Society of Medicine*, 85, 541–544.

Vlachopoulos, S., Biddle, S., & Fox, K. (1996). A social-cognitive investigation into the mechanisms of affect generation in children's physical activity. *Journal of Sport and Exercise Psychology*, 18, 174–193.

Wankel, L.M. (1993). The importance of enjoyment to adherence and psychological benefits from physical activity. *International Journal of Sport Psychology*, 24, 151–169.

Wankel, L.M., & Berger, B.G. (1990). The psychological and social benefits of sport and physical activity. *Journal of Leisure Research*, 22, 167–182.

Warr, P. (1990). The measurement of well-being and other aspects of mental health. *Journal of Occupational Psychology*, 63, 193–210.

Watson, D., Clark, L.A., & Carey, G. (1988). Positive and negative affectivity and their relation to anxiety and depressive disorders. *Journal of Abnormal Psychology*, 97, 346–353.

Watson, D., Clark, L.A., & Tellegen, A. (1988). Development and validation of brief measures of positive and negative affect: The PANAS scales. *Journal of Personality and Social Psychology*, 54, 1063–1070.

Watson, D., & Tellegen, A. (1985). Toward a consensual structure of mood. *Psychological Bulletin*, 98, 219–235.

Weiner, B. (1995). *Judgments of responsibility: A foundation for a theory of social conduct*. New York: The Guilford Press.

Weismann, M.M., & Klerman, G.L. (1992). Depression: Current understanding and changing trends. *Annual Review of Public Health*, 13, 319–339.

Weyerer, S. (1992). Physical inactivity and depression in the community: Evidence from the Upper Bavarian Field Study. *International Journal of Sports Medicine*, 13, 492–496.

White, A. (1974). The interrelationships between measures of physical fitness and measures of self-concept of selected Mississippi State University male students (Doctoral dissertation, Mississippi State University, 1973). *Dissertation Abstracts International*, 34, 4849A.

Whiting, J. (1981). The effect of a mild exercise program on the psychological treatment of in-patient alcoholics. *Dissertation Abstracts International*, 42, 394B–395B.

Wichmann, S., & Martin, D.R. (1992). Exercise excess. *The Physician and Sportsmedicine*, 20, 193–200.

Williamson, D.A., Netemeyer, R.G., Jackman, L.P., Anderson, D.A., Funsch, C.L., & Rabalais, J.Y. (1995). Structural equation modeling of risk factors for the development of eating disorder symptoms in female athletes. *International Journal of Eating Disorders*, 17, 387–393.

Wolf, E.M., & Akamatsu, T.J. (1994). Exercise involvement and eating disordered characteristics in college students. *Eating Disorders*, 2, 308–318.

Worcester, M.C., Hare, D.L., Oliver, R.G., Reid, M.A., & Goble, A.J. (1993). Early programmes of high and low intensity exercise and quality of life after acute myocardial infarction. *British Medical Journal*, 307, 1244–1247.

World Health Organisation (1993). *The ICD-10 classification of mental and behavioural disorders: Diagnostic criteria for research*. Geneva: WHO.

World Health Organisation (1995). Exercise for health. WHO/FIMS Committee on Physical Activity for Health. *Bulletin of the World Health Organisation*, 73, 135–136.

Wykoff, W. (1993). The psychological effects of exercise on non-clinical and clinical populations of adult women: A critical review of the literature. *Occupational Therapy in Mental Health*, 12, 69–106.

Wylie, R.C. (1979). *The self-concept, Volume 2. Theory and research on selected topics*. Lincoln, NE: University of Nebraska.

Wylie, R.C. (1989). *Measures of self-concept*. Lincoln, NE: University of Nebraska.

Yates, A., Leehey, K., & Shisslak, C.M. (1983). Running: An analogue of anorexia? *New England Journal of Medicine*, 308, 251–255.

Yates, A., Shisslak, C.M., Crago, M., & Allender, J. (1994). Overcommitment to sport: Is there a relationship to the eating disorders? *Clinical Journal of Sport Medicine*, 4, 39–46.

Yeagle, G.W. (1982). The effect of a physical recreation program on the self-concept and flexibility of senior citizens (Doctoral dissertation, University of Utah). *Dissertation Abstracts International*, 42, B3184.

Youngstedt, S.D., Dishman, R.K., Cureton, K.J., & Peacock, L.J. (1993). Does body temperature mediate anxiolytic effects of acute exercise? *Journal of Applied Physiology*, 74, 825–831.

Youngstedt, S.D., O'Connor, P.J., & Dishman, R.K. (1997). The effects of acute exercise on sleep: A quantitative synthesis. *Sleep*, 20, 203–214.

Zaitz, D. (1989). Are you an exercise addict? *Idea Today*, 7, 44.

Zuckerman, M., & Lubin, B. (1965). *Manual for the Multiple Affect Adjective Checklist*. San Diego, CA: Educational and Industrial Testing Service.

Zung, W. (1965). A self-rating depression scale. *Archives of General Psychiatry*, 12, 63–70.

Zung, W.W.K., Richards, C.B., & Short, M.J. (1965). Self-rating depression scale in an out-patient clinic. *Archives of General Psychiatry*, 13, 508–515.

Index